Stalin and Stalinism

Stalin and Stalinism

Revised third edition

Martin McCauley

PEARSON
Longman

Harlow, England • London • New York • Boston • San Francisco • Toronto
Sydney • Tokyo • Singapore • Hong Kong • Seoul • Taipei • New Delhi
Cape Town • Madrid • Mexico City • Amsterdam • Munich • Paris • Milan

PEARSON EDUCATION LIMITED

Edinburgh Gate
Harlow CM20 2JE
Tel: +44 (0)1279 623623
Fax: +44 (0)1279 431059
Website: www.pearsoned.co.uk

First edition published in 1983
Second edition published in 1995
Third edition published in 2003
Revised third edition published in Great Britain in 2008

ISBN: 978-1-4058-7436-6

British Library Cataloguing-in-Publication Data
A catalogue record for this book is available from the British Library

Library of Congress Cataloging-in-Publication Data
McCauley, Martin.
    Stalin and Stalinism / Martin McCauley. – Rev. 3rd ed.
        p. cm.
    Includes bibliographical references and index.
    ISBN-13: 978-1-4058-7436-6
    1. Soviet Union – Politics and government – 1917-1936.   2. Soviet Union – Politics and government – 1936–1953.   3. Stalin, Joseph, 1879–1953.   I. Title.
    DK267.M39 2008
    947.084'2–dc22

2008005989

10   9   8   7   6   5   4   3
12   11   10   09

Typeset in 10/13.5pt Berkeley Book by 35
Printed and bound in Malaysia (CTP-VVP)

The publisher's policy is to use paper manufactured from sustainable forests.

Introduction to the Series

History is a narrative constructed by historians from traces left by the past. Historical enquiry is often driven by contemporary issues and, in consequence, historical narratives are constantly reconsidered, reconstructed and reshaped. The fact that different historians have different perspectives on issues means that there is also often controversy and no universally agreed version of past events. *Seminar Studies in History* was designed to bridge the gap between current research and debate, and the broad, popular general surveys that often date rapidly.

The volumes in the series are written by historians who are not only familiar with the latest research and current debates concerning their topic, but who have themselves contributed to our understanding of the subject. The books are intended to provide the reader with a clear introduction to a major topic in history. They provide both a narrative of events and a critical analysis of contemporary interpretations. They include the kinds of tools generally omitted from specialist monographs: a chronology of events, a glossary of terms and brief biographies of 'who's who'. They also include bibliographical essays in order to guide students to the literature on various aspects of the subject. Students and teachers alike will find that the selection of documents will stimulate discussion and offer insight into the raw materials used by historians in their attempt to understand the past.

Clive Emsley and Gordon Martel
Series Editors

Contents

Foreword to the Third Edition

The demise of the Soviet Union revealed one truth about Stalinism: it was flawed and its internal contradictions led to its own destruction. However, elements of this extraordinary phenomenon survive in post-1991 Russia and provide inspiration to many communists. Stalin appears a great leader, given the modest role being played by Russia in the modern world. Over 70 per cent of the present Russian population lived better under communism, the foundations of which were laid by Stalin. Given the political, economic and social problems of Russia today, how did Stalin achieve what he did? After all, it was number two to America when he died in 1953. Fascinating aspects of Stalinism are its brutality and cruelty, but this is counterbalanced by its magnificent and stunning scientific and military achievements.

Since the second edition of this book, there has been an explosion of published materials. Very revealing are the documents which permit a greater insight into the day-to-day decision making of the Stalinist state. The blood and brutality are there on show. Also there have been some revealing glimpses into Stalin the man, on which this study draws. The Soviet dictator was careful to destroy evidence which could have thrown too much light on him personally and on his policies. Vyacheslav Molotov and Andrei Gromyko have provided memoirs which, unfortunately, only dispel part of the mystery which still surrounds Stalin. An aspect which has come to the fore recently is culture. Personal memoirs provide some remarkable insights into what it was like to live and struggle to build a socialist society in the 1930s. A wave of young scholars is expanding Stalinist studies and the fruits of their labour are being eagerly digested by the expanding community of Stalin watchers.

Martin McCauley

Acknowledgements

We are grateful to the following for permission to reproduce copyright material:

Financial Times Limited for extracts from a report by Chrystia Freeland published in the *Financial Times* 13–14 August 1994; Harcourt Inc. for extracts from *Conversations with Stalin* by Milovan Djilas, English translation copyright © 1962 and renewed 1990 by Harcourt Inc., reprinted by permission of the publisher; Taylor & Francis Ltd for extracts from 'Soviet Growth Since 1928: The Alternative Statistics of G.I. Khan' by M. Harrison, *Europe Asia Studies* vol 45: 1 (1993), pp. 141–167 and from 'Soviet Deaths in the Great Patriotic War, a Note' by M. Ellman and S. Maksudov, *Europe Asia Studies* vol 46: 4 (1994), p. 674, reprinted by permission of the publisher (Taylor & Francis Ltd, www.informaworld.com); University of North Carolina Press for extracts from Stalinist Planning for Economic Growth, 1933–1952 by Engène Zaleski, copyright © 1980 by the University of North Carolina Press, used by permission of the publisher.

Plates 1, 2, 3 and 4 copyright © David King Collection, reproduced by permission of David King.

In some instances we have been unable to trace the owners of copyright material and we would appreciate any information that would enable us to do so.

Chronology

1917

25 February   A strike in Petrograd becomes a general strike. The Tsar orders the demonstrations to be dispersed by any means necessary. The troops fire on the demonstrators, causing many casualties

26–27 February   The Petrograd garrison mutinies and joins the demonstrators. This results in the victory of the February revolution

12 March   Stalin, Kamenev and other Bolsheviks, in exile in various parts of Russia, return to Petrograd. They immediately support the policy of the Petrograd soviet and Provisional government

3 April   Lenin, his wife Krupskaya, and other Bolsheviks return to Petrograd from Zürich

4 April   Lenin addresses Bolsheviks and members of the soviet on the tasks of the proletariat, known as the April Theses

10 October   Bolsheviks achieve an absolute majority in the Petrograd and Moscow soviets. A secret meeting of the Central Committee of the RSDRP (Bolsheviks) resolves to launch an armed uprising. Only Kamenev and Zinoviev oppose this

12 October   The Petrograd soviet sets up a Military Revolutionary Committee (MRC) to combat counter-revolution. This then permits the Bolsheviks to organise an uprising through the MRC

25–26 October   During the night Bolshevik units take the Winter Palace, arrest 13 Provisional government ministers but Kerensky escapes dressed as a female nurse. The IInd All-Russian Congress of Soviets convenes in Petrograd and confirms the seizure of power as Bolsheviks and left SRs are in the majority. Right SRs and Mensheviks leave the Congress in protest. The Congress then declares that power has passed to the soviets

26–27 October   During an all-night sitting the Congress passes the decree on peace and the decree on land. A provisional Council (Soviet) of People's Commissars (*Sovnarkom*) is confirmed, headed by Lenin, consisting only of Bolsheviks

1918

3 March Brest-Litovsk Peace is signed between Russia and Germany, Austria-Hungary, Bulgaria and Turkey

6–8 March At the VIIth Bolshevik Congress the name of the party is changed from Russian Social Democratic Labour Party (Bolsheviks) to Communist Party of Russia (Bolsheviks) RCP(B)

1919

2–6 March The Communist International, the Comintern or IIIrd International, is founded in Moscow, Zinoviev is elected President

1921

2–18 March The Kronstadt uprising against Bolshevik rule. The island base, in the Gulf of Finland, was of great strategic importance and the Bolsheviks suppress the uprising of the sailors with huge losses on both sides

8–16 March The Xth Congress of the RCP(B) is shocked by the uprising and under Lenin's leadership introduces the New Economic Policy (NEP) and bans factionalism (organised opposition) in the party

1922

3 April Stalin is elected Secretary-General (*Gensek*) of the RCP(B)

1923

4 January Lenin, very ill, adds a postscript to his Testament, advising that Stalin be removed from positions of power at the centre because of character defects

15 December Stalin opens a campaign against 'Trotskyism' in *Pravda* in response to Trotsky's attacks against bureaucratisation (too much bureaucracy) in the party and the lack of inner party democracy

1924

21 January Lenin dies in Gorky, near Moscow, and is succeeded by three men, the triumvirate, Stalin, Kamenev and Zinoviev

26 January– 2 February At the IInd All-Union Congress of Soviets Stalin swears to uphold Lenin's legacy and presents himself as the leading follower of the dead leader

23–31 May At the XIIIth Congress of the RCP(B) Zinoviev and Kamenev attack Trotsky with Stalin keeping his counsel. Lenin's Letter to the Congress, in which he comments on the qualities of the leading Bolsheviks, and his postscript, in which he speaks of Stalin's character defects, are read to the Congress

1925

10 April   Tsaritsyn is renamed Stalingrad

27–29 April   At the XVth Conference of the RCP(B) Stalin's concept of socialism in one country is adopted against the opposition of Trotsky, Kamenev and Zinoviev

18–31 December   The XIVth Party Congress in Moscow adopts Stalin's views on industrialisation and a new party statute, renaming the party the Communist Party of the Soviet Union (Bolsheviks)

1926

14–23 July   At a joint plenum of the CC and the Central Control Commission (CCC) Trotsky presents the 'Declaration of the 13', opposing the Stalin group in the leadership. The argument for more rapid industrialisation is rejected and Zinoviev is removed from the Politburo

1927

2–19 December   The XVth Party Congress confirms the expulsion of Trotsky and Zinoviev from the party and Kamenev and another 74 opposition figures lose their party membership. The Congress decides on the collectivisation of agriculture and the drafting of a five-year plan for the Soviet economy. The main victor is Stalin

1929

18 January   Stalin succeeds in the Politburo in forcing through the banishment of Trotsky from the Soviet Union, against the opposition of Bukharin, Rykov and Tomsky

23–29 April   The XVIth Party Congress adopts the first Five-Year Plan (FYP) for the development of the economy and condemns the right deviation (Bukharin and Rykov) as a great danger to the party

1930

2 March   In an article in *Pravda*, 'Dizzy with Success', Stalin chastises those who have forced peasants into collectives and permits them to leave if they so desire. They rush out of the *kolkhozes* but Stalin's move is only tactical in order to ensure that the spring sowing would not be interrupted. Later the peasants are recollectivised

1934

1 January   The second FYP (1933–37) is published which foresees the completion of socialist reconstruction

12 January   The party purge reveals that about 300,000 members in Siberia and the Soviet Far East (15.6 per cent of the total membership) have been expelled

26 January– *10 February*	The XVIIth Party Congress (the Congress of the Victors) meets in Moscow; Stalin delivers the main speech and states that the Soviet Union has been transformed from an agrarian country into an industrial state
1 December	Sergei Kirov, party leader in Leningrad, is murdered, and Stalin uses this act to begin a period of mass terror

1935

15–17 January	Kamenev, Zinoviev and others are accused of treason but Kamenev gets only 5 years' imprisonment and Zinoviev 10 years; 76 supporters of Zinoviev are exiled to Siberia
21 March	The NKVD states that 1,074 persons from Leningrad have been exiled for life to Siberia
29 March	British Foreign Secretary Anthony Eden (later Lord Avon) arrives in Moscow to see Stalin who attempts to convince him and the western powers to enter a collective security system against Hitler
25 July–20 August	The VIIth Comintern Congress meets in Moscow, attended by 510 delegates. The dangerous international situation leads to the adoption of a popular front strategy

1936

27 June	Decree banning abortion and promoting the family. The family becomes again the basis of society
19–24 August	First Moscow Show Trial (the Trial of the 16) against the terrorist Trotsky–Zinoviev centre. The main accused are Kamenev and Zinoviev and are sentenced to death and executed, Tomsky commits suicide on 23 August
26 September	Genrikh Yagoda is replaced by Nikolai Ezhov as People's Commissar for Internal Affairs
5 November	Germany and Japan sign the Anti-Comintern Pact in Berlin which includes the agreement not to sign a treaty with the Soviet Union without the permission of the other country
5 December	A new Soviet constitution is adopted at the VIIIth Congress of Soviets which abolishes the three-class elector system (workers, peasants, intelligentsia) and introduces the general and equal right to vote and direct elections to all soviets. The USSR Supreme Soviet is to consist of two houses, Soviet of the Union and Soviet of Nationalities. The number of Soviet republics increases from 7 to 11 with the dissolution of the Transcaucasian Federal Socialist Republic and the appearance of Azerbaidzan, Armenia and Georgia as Soviet republics. Kazakhstan and Kirgizia are upgraded from Autonomous Republics to Union Republics

1937

23–30 January Second Moscow Show Trial against 17 members of the 'anti-Soviet Trotskyist parallel centre'; 13 are sentenced to death (and shot, 1 February) and the others to 10 years' imprisonment

11 June The arrest of leading military officers (Marshal Tukhachevsky, Deputy People's Commissar for Defence, and six generals) is announced. In a secret trial they are sentenced to death and executed. This begins a mass purge of the military

16 December Eight Soviet officials, mainly leaders of national minorities (Jews, Armenians), are accused of spying and treason, sentenced to death and executed

1938

2–13 March Third Moscow Show Trial against the 'anti-Soviet bloc of the right and the Trotskyists' involving 21 accused, including Rykov and Bukharin. On 13 March 18 are sentenced to death and executed on 15 March

8 December Nikolai Ezhov, notorious for his role in the Moscow Show Trials, resigns as People's Commissar for Internal Affairs and is succeeded by Lavrenty Beria

29 December A decree on raising labour discipline withdraws many of the social gains of the previous years (reduction of wages and holidays, including maternity leave, and the removal of benefits from those who change jobs twice). All workers and employees are to be given labour books (a record of their work performance)

1939

17–26 June Second Soviet census reveals a population of 190,687,000 on 17 June

10–21 March The XVIIIth Party Congress (the Party Congress of the Completion of the Victory of Socialism) adopts the guidelines for the third FYP and a new party statute. Stalin states that the goal is to catch up and surpass the developed capitalist countries and the construction of a classless socialist society

11 May Beginning of battle of Khalkin-Gol, on the Soviet–Mongolian border, with Japan; Moscow emerges the winner on 15 September

23 August Molotov and von Ribbentrop, German Foreign Minister, sign in Moscow the German–Soviet Non-Aggression Pact, having already signed a trade and credit agreement (19 August). In a secret protocol the two sides divide up east central Europe

1 September	Germany attacks Poland and penetrates up to the line agreed in the secret protocol and the Second World War begins
17 September	Soviet troops begin their march into eastern Poland (as agreed by the secret protocol)
28 September– *10 October*	The Soviet Union signs agreements with Estonia (28 September), Latvia (5 October) and Lithuania (10 October) which permit Soviet bases on their territories. A similar agreement with Finland is not reached (11–12 October)
26–28 October	The Soviet-occupied west Ukraine, formerly in east Poland, votes to introduce Soviet power and to join the Ukrainian Soviet Socialist Republic. The Belorussian population of former east Poland do the same and become part of the Belorussian Soviet Socialist Republic on 28–30 October
27 November	After the failure of Finnish–Soviet negotiations to establish a mutual assistance pact (Finland refused to permit Soviet bases on its territory), Moscow declares the non-aggression of 21 January 1932 null and void and breaks off diplomatic relations on 28 November
30 November– *12 March 1940*	The Soviet–Finnish (or Winter) war begins with an air raid over Helsinki and the march of Soviet troops into Karelia

1940

12–17 June	Soviet demands to Lithuania (12 June), Estonia and Latvia (16 June) to permit more Soviet bases and to elect governments according to Soviet wishes lead to the transformation of the Baltic States into Soviet republics (21–22 July) and then as part of the Soviet Union (3–6 August)
22 June 1940	France agrees an armistice with Germany, after failing to stem German advances since May: Britain is now alone against Germany; Italy is allied to Germany
26 June	The Soviet government demands that Romania secede Bessarabia and northern Bukovina to it. When Romania does not concur, Red Army units occupy both regions on 28 June
21 July	Field Marshal von Brauchitsch, Commander in Chief of the army, is ordered by Hitler to begin preparing for war against the Soviet Union. Hitler envisages a five-month campaign in the spring of 1941
21 August	Trotsky dies in Mexico after an attempt on his life (20 August)
12–13 November	Molotov arrives in Berlin for negotiations concerning the division of the world. Moscow wants Finland, Romania and Bulgaria
18 December	Hitler signs instruction no. 21, Operation Barbarossa, which envisages all preparations for an attack on the Soviet Union to be finished by 15 May 1941

1941

22 June — German units attack the Soviet Union across a broad front without a declaration of war. Churchill offers Stalin help, as does Roosevelt (23 June); Molotov, not Stalin, announces to the Soviet people that Germany has invaded

30 June — The State Committee for Defence (GKO) is set up and Stalin becomes its head (1 July)

3 July — Stalin, in a radio broadcast, proclaims the Great Patriotic (Fatherland) War and orders that no territory shall be conceded to the enemy

8 September– 20 January 1944 — 900-day siege of Leningrad

26 September — The battle of Kiev ends with 665,000 Red Army prisoners

30 September– 20 April 1942 — Battle for Moscow; Hitler calls it Operation Typhoon and it is codenamed Moscow Cannae (the battle in 216 BC in south-eastern Italy where the Roman legions were destroyed by Hannibal). The German offensive comes to a stop in December and on 5 December a Soviet counter-offensive forces the Germans back

16 October — The Soviet government and diplomatic corps moves from Moscow to Kuibyshev (now Samara) but Stalin stays in Moscow

7 December — Japanese forces attack Pearl Harbor, Hawaii, thus bringing the US into the war

1942

26 May — In London, Molotov signs an Anglo-Soviet alliance and friendship treaty for 20 years

29 May–1 June — Molotov holds talks in Washington on a second front in west Europe (Britain had already agreed to this on 26 May) and economic aid

17 July– 2 February 1943 — The battle of Stalingrad

25 July– 9 October 1943 — The battle for the Caucasus

1943

31 January– 2 February — The southern part of the German army at Stalingrad surrenders on 31 January (General Paulus) and the northern part on 2 February (General Strecker)

22 February– 21 March — German offensive recovers much lost ground; recapture of Kharkov on 16 March and Belgorod on 21 March

14 April — Stalin's son, Yakov, a prisoner of war in the German concentration camp Sachsenhausen, deliberately seeks death by entering a prohibited zone and is shot dead

15 May	Stalin dissolves the Cominform to demonstrate that the Soviet Union has no expansionary aims; the functions of the Cominform are taken over by the Central Committee Secretariat and a department of international affairs is set up
12 July	Greatest tank battle of the Second World War at the Kursk salient involving over 1,200 tanks. The Germans later break off the battle and retreat
28 November–1 December	Stalin, Churchill and Roosevelt agree, in principle, on the partition of Germany at Tehran

1944

4 March–10 April	Spring offensive of the Red Army in the southern Ukraine along a 1,100 km front. Kherson is liberated on 13 March, Vinnitsa on 20 March and Nikolaev on 28 March
26 March	Soviet troops reach the Romanian border on the river Pruth
6 June	D-Day landing of allied troops in Normandy, codenamed Operation Overlord
19–20 June	Soviet partisans interrupt railway communications of the German army group centre at 9,600 places in the greatest act of sabotage of the war
22 June–1 August	Soviet summer offensive against the German army group centre
24 August–2 September	The German 6th army is encircled and annihilated near Kishenev
12 September	London protocol, signed by the United States, the Soviet Union and Great Britain, on future occupation zones in Germany and the administration of Greater Berlin
19 September	A ceasefire is agreed by the Soviet Union, Great Britain and Finland in Moscow. Finland is to withdraw to the 1940 frontiers
7 October	At Dumbarton Oaks, the United States, Great Britain, the Soviet Union and China agree to establish the United Nations (and a draft UN charter) as the successor organisation to the League of Nations
9–18 October	Stalin and Churchill meet in Moscow and negotiate on a post-war settlement, especially on eastern and south-eastern Europe. Stalin agrees in principle to Churchill's 'percentages' deal', apportioning zones of influence in the Balkans

1945

4–11 February	Stalin, Churchill and Roosevelt discuss future military operations and the post-war world at Yalta
12 April	President Roosevelt dies and Vice-President Harry Truman becomes President

16 April   Great offensive of the 1st Ukrainian and 1st Belorussian fronts towards
                Berlin, which is encircled on 25 April

2 May   Berlin capitulates to the Red Army

8 May   General Field Marshal Keitel, Admiral von Friedeburg and Colonel General
                Stumpff sign the unconditional surrender of German forces at the Soviet
                headquarters at Berlin Karlshorst. The document is dated 8 May but it is
                signed at 0.16 on 9 May

24 May   At a victory reception in the Georgevsky Hall, in the Kremlin, for over a
                thousand officers, Stalin lauds the Russian nation and places it above all
                other nations in the Soviet Union

17 July–2 August   The United States, the Soviet Union and Great Britain agree on the political
                and economic goals of their occupation policy in Germany at the Potsdam
                Conference

6 August   US drops atomic bomb on Hiroshima, Japan

9 August   US drops atomic bomb on Nagasaki, Japan

21 August   Japanese troops capitulate to the Red Army, including over
                600,000 prisoners

2 September   Japan surrenders to the Allies on board USS *Missouri* (V-J Day)

11 September–   London conference of the foreign ministers of the Soviet Union,
2 October   United States, Great Britain, France and China finds agreement difficult.
                Discussions on peace treaties for defeated states and reparations for the
                Soviet Union

24 October   The Soviet Union, Belorussia and Ukraine join the UN as founding
                members

1946

9 February   Stalin launches a new Five-Year Plan and celebrates the Great Patriotic War
                as a victory of 'our Soviet social system' and of 'our Soviet state'

25 February   The Red Army is renamed the Soviet Army

5 March   Churchill's speech at Fulton, Missouri, speaks of an 'iron curtain'
                descending in Europe from Stettin (Szczecin) in the north to Trieste in the
                south. He calls for an Anglo-American alliance. Stalin sharply criticises the
                speech on 13 March

25 April–15 May;   The 2nd conference of the four powers (the USSR, USA, Great Britain and
15 June–12 July   France) discusses European security and Germany, the Trieste problem and
                a peace treaty with Austria

1947

12 March President Harry Truman proclaims the Truman Doctrine which promises US help to countries threatened by communism

5 June General George Marshall, US Secretary of State, announces the Marshall Plan, the European recovery programme

22–27 September An information bureau of communist and workers' parties (Cominform) is set up in Szklarska Poreba, Poland, by communist and workers' parties from the Soviet Union, Hungary, Romania, Bulgaria, Poland, Czechoslovakia, France, Italy and Yugoslavia (until 1948). Its headquarters are in Belgrade, and in Bucharest from 1948

1948

20 March The Allied Control Commission in Berlin is paralysed by the withdrawal of Marshal Sokolovsky

24 June–
12 May 1949 Berlin Blockade: all land and waterways to west Berlin and east Germany are blocked. Berlin is supplied by air lift from 26 June 1948 to 29 June 1949

28 June The Communist Party of Yugoslavia is expelled from the Cominform at a conference in Bucharest and Cominform's headquarters are moved to Bucharest

1949

25 January The Council for Mutual Economic Assistance (Comecon or CMEA) is set up by the Soviet Union, Bulgaria, Hungary, Poland, Romania and Czechoslovakia

4 April NATO is set up in Washington

4 May Four-power agreement in New York ending the Berlin Blockade, to be effective on 12 May

25 September TASS reports the explosion of the first Soviet atomic bomb

7 October The German Democratic Republic (DDR) is established

1950

13 January The Soviet Union ceases to participate in the UN Security Council and UN agencies (until 1 August 1950)

31 January President Truman announces that the US is to build a hydrogen bomb

14 February The Soviet Union and China conclude a treaty of friendship and mutual assistance for 30 years

25 June The Korean war begins

1952

10 March	Stalin proposes, in a note to the US, Britain and France, a peace treaty which would result in a unified, neutral Germany; the west sends a non-committal reply on 25 March
September	Stalin's *Economic Problems of Socialism* is published
16 September	The Soviet Union agrees to restore Port Arthur and their rights over railways to China
3 October	Britain explodes successfully its first atomic bomb in the Montebello islands
5–14 October	The XIXth Congress of the CPSU(B) adopts a new statute. The Politburo is replaced by a Presidium of the CC. The CC secretariat, headed by Malenkov, is expanded to 10 members. The term Bolsheviks in the name of the Party is dropped. In future the Party will be called the CPSU
1 November	The US explodes its first hydrogen bomb successfully in the Marshall Islands

1953

9 January	Nine Kremlin doctors are arrested and held responsible for the deaths of leading Soviet politicians. An anti-Semitic campaign begins with the announcement of the Doctors' Plot on 13 January
5 March	Stalin dies from a heart attack suffered on 1 March

Who's Who

Alliluyeva, Nadezhda Sergeevna (1902–32): She married Stalin as his second wife at the age of 17 and was a student at the Industrial Academy where she met Nikita Khrushchev. She committed suicide, mainly because she could not cope with the harsh political reality of the time.

Beria, Lavrenty Pavlovich (1899–1953): A political gangster who was kind to his family. A fellow Georgian, he was Stalin's butcher in the Caucasus and succeeded Ezhov in 1939. He headed the Soviet atomic programme. He lost out to Khrushchev and others after Stalin's death and was executed.

Budenny, Marshal Semen Mikhailovich (1883–1973): He became one of Stalin's favourite military men. A cavalry man, mechanised warfare in 1941 totally bewildered him. Stalin shunted him sideways. His intellect may have saved him during the purges.

Bukharin, Nikolai Ivanovich (1888–1938): In Lenin's phrase, the 'darling of the party', Bukharin was a sophisticated, urban intellectual who was a major economic theorist but, politically, was no match for Stalin. He was associated with the right and a slow transition to socialism. Victim of a Show Trial.

Bulganin, Marshal Nikolai Aleksandrovich (1895–1975): A political marshal who occupied many high-ranking posts connected with defence and security. His task at the beginning of the Second World War was to ensure that the military obeyed Stalin and implemented his orders. He was Minister for the Armed Forces 1947–49. Then he became Deputy Prime Minister until Stalin's death. The fact that Stalin never became suspicious of his motives reveals his high political skill.

Ezhov, Nikolai Ivanovich (1895–1940): A 'bloody dwarf' and 'iron people's commissar', Ezhov gave his name to the bloodiest period of the purges, the Ezhovshchina. He succeeded Yagoda in September 1936 and, in turn, gave way to Beria in April 1939. In his desk, Ezhov kept the bullets, wrapped in paper, with the victim's name on each, which had terminated the lives of Bukharin, Zinoviev and other top leaders.

Gorky, Maxim (1868–1936): Seen by many as the father of Soviet literature, he became the most famous communist writer in the world, while living, of all places, in fascist Italy. He returned to Moscow in 1931 and his death may have been due to natural causes or Stalin may have helped him into the next world.

Kaganovich, Lev Moiseevich (1893–1991): True to Stalin to the end; he even denied he was a Jew. He was party leader in Moscow in 1930 and helped Khrushchev's career. He did not intercede on behalf of his brother, Minister for Aviation, who committed suicide on hearing that he was going to be arrested by Beria and shot. Jews complained of his anti-Semitism. Stalin told him to shave off his beard because he did not want a rabbi near him.

Kamenev, Lev Borisovich (1883–1936): The eternal moderate of the Bolshevik party. He was Lenin's deputy as Prime Minister and sided with Stalin against Trotsky even though his wife was Trotsky's sister. Later he sided with Trotsky and Zinoviev against Stalin. He was sacked from the Politburo and became Soviet ambassador to Italy, 1926–27. He was a victim of the first Show Trial in Moscow.

Khrushchev, Nikita Sergeevich (1894–1971): A rumbustious, intelligent but uneducated party official who was entranced by Stalin. The spell was only broken after Stalin's death and he demolished Stalin's reputation in 1956. Khrushchev was party leader in Ukraine and Moscow and enthusiastically participated in the purges.

Kirov, Sergei Mironovich (1886–1934): His assassination in December 1934 was seized upon by Stalin to begin what later became known as the purges. He had been approached by some delegates at the party congress in 1934 to stand against Stalin as party leader. This may have sealed his fate.

Konev, Marshal Ivan Stepanovich (1897–1973): One of the most successful Red Army commanders during the Great Fatherland War. Commander of the Kalinin Front, October 1941–December 1942. He commanded the Steppe Front, 1943–44 and became a Marshal of the Soviet Union in 1944. His front advanced to the Vistula and then Berlin. He continued to Torgau where he linked up with US forces. His forces then moved south and entered Prague in May 1945. He was First Deputy People's Minister of Defence and commander of Soviet ground forces, 1946–50.

Krupskaya, Nadezhda Konstantinovna (1869–1939): Lenin's wife but not his great love. She was a faithful wife who worked for the cause but her memoirs are disappointingly shallow. She was advised to pay more attention to

Lenin to save him from seeking satisfaction with his secretaries. She was browbeaten by Stalin who warned her that if she were not careful the party would appoint someone else as Lenin's widow.

Lenin, Vladimir Ilich (1870–1924): One of the great political actors of the twentieth century in world politics. Inspired by the Enlightenment vision of a just, harmonious society, he brooked no opposition in his quest for revolution. Stalin was a key aide in 1917 and afterwards Lenin tried to smooth the acrimonious relationship between Stalin and Trotsky. In his Testament he warned the party against Stalin's inclination to abuse power. Stalin's associates rallied to his cause after Lenin's death and Trotsky fluffed his lines. Stalin never looked back and repaid his opponents with death.

Malenkov, Georgy Maksimilianovich (1902–88): A skilled administrator, he played a key role during the war as a member of GKO. He was elected to the Politburo in 1946 and was also Deputy Prime Minister. Stalin poked fun at his excess flab.

Molotov, Vyacheslav Mikhailovich (1890–1986): Ever faithful to Stalin, 'bootface' Molotov played a major role in foreign affairs and was greatly disliked in the West. His memoirs are disappointing and reveal little of Stalin's real thinking. He found the Khrushchev era soft because it was not Bolshevik enough, meaning not enough coercion was being used to mould the new society.

Ordzhonikidze, Grigory Konstantinovich (Sergo) (1886–1937): A prominent Georgian revolutionary who was influential in the 1930s during industrialisation. He was a supporter of Stalin and moved to Moscow in 1926 to become chair of the Central Control Commission and Rabkrin. In 1930 he became chair of VSNKh and in 1932 Commissar for Heavy Industry. He became a full member of the Politburo in 1930. He fell out with Stalin over the purges, in which his brother was tortured and shot. He committed suicide.

Pyatakov, Georgy Leonidovich (1890–1937): He was always on the left of the party (his father was a sugar merchant) and he supported Trotsky against Stalin. He was Deputy Commissar for Heavy Industry (under Ordzhonikidze) 1932–36. He was the chief accused at the second great Moscow Show Trial in 1937. He was found guilty and shot.

Rykov, Aleksei Ivanovich (1881–1938): Stalin's ally in the battle against Trotsky after Lenin's death, Rykov reaped the whirlwind later. He became a leading member of the right opposition, with Bukharin, against Stalin's policies, especially forced collectivisation. In 1930 he was sacked from all his posts and from the Politburo. He was tried for treason in the third great Show Trial in 1938 and executed.

Stalin, Iosef Vissarionovich (1878–1953): A brilliant but flawed politician who was one of the most important leaders of the twentieth century. He revealed matchless skill at political tactics and had a superb memory. He never forgot a slight. He relentlessly pursued the goal of making Soviet society socialist and the Soviet Union the leading country in the world. Although a Georgian he became an assimilated Great Russian and remorselessly suppressed non-Russian nationalism. He was willing to sacrifice anyone in the pursuit of moral–political unity (a harmonious society).

Timoshenko, Marshal Semen Konstantinovich (1895–1970): He occupied many top military posts during the Great Fatherland War but it was his friendship with Stalin, going back to the Civil War, which saved him from retribution for failure. He was a cavalry man and replaced Voroshilov as Commissar for Defence, in May 1940, with special responsibility to reorganise the Red Army after defeat in the Winter War with Finland. He became commander of the western front when the Germans invaded and could do little to stem the tide. He was defeated by the Germans at Kharkov, May 1942. This cost him his command and he was transferred to the north-western front, his last operational command. He then moved to *Stavka* for the rest of the war.

Trotsky, Lev Davidovich (1879–1940): The most brilliant speaker and writer of the revolution, he failed as a politician. He thought that intrigue was beneath him and this cost him dear against Stalin. He was in Lenin's mind as his successor and this meant that Stalin and the others ganged up against him. On the left, he played a major role in the Civil War as Commissar for Defence. Trotsky ridiculed Stalin's socialism in one country and typically failed to see its nationalist appeal. He was driven to open opposition in 1927 and exiled in 1928. Stalin's hitman finished him off in Mexico, in 1940.

Tukhachevsky, Marshal Mikhail Nikolaevich (1893–1937): One of the architects of the Red Army, his brilliant career was cut short because of suspicions about his loyalty to Stalin. Autocratic by nature, he was of aristocratic Polish origin, his hauteur made many enemies. He became a Marshal of the Soviet Union in 1935. In 1936 he was First Deputy Commissar for Defence. Tortured and executed, he was exonerated and rehabilitated under Gorbachev.

Voroshilov, Marshal Klimenty Efremovich (1881–1969): Close to Stalin from the Civil War, he proved himself a great survivor. He was Commissar for Defence, 1934–40. He gave way to the more able Timoshenko, in May 1940, as part of the reorganisation of the Red Army. He then became a deputy chair of *Sovnarkom* and the chair of the defence committee. He was appointed to the GKO, responsible for the overall running of the war. He was put in command of the armies of the north-western front, but could do little to stem the German advance. He was a member of *Stavka*. He signed the armistice for the Allies with Hungary and headed the Allied (Soviet) Control Commission in Hungary, 1946–47. He was USSR Deputy Prime Minister, 1946–53.

Vyshinsky, Andrei Yanuarevich (1883–1954): A venomous, merciless state prosecutor who gained worldwide notoriety for his courtroom behaviour during the great Show Trials. A former Menshevik, he always had to prove his loyalty to Stalin. He came out with the famous line, in closing for the prosecution, during the first great Show Trial: 'I demand that these mad dogs be shot, every last one of them!' He was Deputy Commissar for Foreign Affairs, 1940, and deputy chair of Sovnarkom, 1939–44. In 1949, he replaced Molotov as Minister of Foreign Affairs (he was reputed to have reported to Stalin over Molotov's head) and was permanent Soviet representative at the United Nations. He turned his venom on the United States, especially during the Korean War, 1950–53. In a memorable phrase, Leonard Schapiro described him as the nearest thing to a human rat he had ever seen!

Yagoda, Genrikh Grigorevich (1891–1938): One of Stalin's bloodiest police chiefs, he himself fell victim to the executioner's bullet. Some referred to him as the Mephistopheles from the (Jewish) Pale. Stalin made him head of the NKVD, 1934–July 1936. Just to keep him dangling, Stalin appointed him Commissar for Posts and Telegraph, 1936–37, and then had him arrested. He commented: 'I have long been expecting you.'

Zhdanov, Andrei Aleksandrovich (1896–1948): The guardian of Stalinist cultural orthodoxy, from socialist realism to the xenophobia of the late 1940s, known as the Zhdanovshchina, he became a member of the Politburo in 1939. In 1934, he laid down the rules for writers – socialist realism: all published work was to be didactic and optimistic. He led the defence of Leningrad, 1941–44. He died suddenly in 1948, probably naturally – he was a heavy drinker. Malenkov and Beria seized the opportunity to settle scores with the Leningrad leadership in what became known as the Leningrad Affair. This resulted in many officials being executed and many hundreds being dismissed.

Zhukov, Marshal Georgy Konstantinovich (1896–1974): The most prominent and successful Red Army commander during the Great Fatherland War. He defeated the Japanese at Khakin-Gol, Mongolia, 1939. He was made chief of the General Staff and Deputy Commissar for Defence, January–July 1941. In October 1941, he replaced Voroshilov as commander of the northern sector and was personally responsible for the defence of Leningrad. He then moved to Moscow and became commander-in-chief of the entire western front. He was responsible for the defence of Stalingrad. He participated in the battle of Kursk and became commander of the 1st Belorussian front, November 1944. His troops reached Berlin in April 1945. He then became commander of Soviet occupation forces in Germany. Stalin was wary of his popularity and in April 1946 demoted him to commander of the Odessa military district. After Stalin's death, he returned to Moscow as Deputy USSR Minister of Defence. A brilliant but rude and abrasive man, he was undoubtedly the leading military man of his generation.

Zinoviev, Grigory Evseevich (1883–1936): In Trotsky's memorable phrase, Zinoviev was either in seventh heaven or in the depths of despair. His Jewish family owned a dairy farm. A passionate orator and volatile politician, Stalin made mincemeat of him. Stalin drew him into a tactical alliance against Trotsky after Lenin's death but after Trotsky's defeat Stalin turned on Zinoviev. In 1926, he lost his place on the Politburo and his Comintern post, and was expelled from the party, in November 1927, after going on to the streets with Trotsky to protest, in vain, against Stalin's policies. He was readmitted to the party in 1928, after praising Stalin to the skies. He was expelled again in 1932. He (and Kamenev) were tried in secret in January 1935, and sentenced to ten years' imprisonment. In April 1936, he was the main accused in the first great Show Trial. He was a pathetic figure before execution. He was rehabilitated under Gorbachev.

Glossary

ASSR: Autonomous Soviet Socialist Republic; an administrative unit of a republic which is populated by a nationality other than the titular nationality: e.g. the Tatars made up the Tatar ASSR in the RSFSR. Although they had their own government, they were ruled from the titular nationality's capital; in the Tatars' case, Moscow. Hence 'autonomous' here does not mean independent.

AUSW: All-Russian Union of Soviet Writers; *see also* AUW and RAPP.

AUW: All-Russian Union of Writers; *see also* AUSW and RAPP.

Bolsheviks: When the All-Russian Social Democratic Labour Party (RSDRP), founded in 1898, split in 1903, those in the majority became known as Bolsheviks; in October 1917 the Bolshevik or Communist Party seized power.

Brest-Litovsk: Brest-Litovsk Treaty with Germany, March 1918, recognised Soviet Russia in international law; fulfilled the Bolshevik pledge to bring peace; revealed how split the Bolshevik leadership could be on a major issue.

Candidate member: (a) Before a person could become a full member of the Communist Party he had to serve a probationary period during which he was called a candidate member; (b) candidate members of the Central Committee and Politburo might attend meetings, speak but not vote.

CC: Central Committee of the Communist Party; this organisation acted in the name of the Party Congress when the latter was not in session; it contained all the important party officials, government ministers, leading army and naval personnel, key ambassadors, etc.

CEC: All-Russian Central Executive Committee of the soviets; the body which acted in the name of the Congress of Soviets when that body was not in session; theoretically, it was the supreme organ in the state but it rapidly lost power to *Sovnarkom* after December 1917. The Bolsheviks had a majority in the CEC but in the Presidium or inner council of the CEC there were only Bolsheviks; the chairman of the CEC was, in practice, the president of the country; in 1922 it changed its name to the CEC of the USSR; the 1936 constitution replaced it with the USSR Supreme Soviet. It was headed by L.B. Kamenev, October 1917–January 1918; Ya.M. Sverdlov, January 1918–March 1919; M.I. Kalinin, March 1919–36.

Cheka: All-Russian Extraordinary Commission to Fight Counter Revolution, Sabotage and Speculation; established December 1917; renamed OGPU in 1922; later KGB.

Collectivisation: Establishment of *kolkhozes* and *sovkhozes*, which meant the end of private farming. Collectivisation began in 1917 but had made little impact by 1929 when it really got under way; was completed by 1937. In practice several villages were lumped together and declared a *kolkhoz*; peasant opposition was dealt with brutally, by using military force, deportation or expulsion; initially almost everything was collectivised, but in March 1930 the private plot around the peasant's cottage was legalised; as of May 1932 he could legally sell any surplus (after paying taxes) in an urban *kolkhoz* market where demand and supply determined prices.

Cominform: Communist Information Bureau; established in 1947 and disbanded in 1955.

Comintern: Communist International; international communist organisation established in 1919 and disbanded in 1943.

Commissar: (a) Government minister; (b) official representing party, government or soviet.

Conference: Differed from a Party Congress in that not all organisations were represented (an exception was the XIXth Party Conference in 1988). In the early years the problems of logistics were such as to make it difficult to call a Congress at short notice. A Conference did not have the right to elect members to the Central Committee and Politburo.

Congress: Most important meeting of party, soviet, trade union or other organisation; at a congress the Communist Party reviewed its past record and laid down goals for the future; a new Central Committee was elected and it, in turn, elected a new Politburo and Secretariat.

FYP: Five-Year Plan; first FYP ran from October 1928 to December 1932; second from January 1933 to December 1937; third from January 1938 to June 1941; fourth from January 1946 to December 1950; fifth from January 1951 to December 1955.

GKO: State Committee of Defence during the Great Fatherland War (1941–45).

Gosplan: State Planning Commission of the USSR Council of Ministers; responsible for drafting economic plans and checking on their implementation; founded February 1921; headed by G.M. Krzhizhanovsky, 1921–23, 1925–30; A.D. Tsyurupa, 1923–25; V.V. Kuibyshev, 1930–34; V.I. Mezhlauk, 1934–37; N.A. Voznesensky, 1938–49.

Kolkhoz: Collective farm; members farmed the land as a cooperative but in reality had little say in what was to be produced; this was laid down in the annual state plan. Under Stalin payment was based on the number of labour days worked (it was possible to acquire several labour days during a day's work) and rewards came at the end of the harvest. If the farm recorded a loss no wages were paid. A basic guaranteed wage was only introduced in 1966.

Kolkhoznik: Collective farm peasant; between 1929 and 1966 there was no guaranteed basic wage; wages were paid out at end of harvest according to the profitability of the farm; the private plot kept the *kolkhoznik* and his family alive until the 1950s.

Kombedy: Committees of poor peasants; established by the Soviet government in June 1918 to seize grain from richer peasants who held surpluses; the state was to get most of grain (to feed cities) but in fact received little. In November 1918 there were 122,000 *kombedy* but in the same month all were disbanded.

Komsomol: Communist youth movement for those between ages 14 and 28.

KPD: Communist Party of Germany; founded in December 1919; refounded in Soviet Zone of Germany June 1945; fused with Soviet Zone SPD in April 1946 to form Socialist Unity Party of Germany (SED).

Kulak: Peasants were divided into poor, middle and rich by the Bolsheviks; the poor peasant did not have enough land to live off, the middle peasant did, and the rich peasant had enough to produce a surplus; in west-European terms the *kulak* would have been classified as a modestly well-off farmer.

Left communists: Bukharin was the leader of this group on the Central Committee (October 1917–18); they favoured the immediate introduction of socialism and a revolutionary war against imperial Germany. Lenin wanted a slow march to socialism and peace with Berlin; he eventually won over a majority of the Central Committee.

Lend-Lease: US military and food aid to Allies during the Second World War; authorised by Congress in March 1941 to aid Great Britain, it was extended to include China in April and the USSR in September 1941; about 22 per cent of aid or US$10,000 million went to the Soviet Union.

Mensheviks: When the All-Russian Social Democratic Labour Party (RSDRP), founded in 1898, split in 1903, those in the minority became known as Mensheviks; in October 1917 the Mensheviks opposed the Bolshevik seizure of power since they believed that Russia was not ready for socialism; they thought that the country had to become strong economically and a large working class come into being before a socialist revolution became a possibility.

Mir: Peasant commune.

Moderate socialists: Mensheviks and right Social Revolutionaries; they were called moderate to contrast them with the radical Bolsheviks.

Muzhik: Russian peasant.

NEP: New Economic Policy, introduced in March 1921; it brought back the market economy with money again being backed by gold; during NEP peasants could dispose of their produce as they liked; light industry also passed into private hands but heavy engineering, energy and transport stayed in state hands; in practice ended in 1929.

NKVD: People's Commissariat of Internal Affairs; renamed Ministry of Internal Affairs (MVD) in April 1946.

NSDAP: National Socialist German Workers' Party or Nazi Party.

Oblast: The principal territorial subdivision of a republic.

Orgburo: Organisational Bureau of the CC; handled all matters of an organisational and administrative nature, domestic and foreign, except those deemed important enough to be passed over to the Politburo; abolished in 1952.

Politburo: Political Bureau of the CC; key decision-making body of the Communist Party; established in 1919; prior to that the Central Committee was the most significant body; called the Presidium between 1952 and 1966.

Presidium: Inner council or cabinet, hence supreme body; the Politburo of the Communist Party was also known as the Presidium between 1952 and 1966.

Rabkrin: People's Commissariat of Workers and Peasants Inspection; founded in 1920 to supervise all government organs; dissolved in 1934 when functions were transferred to Commission of Soviet Control; in 1940 became People's Commissariat of State Control and from 1946 Ministry of State Control. Headed by I.V. Stalin, 1920–22; A.D. Tsyurupa, 1922–23; V.V. Kuibyshev, 1923–26; S. Ordzhonikidze, 1926–30; A.A. Andreev, 1930–34.

RAPP: All-Russian Association of Proletarian Writers; founded 1928 and dissolved in 1932; *see also* AUSW and AUW.

RCP: All-Russian Communist Party (Bolsheviks) 1918–25; formerly All-Russian Social Democratic Labour Party (RSDRP) 1898–1918; renamed All-Union Communist Party (Bolsheviks) 1925–52; renamed Communist Party of the Soviet Union (CPSU) 1952–91.

Right Opposition: Bukharin, Rykov, Tomsky and their supporters came together in the summer of 1928 to oppose the headlong rush towards industrialisation which was then beginning to gain momentum; they favoured voluntary collectivisation which meant in practice very slow collectivisation; by early 1929 they had been defeated by Stalin.

RSFSR: Russian Soviet Federated Socialist Republic; constitution adopted July 1918; between October 1917 and July 1918 the state was referred to as Soviet Russia or the Russian republic – in essence it amounted to the RSFSR; when the USSR was formed in December 1922 the RSFSR became the largest republic; between June 1918 and December 1922 the RSFSR concluded treaties with Belorussia, Ukraine, Georgia, Armenia, Azerbaidzhan and Central Asia – together they formed the Soviet state.

Secretariat: The administrative centre of the Communist Party; its key officials were called secretaries and the leading one Secretary-General (1922–53, 1966–) or First Secretary (1953–66); only from 1929 was the Secretary-General the leader of the Soviet Union.

SED: Socialist Unity Party; ruling communist party in the German Democratic Republic; founded in April 1946.

Sovkhoz: State farm; run like a factory with guaranteed minimum wages higher than those of *kolkhozniks*; operatives were classified as workers and enjoyed their social benefits.

Soviet: Name of state – Soviet Union; also elected council.

Sovnarkom: The Council of People's Commissars; the government of Soviet Russia and later of the USSR; it was appointed by the IInd Congress of Soviets in October 1917 and was to be subordinate to it but soon proved stronger; all the members of the first *Sovnarkom* were Bolsheviks and picked by Lenin himself; there was a brief coalition government between December 1917 and March 1918 when some left SRs joined; since March 1918 only Bolsheviks or communists have been commissars or ministers; was renamed USSR Council of Ministers in April 1946; according to the 1936 and 1977 constitutions the government should resign at the end of each legislative period, but this was a mere formality. These constitutions also laid down that each republic and autonomous republic (ASSR) was to elect its own government or Council of Ministers to underline the federal nature of the Soviet state, but in reality the USSR Council of Ministers dominated; *Sovnarkom* was the dominant body in the state while Lenin was well, but it was superseded by the Politburo in 1922. Headed by V.I. Lenin, October 1917–January 1924; A.I. Rykov, February 1924–December 1930; V.M. Molotov, December 1930–May 1941; I.V. Stalin, May 1941–March 1953.

SPD: Social Democratic Party of Germany; refounded in 1945 and fused with KPD in Soviet Zone of Germany in April 1946 to form SED; *see also* KPD.

SRs: Socialist Revolutionaries; the SRs constituted an agrarian socialist party; they had great support among the peasants since they advocated the handing over of the land to the peasants; as agrarian socialists they were not Marxists – they sought to influence and represent the urban working class; the party split in 1917 into right and left SRs, the latter supporting the Bolshevik seizure of power in October 1917; the left SRs joined *Sovnarkom* in December 1917 to form the first coalition government but left after refusing to be associated with the Treaty of Brest-Litovsk signed in March 1918; they then joined the anti-Bolshevik opposition, some even resorting to armed violence; the SR parties were banned in the early 1920s.

State capitalism: The economic order in existence between October 1917 and June 1918.

Stavka: General Staff of the Red Army and Navy during the Great Patriotic War (1941–45).

Supreme Soviet: Set up by the 1936 constitution; the USSR Supreme Soviet was bicameral: Soviet of the Union and Soviet of Nationalities; the number of deputies of the former was based on population, while the number of the latter was fixed; the houses were of equal status and often met in joint session; a parliament only in name, the key decisions were taken by the government and the party; the chairman of the presidium of the USSR Supreme Soviet was the president of the country; each republic and autonomous republic had its own Supreme Soviet but they were unicameral.

United Opposition: Trotsky, Zinoviev, Kamenev and their supporters combined in the summer of 1926 to form the United Opposition – to oppose socialism in one country and the policy of allowing *kulaks* free rein; they favoured a more rapid growth of industry and more weight to be accorded the world socialist revolution; this opposition was directed essentially against Bukharin and Stalin.

USSR: Union of Soviet Socialist Republics.

VSNKh: (*Vesenkha*) Supreme Council of the National Economy; founded December 1917 and responsible for the whole economy and state finances; as of June 1918 it became in effect the commissariat of nationalised industry;

there were local VSNKh to run industry; during the Civil War the main function of VSNKh was to provide the Red Army with war material and clothing; under NEP, factories producing similar products were grouped together in trusts but still managed by VSNKh; in 1924 a VSNKh was created in each republic and made responsible for industry there; VSNKh was headed by N. Osinsky, 1917–18; A.I. Rykov, 1918–20, 1923–24; P.A. Bogdanov, 1921–23; F.E. Dzerzhinsky, 1924–26; V.V. Kuibyshev, 1926–30; S. Ordzhonikidze, 1930–32; then it was divided into the Commissariats of Heavy Industry, Light Industry and the Timber Industry.

War communism: The economic order in existence between June 1918 and March 1921.

Workers' or food requisition detachments: Established in August 1918; they were highly successful in requisitioning grain since they were composed of workers who desperately needed the food for their urban families and the army and because they had machine guns. Forced requisitioning lasted until March 1921.

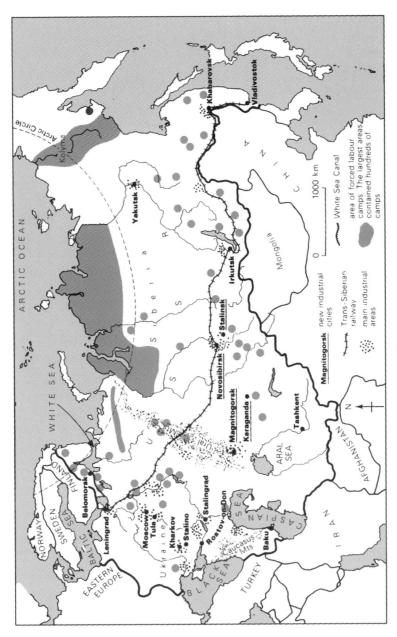

Map 1 The expansion of Soviet industry under Stalin

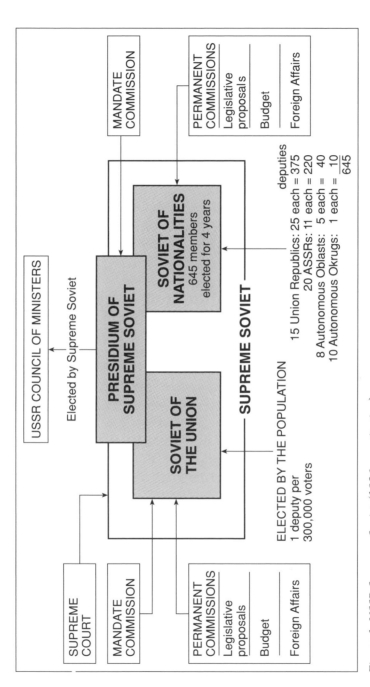

Figure 1 USSR Supreme Soviet (1936 constitution)

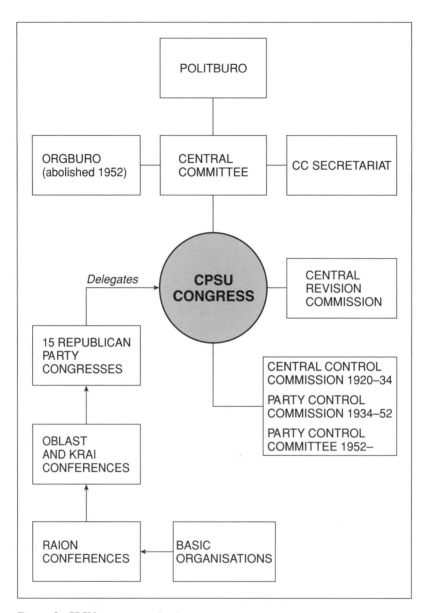

Figure 2 CPSU party organisation

Part 1

THE CONTEXT

1

Introduction: The Problem

Half a century has now passed since **Stalin** died but he and the mode of rule which bears his name, Stalinism (defined as the system which came into being between 1929 and 1953), still exert a fascination inside and outside Russia. Indeed, more research is now being conducted on these twin phenomena than ever before. Russia was number eight in the world rankings in 1914 but then succumbed to defeat in the First World War, revolution and civil war. The Stalin revolution revitalised the country and it defeated national socialist Germany in the Second World War. On Victory Day, 9 May 1945, Russia was a great power, the leading power in Europe and second only to the United States throughout the world. Its power waxed as it acquired an empire in eastern and south-eastern Europe, the spoils of victory, after 1945. China became a communist state in 1949 and soon afterwards about one-third of humankind was attempting to implement the teachings of Karl Marx. In the early 1960s some western commentators thought that Russia would eventually become the leading world power. Moscow would be the centre of the universe. Then in the 1970s the United States recognised Russia as an equal nuclear power. At this moment things began to unravel. At the end of the decade Russia became involved in a disastrous war in Afghanistan. The military burden became onerous and the country began a slow descent which accelerated under Gorbachev. Russia collapsed in 1991. Thus the Stalinist system met an ignominious end. Conceived as a world model which could outperform capitalism, it proved quite incapable of competing successfully with the United States. Was this the fault of Stalin's successors or was its failure inevitable?

Karl Marx (1818–83) was inspired by the philosophy of Georg Wilhelm Friedrich Hegel (1770–1831). He, in turn, had been inspired by the Enlightenment (so called because it lit up human perception), which had swept through Europe in the seventeenth and eighteenth centuries, and the French Revolution. Central to the Enlightenment was the use and celebration of reason. Reason could be used to understand the universe and improve

Stalin, Iosef Vissarionovich: One of the most important leaders of the twentieth century. He relentlessly pursued the goal of making Soviet society socialist and the Soviet Union the leading country in the world. Although a Georgian he became an assimilated Great Russian and remorselessly suppressed non-Russian nationalism.

the lot of men and women. The goals of the rational human being were knowledge, freedom and happiness. The Enlightenment had a revolutionary impact on art, philosophy and politics. Modern science dates from this time. Thinkers set about applying the laws of science to nature and society. The hunt was on for a rational social order. Science would transform the social world and it was taken for granted that the result would be a just and fair social order which would bring happiness to everyone. Science would not only bring a once and for all improvement, it contained the seeds of constant progress. These ideals inspired the French revolutionaries and for the first time men and women became aware that politics could change society. The existing order was not static but potentially dynamic. The revolution, of course, did not give birth to one model but offered a choice. Liberalism, republicanism and the Bonapartist dictatorship all emerged claiming the same parentage. There were left- and right-wing visions of the new order. Revolutionary politics had been born.

The leading Russian revolutionaries were almost obsessed with the course of the French Revolution and saw themselves as continuing the great experiment which had begun in 1789. They were convinced that by learning the lessons of the revolution they would not repeat its mistakes. They would succeed in laying the foundations of a socialist society which would, of course, be a society based on reason. As such, it would be socially just.

Bolsheviks: When the All-Russian Social Democratic Labour Party (RSDRP), founded in 1898, split in 1903, those in the majority became known as Bolsheviks; in October 1917 the Bolshevik or Communist Party seized power.

The French Revolution had based itself on the nation but the **Bolsheviks** narrowed this to the working class. The proletariat would be the bearer of the new order and it would be internationalist. Where Russian workers boldly went, workers in the rest of the world would swiftly follow. There were two reasons for this belief. A single socialist revolution could not survive surrounded by a capitalist sea. More importantly, the new, rational order would prove absolutely irresistible. Reason was bound to triumph. The Bolsheviks were convinced that they had found the keys to the new kingdom of plenty, Marxist class analysis. Their revolution would be a class revolution which would destroy all other classes and sub-classes.

Their bible was the gospel according to Karl Marx. He had married Enlightenment philosophy, epitomised in the writings of Hegel, to French revolutionary politics. Theory and practice were fused to provide cast-iron certainty. Apply his ideas constructively and paradise awaited. The industrial revolutions in England and France had given him the raw materials to fashion his view of the inevitable victory of justice in the world. The wretched, oppressed proletariat was identified as the irresistible force which would smash capitalism and usher in the socialist revolution. Part of Marx's attractiveness was that he presaged a moral and a material revolution. Russia was only just beginning industrialisation in the 1890s so Russian Marxists had little home-grown experience of capitalism. At a time when German Marxism was retreating from the concept of the inevitable violent conflict between workers and capitalists to usher in the dictatorship of the proletariat, Russian Marxists began to defend Marxist orthodoxy passionately. They became the fundamentalists of their day. They viewed the slightest deviation from the master's teachings as putting at risk the inevitability of the kingdom of heaven on earth.

THE BOLSHEVIKS COME TO POWER

The French Revolution came like a bolt from the blue. So did the Russian. The February Revolution, quickly followed by the abdication of Tsar Nicholas II, provided a stage for all the pent-up revolutionary ideas to compete for primacy. Millenarian (period of good government, great happiness and prosperity), utopian (ideal place with perfect social and political system), messianic (inspired by the belief or hope of a Messiah), liberal, conservative, nationalist and a host of other views competed for attention. Nothing was too outlandish in Russia in the spring of 1917. One has to remember that Russia did not experience the Renaissance, the Reformation and the Enlightenment along with the rest of Europe. It was now experiencing all three simultaneously. Scepticism, induced by reason, had not invaded Russia as yet. This is one explanation for the wild extremism of politics at this time. Rational politics was soon swept aside and replaced by emotional politics. The Bolsheviks, inhabiting the kingdom of certainty, soon became the masters of emotional politics. In this new world everything was possible. All one had to do was to believe it was feasible. Everyone (except the bourgeois) could have everything they wanted. This was popular, not populist, politics at its most naked. All this was not peculiarly Russian. It flowed from the traditions of the Enlightenment and the French Revolution. Russians always want to show Europeans the way ahead. They thought their opportunity had now come.

All Provisional governments were centre–moderate left coalition governments. This led to a situation where they talked endlessly but never acted decisively. All the problems of war, peace, land, nationality and so on were left for the future. The Constituent Assembly, the most democratically elected parliament Russia would have up to that time, would address all the thorny problems. The governments were hopelessly split on two key questions: war and land. The liberals wanted to prosecute and win the war but their socialist partners only wanted to defend Russia. The liberals would not countenance handing land (their land) over to peasants. The socialists wanted the land. While the government fiddled, the peasants seized land. There would have been a revolution in October even without the Bolsheviks. The government was at the end of its tether and the Socialist Revolutionaries, the large peasant party, was poised to play a leading role in reshaping Russia. Then the government committed an act of crass misjudgement. It set out, on 24 October 1917, to close down the Bolshevik presses. It failed and propelled the Bolsheviks to power.

Socialists of all hues expected a socialist coalition government but **Lenin** thought otherwise. He set out to establish a Bolshevik dictatorship. The October seizure of power was not decisive in shaping Bolshevism. The Civil War transformed Lenin's comrades into military fighters and liquidators of opposition. The ebb and flow of the conflict allowed them a hit-and-miss attitude to power. Through experimentation they discovered the most effective way of gaining and retaining control over an area. Militarised socialism was the result. Russia paid a heavy price in blood for this experiment. About 13 million died on the Red and White sides during the Civil War and another 2 million moved abroad.

An army only remains successful if subordinates carry out orders from above to the letter. This became the rule in the Bolshevik Party, the government and indeed all walks of life. Those above issued orders and held their subordinates responsible. They, in turn, issued orders and were held responsible by their superiors. By 1921 the Civil War had been won but the country could not sustain militarisation much longer. The supremely tactical Lenin compromised and retreated from the goal of a rapid move to socialism. Many of his followers felt betrayed. The post-1917 years had seen wild experimentation in all walks of life. Even money was being abolished. The New Economic Policy (**NEP**) was a retreat to a market economy, free trade and a new bourgeoisie. Lenin died in 1924 but had played little or no part in government for the previous two years. The country drifted. Who would seize Lenin's mantle and steer the ship of state back towards socialism? It turned out to be Stalin. Beginning in 1929 he launched a violent, phenomenally ambitious economic modernisation of the country. Forced industrialisation and forced collectivisation transformed the country and a new ruling elite emerged – bureaucrats, engineers, scientists – all those who could contribute much to the building of Russia into the strongest power on earth. Stalin and his élites were nothing if not ambitious. There was logic in this seeming madness. Only when Soviet Russia was the strongest state in the world could it feel secure.

Hand in hand with industrialisation went the expansion of the military economy. Indeed the Soviet Union was being run on a war footing. War was held to be inevitable so the country had to be ready at a moment's notice. Military doctrine included one concept which turned out to be false. When war came it would be fought on the territory of other countries. It was never envisaged that there would be a home front, that Soviet Russia would be invaded.

Lenin, Vladimir Ilich: One of the great political actors of the twentieth century in world politics. Inspired by the Enlightenment vision of a just, harmonious society, he brooked no opposition in his quest for revolution. Stalin was a key aide in 1917 and afterwards Lenin tried to smooth the acrimonious relationship between Stalin and Trotsky.

NEP: New Economic Policy, introduced in March 1921; it brought back the market economy with money again being backed by gold; during NEP peasants could dispose of their produce as they liked; light industry also passed into private hands but heavy engineering, energy and transport stayed in state hands; in practice ended in 1929.

All the efforts and sacrifices turned out to be worth while. The Red Army occupied Berlin in May 1945 and the Soviet Union was second only to the United States as a military power. An empire was added in eastern and south-eastern Europe and when Stalin died, in March 1953, the Soviet Union appeared to be impregnable. The political, economic and social system which drove the Stalin revolution forward is called Stalinism. It was phenomenally successful and eventually a crashing failure. This book is an attempt to understand this incredible phenomenon. Why was it so seemingly strong yet so potentially fragile? Was it essentially Stalin's creation? Could it have come into existence without him? Given the violence and the exploitation of the population in the 1930s why did it not unravel? What kept it going – terror, or a commitment to a better tomorrow? Did Russia's addiction to socialism save Stalin?

The Soviet Union was little studied before 1941. It did not appear to pose a threat to the main capitalist powers. Anyway the 1930s had seen the Great Depression, when it appeared that capitalism might expire. The regeneration of capitalism took two opposing forms: fascism and Roosevelt's New Deal. In both, the state played a major role in shaping the market. Hitler saw communism as his greatest threat and knew that world domination, his goal, could not be achieved without a war against the Soviet Union. German intelligence on the Soviet Union was not particularly good but Berlin realised that war had to come sooner rather than later. As it turned out, Germany waited too long to attack.

The wartime alliance with the Soviet Union was forced upon the British and Americans. They knew little about the Soviet regime and what they knew they did not like. Winston Churchill, the British war leader, always remained an ideological enemy of Soviet socialism. He had been involved in the ill-starred allied intervention in Russia after 1918. The goal, topple the Bolsheviks, had not been attained. As a perceptive politician he realised that Soviet socialism could eventually become a dangerous foe of capitalism. However, Churchill was a statesman and took the view that he would ally himself to the devil if needs demanded. They did in 1941 and he immediately offered Stalin Britain's unconditional support. An alliance was negotiated in 1942 but it was rather distasteful to some British negotiators. One referred to 'bootface' **Molotov**, the Soviet Foreign Minister. Others talked about the 'oriental barbarism' of the Russians.

The Americans had not bothered to establish diplomatic relations with the Soviet Union until 1933. Until then, the Russian watchers were parked in Riga, Latvia. Several of those who were to influence American thinking about the Soviet Union honed their analytical skills in Riga. One of these was George Kennan. They then moved to Moscow and found the atmosphere of distrust and terror not to their liking. Their contacts had a distressing tendency to disappear.

Molotov, Vyacheslav Mikhailovich: Ever faithful to Stalin, 'bootface' Molotov played a major role in foreign affairs and was greatly disliked in the West. He found the Khrushchev era soft because it was not Bolshevik enough, meaning not enough coercion was being used to mould the new society.

APPROACHES TO THE STUDY OF STALINISM

Wartime experience of negotiating with Stalin and his cohorts left indelible marks on the Allies. The pugnacious Churchill thought that he could do deals with Stalin and outsmart the 'wonderful Georgian' (Lenin's phrase). As it turned out, Stalin won almost every trick. The Russians caught on quickly that the perpetually cigar-smoking British Prime Minister could be read like a book. The more frustrated he became the more cigars he smoked. Anthony Eden (Lord Avon), his suave Foreign Minister, did not like rows so always took the line of least resistance with the Soviets. The ailing Roosevelt was never a match for the wily Soviet dictator. The Allies found it very difficult to gauge who made Soviet policy. Stalin was always talking about his colleagues and the need to assuage them. This was because the British and Americans stressed that they could not act unilaterally. Public opinion was also a constraint. Stalin played along with this and pretended he had the same problems. In reality he was the boss and made foreign and defence policy. Very few western analysts picked this up.

Given the experiences of the British and American policy-makers before and during the war it is not surprising that analyses about future moves placed little trust in Soviet conduct and motives. Churchill, in 1944, came up with Operation Unthinkable, the object of which was the 'elimination of Russia'. It involved hundreds of thousands of British and American soldiers, supported by 100,000 rearmed German soldiers, unleashing a surprise attack upon the war-weary Russian ally. The RAF would bomb Soviet cities from northern Europe (Aldrich, 2001: 58). The proposal was soon scotched by Churchill's top military advisers (they were only consulted after it had been drafted) who informed him that such a plan had clearly been drafted in a lunatic asylum.

After the war, the school of thought which emphasised the danger that Soviet communism posed for western democracies became known as the totalitarian (Kotkin, 1995: 2). A basic problem was what to research as the Soviet Union was almost completely closed to academic research. Diplomats were severely restricted in their contacts and even the servants were hand-picked by the **NKVD**, the predecessor of the KGB. Could one actually believe anything which one read in the newspapers? A joke was that there was no *Izvestiya* (news – the government newspaper) in *Pravda* (truth – the Communist Party's newspaper) and no *Pravda* in *Izvestiya*. How did one glean information? One source was the group of Soviet émigrés who had managed to evade the net which had swept so many of their compatriots back to the Soviet Union and to their death. They were quizzed in depth in an attempt to find the hidden or suppressed secrets which would provide an

NKVD: People's Commissariat of Internal Affairs; renamed Ministry of Internal Affairs (MVD) in April 1946.

understanding of the Soviet system. Once debriefed, problems arose about the objectivity of the interviewees. Were they so hostile to the Soviet system that their evidence was too subjective? The Smolensk archives, captured by the Germans and in turn by the Americans, were a major boon. They provided detailed information on the course of Soviet policy in Smolensk **oblast**. Merle Fainsod did a magnificent job and produced a classic account, appropriately entitled *How Russia Is Ruled*.

> **Oblast:** The principal territorial subdivision of a republic.

Eventually the totalitarian school concluded that the system was totally controlled from the top – hence the term totalitarian. All the institutions, all the economy, all means of communications etc. were controlled by Stalin and the Communist Party. Hence there was little else to study besides politics. How did one explain the fact that the regime continued to function – indeed it appeared impregnable? The conclusion reached was that it was all due to repression. Hence the study of the Great Terror of the 1930s became an important subject. Many similarities were drawn between Soviet communism and German fascism. Much excellent work was done but the reason adduced for the continued existence and strength of the Soviet Union remained coercion. This approach was dealt a blow on Stalin's death. The country did not fall apart or even revolt. The **Khrushchev** era produced more fine research but the approach was mainly that of high politics. One fertile source was the history of the Communist Party and its myriad schisms and ferocious infighting. Great names such as Leonard Schapiro, Richard Pipes, Robert Conquest and Hugh Seton-Watson dominated the field.

> **Khrushchev, Nikita Sergeevich:** A rumbustious, intelligent but uneducated party official who was entranced by Stalin. The spell was only broken after Stalin's death and he demolished Stalin's reputation in 1956. Khrushchev was party leader in Ukraine and Moscow and enthusiastically participated in the purges.

The Vietnam War and the 'generation of 1968' took a different route to understanding Stalinism. Self-proclaimed revisionists, led by Sheila Fitzpatrick, rejected the view that the most effective tool for explaining the phenomenon was coercion. They were, in the main, social historians and began researching a much wider range of sources, including archives. They set out to demonstrate that many citizens had accepted and adopted the values of Stalin's Russia. Fitzpatrick devoted great energy and skill to tracing those who benefited from the 'Cultural Revolution' and the educational opportunities it offered. Foremost among these were engineers and managers, indeed the upwardly mobile who benefited and then allied themselves to the system because it had brought them into being.

The generation of 1929, which had seized the chance to study, and were mainly of peasant background, stayed in power until the 1980s. Leonid Brezhnev was one of them and he died in 1982. Indeed it was only the advent of Mikhail Gorbachev, in 1985, which swept aside this cohort. Fitzpatrick regards the Cultural Revolution as ending in 1932 when more orthodox selection criteria for higher education returned. These new élites then settled down and became quite conservative in their attitudes. Bourgeois values were again in vogue. Fitzpatrick never quite makes up her mind whether this new social phenomenon can be labelled socialist or not. Her thoughts bring to mind the work of Nicholas Timasheff who labelled these phenomena the 'Great Retreat' from socialism. **Trotsky's** view that Stalinism represented the 'betrayal' of the revolution is also worth mentioning. The products of Stalin's revolution from above, the new élites supposedly rejected any further radicalism and gradually returned to Russian traditional values. This new middle class was cultured but also technically skilled, an ideal combination to drive forward quickly Stalin's industrialisation programme. The revolution had a social base, the members of which had bourgeois tastes, accepted invasive state control and were loyal to Stalin and the new system. Russia had adopted a stop–go attitude to revolution and socialism. The wild radicalism of the Civil War period (1918–21) gave way to the hiatus of NEP (1921–28). This, in turn, was replaced by socialist utopianism during the first Five-Year Plan (1928–32). Then it ended and traditional Russian values, especially of hierarchy and the dominant role of the state, took over (from 1933 onwards). A revolutionary mentality gave way to a Soviet mentality. Was the new society socialist? Fitzpatrick never comes to any concrete decision. Even Trotsky, at his most corrosively critical, could not bring himself to qualify the Stalinist system as non-socialist.

Moshe Lewin, who had worked on a **kolkhoz** (collective farm) in Kazakstan, brought hands-on expertise to the study of Stalin's new creation (Kotkin, 1995: 4). Starting from basically Trotskyist premises, he roundly condemned the new order as a move away from socialism. The new creation, called the Stalinist system, resulted from the 'degeneration' of the Communist Party into a hierarchical, administrative body which felt it could apply unlimited coercion to achieve its goals. However, the more force it used the more confused the situation became. The consequence of forced collectivisation was that the peasants were driven into the cities but once there 'ruralised' them. They retained their social values (patriarchal, family networks), a rural attitude to work (short bursts followed by periods of inactivity) and time (regular timekeeping was alien to them) and thereby overwhelmed the state. Lewin writes of the 'quicksand society' and the 'demonisation' of the authoritarian political system. The state bureaucratised society but the values of the village predominated. The village exacted its revenge by turning Russia backwards in its quest for modernisation. The attempt to destroy village values, so prevalent in collectivisation, produced confusion and alienation and led to a sense of permanent crisis. The nervousness of the leadership and its fear of instability led to the cruel, elemental violence of the Great Terror. Lewin was in no doubt about whether the Soviet system was socialist or not. He passionately rejected the new order, from a socialist point of view, and saw it as a bastard who had wreaked havoc in Russia. Fitzpatrick and Lewin never entered into debate and, indeed, ignored

Trotsky, Lev Davidovich: The most brilliant speaker and writer of the revolution, he failed as a politician. Trotsky ridiculed Stalin's socialism in one country and typically failed to see its nationalist appeal. He was driven to open opposition in 1927 and exiled in 1928. Stalin's hitman finished him off in Mexico, in 1940.

Kolkhoz: Collective farm; members farmed the land as a cooperative but in reality had little say in what was to be produced; this was laid down in the annual state plan. Under Stalin payment was based on the number of labour days worked.

one another's work in public and in print. However, their work does reveal some similar tendencies. Both see the 1930s as a reversal of the revolution. For Lewin, NEP was a false path which then led to forced industrialisation and collectivisation. For Fitzpatrick, the end of the Cultural Revolution, in 1932, called a halt to the revolutionary impulse of socialism. Just like the totalitarian approach, these two vistas have now run their course.

Remarkable changes occurred in the 1990s. The collapse of the Soviet Union ended the decades-long separation of Russian and Soviet scholarship from western studies of the largest country in the world. The way was open for the integration of Russian scholars, especially the younger generation, into the mainstream scholarly community. Even more exciting, it opened up Soviet archives to historians and permitted anthropologists, sociologists, political scientists and even economists to engage in on-the-spot research and inundate themselves in public opinion-polling and oral testimony.

Social history gave way to cultural studies. Social theory became a hot subject and the French Michel Foucault and Jacques Derrida and the German Jürgen Habermas exerted considerable influence. The excitement about theory and the opening of the archives came together to produce studies framed by theory but substantiated by empirical archival research. Stalinism became the centre of the new studies. It represented a mystery, an extraordinary political, economic, social and cultural experiment which had captured the imagination of millions inside and outside the Soviet Union, was then exported to eastern and south-eastern Europe, was adopted by the Chinese after 1949 and by other new communist states and seemed to be the wave of the future. This was the façade but what was the reality? Eventually the whole system collapsed, to quote Marx, under its own contradictions. Born of the Enlightenment, Stalinism was exported to Asia and Africa. Was it bound to fail because it was Europocentric or was it a universal paradigm? This question cannot be answered yet and will probably have to wait until China becomes a post-Marxist state.

Cultural studies are an attempt to understand the processes at work from below. Hence everyday discourse, ritual and practices are very relevant. Diaries and oral testimony provide valuable insights. Examining national and social identity, the world of informers, the personal battles to become accepted in the new society, the pull of consumption, the terror and the battle to understand the logic behind it, the desire of people to remain individuals and not to be treated as part of the mass – all these and more now delight the interested reader.

Cultural studies have already produced a host of important and influential research. Sarah Davies on social identity, Jochen Hellbeck on a diary, Alexei Kojevnikov on the battles within the scientific community and how they affected science policy, Yuri Slezkine on ethnic particularism and Terry

Martin on a scribed nationality, to name only a few, have mined deep in Soviet archives. Jeffrey Brooks' book on Soviet public culture, *Thank You, Comrade Stalin! Soviet Public Culture from Revolution to Cold War*, provides valuable insights.

Another outstanding product of the influence of social theory (Foucault) is Stephen Kotkin's *Magnetic Mountain*, about the building of the industrial city of Magnitogorsk. His subtitle is: *Stalinism as a Civilization*. He does not anguish over whether Stalinist society was socialist or not. Those in Magnitogorsk certainly thought it was and this view was overwhelmingly held throughout the country. Calling Stalinism a civilisation is a bold move and reveals how far Soviet studies have come since the heyday of the totalitarian school. The great warhorses of that era would turn in their graves at the suggestion that Stalinism was a new civilisation. One reason for taking a more relaxed attitude to Stalinism and chronicling its successes (whatever one thinks about the goals and the methods deployed) is that no one fears Stalinism any more. It has failed everywhere except perhaps in North Korea. Kotkin's brilliant work allows the reader to follow the twists and turns of policy and understand how individuals coped by skilfully exploiting the system. They learnt to speak Bolshevik. Survival was the top priority and even those at the top could not feel safe. The regime was adept at turning public anger at low living standards against the bosses of Magnitogorsk who lived in luxury. Despite the exploitation and the terror people still thought they were building socialism, guided by the wise father of the nation, Stalin. The hope of a better socialist tomorrow kept them going. Perhaps those living in hell have to believe in heaven in order to remain sane and not fall into the pit of despair and depression.

Several valuable works on high politics, economics, demography and foreign and military policy have also appeared since the collapse of the Soviet Union. However, they are mainly concerned about how the system functioned and the decision-making process. The Stalinist soul, nevertheless, can only be examined through cultural, literary and social studies. The most exciting discoveries about the Stalin period will probably come through these endeavours.

2

The Russian Revolution and the Soviet State, 1917–29

Russia was addicted to socialism. In the years before the revolution in 1917 there was much speculation about the coming of a new era when the Tsar and his system would be swept away. The overwhelming view was that this would usher in a new age of justice and happiness. Those who questioned the coming utopia were dismissed as apologists of Tsarism. So when the imperial Russian state collapsed and the Tsar departed, the key question was how quickly Russia could move towards socialism. Since socialism was based on democracy and popular sovereignty, everyone with a grievance (almost the whole population) began organising councils, committees and groups, ready to change the world they lived in for the better. Thousands of local soviets or councils (to take control of local government), factory committees (to take over the factories), army committees (to turn it into a people's army), village assemblies, Red Guards, trade unions, nationality and religious organisations, cultural and educational clubs, women's and youth organisations, officers' and industrialists' associations, householders' associations, economic cooperatives and many others (Wade, 2000: 283–4) came into being. One of the reasons for this welter of cooperative activity was the important role the family and the extended family played in Russian society. It was natural for Russians to set up networks of interested persons. It was a society based on personal contacts and self-help.

The massive task facing the Provisional government (all governments before October 1917, and even the first **Soviet**, were provisional or temporary – until the Constituent Assembly met) was how to cooperate with the new organisations, gain authority over them, respond to their aspirations and implement some of their demands. Another major problem was that the February Revolution swept away the parties of the right and left the liberals as the right. Facing them were the socialists on the left. There was nothing else in between. A coalition government had to be composed of liberals and

Soviet: Name of state – Soviet Union; also elected council.

Moderate socialists: Mensheviks and right Social Revolutionaries; they were called moderate to contrast them with the radical Bolsheviks.

Mensheviks: When the All-Russian Social Democratic Labour Party (RSDRP), founded in 1898, split in 1903, those in the minority became known as Mensheviks; in October 1917 the Mensheviks opposed the Bolshevik seizure of power since they believed that Russia was not ready for socialism.

SRs: Socialist Revolutionaries; the SRs constituted an agrarian socialist party; they had great support among the peasants since they advocated the handing over of the land to the peasants; the SR parties were banned in the early 1920s.

socialists. Again the socialists were split three ways: **moderate socialists** (**Mensheviks** or Marxist social democrats), Socialist Revolutionaries or **SRs** (agrarian non-Marxist socialists) and the Bolsheviks (left-wing Marxist socialists).

The Kadets, the liberals, were also split. The right wing, of which the leading figure was Pavel Milyukov, wanted to continue the war but opposed the influence of the Petrograd soviet. The other group favoured working with the moderate socialists in the Petrograd soviet and attempting to find a way out of the war. Mensheviks and SRs dominated the Petrograd and Moscow soviets and most others throughout the country until September 1917. Their policy was labelled 'revolutionary defensism' and consisted of pushing for peace but at the same time defending Russia from attack. This was popular among soldiers. They also cooperated with the government in the interim period before the convocation of the Constituent Assembly. The leaders of the soviets and the government all shared common values. They were representatives of the Russian educated, cultured class, familiar with European languages and culture. By the summer the key politician was Aleksandr Kerensky. Nominally an SR, he was middle class and moderate and was almost indistinguishable from the left wing of the liberals. He became the perfect link man.

A radical left-bloc gradually emerged to challenge the consensual politics of the moderate elites. It consisted of Bolsheviks, left SRs, Menshevik-Internationalists, anarchists and others who demanded an all-socialist government based on the soviets. They became the main beneficiaries of the failure of the Provisional government to resolve the major problems of the time. With pressure from the left the soviet members of the Provisional government became more radical in their demands and this ensured conflict between socialists and liberals which continued until October. Two centres of power had emerged, the government and the Petrograd soviet. This dichotomy was mirrored throughout society: workers against bosses, soldiers against officers, and peasants against landlords. It was us against them, those below against those above. As the government's authority waned, so the influence of the soviets and locals organisations grew. The problem facing the divided government was that much of the country was beyond its control and most of the demands of the population could not be met. Non-Russians became strident in their demands for autonomy. Russia was facing dissolution.

The hopes for a peace conference faded as Russia's allies were determined to fight the war to a victorious conclusion. This bad news was compounded by the bad decision to launch an attack on the Germans and Austrians. Predictably it was a disaster and turned many soldiers and socialists against the government. The massive demonstrations against the failed offensive – called the July Days – could have toppled the government and transferred power to the soviets. However, the moderate socialists did not want power and the left-bloc was not popular enough to take power. The Bolsheviks did attempt at the end to take power but failed.

The final nail in the coffin of the Provisional government was the Kornilov Affair, in August. Timed to coincide with the demi-anniversary of the February Revolution, the object was to use the army to put down the Petrograd soviet. The attack on Petrograd, which was prevented, forced the soviet to set up its own military wing, the Military Revolutionary Committee, and weapons were handed out which were never returned. An armed uprising was now feasible. The radical left now had a winning slogan: All Power to the Soviets. By September they were in the majority not only in the soviets but in many other social organisations. They had great popular appeal: they promised everything people wanted. People wanted to believe them.

Everyone now waited for the Bolsheviks and their allies to attempt to seize power. The expected move was merely a matter of timing. Kerensky was nonchalant and foolishly confident of crushing the Bolsheviks. Moderate socialists were dismayed as they expected the Bolshevik violence to lead to a right-wing dictatorship. This would provoke civil war. Lenin and Trotsky had to wait for a pretext. Soldiers would only come out in defence of the Petrograd soviet and the upcoming **Congress** of Soviets. They would not act as a cat's paw for a Bolshevik seizure of power. Kerensky, again acting foolishly, provided the pretext by ordering the closure of Bolshevik presses on 24 October. Now the soldiers would act as defenders of the revolution. The Bolsheviks were lucky in that the opening of the Congress of Soviets had been put back from 20 October to 25 October because not enough delegates had arrived in Petrograd. When it did convene on 25 October moderate socialists walked out in protest at the street violence orchestrated by the Bolsheviks. Had the Congress convened on 20 October there would have been no walk-out and the moderate socialists would have been in a majority. The history of Russia, Europe and the rest of the world could have turned out differently. The transfer of power to the soviets had, to all intents and purposes, already taken place by 20 October. The understanding was that a pan-socialist government would emerge and rule by consensus. The Bolsheviks skilfully exploited their luck and turned a transfer of power to the soviets into a transfer of power to themselves. Unless the Bolsheviks made concessions, Russia was heading for civil war. This became inevitable after the Bolsheviks dispersed the Constituent Assembly, after one day's deliberations, on 19 January 1918. The Bolsheviks had polled only 22.5 per cent of the national vote in contrast to the Socialist Revolutionaries' 39.5 per cent. To cut down the numbers of the opposition, the liberal party (Kadets) was proscribed in December 1917, thus ensuring that its delegates could not

Congress: Most important meeting of party, soviet, trade union or other organisation; at a congress the Communist Party reviewed its past record and laid down goals for the future; a new Central Committee was elected and it, in turn, elected a new Politburo and Secretariat.

attend. Since the SRs stayed and did not walk out there was no way Lenin could manipulate the vote to obtain a Bolshevik majority. To ensure that the Assembly could not reconvene elsewhere, he had many of the delegates arrested. He gambled that the voters would not rise up in support of the Assembly. The few who did were fired upon. He took an enormous risk but got away with it.

THE OCTOBER REVOLUTION

To the exultant Lenin the chief task after the October Revolution was the building of the 'proletarian socialist state'. However, the proletariat or working class was numerically very small (about 10 per cent of the population in 1917), there were many interpretations of socialism, and Lenin himself had declared in his *State and Revolution*, written in exile in August 1917: 'So long as the state exists there can be no freedom. When freedom exists there will be no state.' The early decrees of the Council of People's Commissars (**Sovnarkom**) did not spell out what the Bolsheviks understood by socialism and by the state. They were mainly devoted to institutionalising the gains of the various segments of the population which welcomed the removal of the Provisional government. October was a Soviet revolution, a proletarian revolution, a peasant revolution and a national revolution. It was Soviet since the Bolsheviks, on taking power, had handed it over to the IInd All-Russian Congress of Soviets of Workers' and Soldiers' Deputies. This had a Bolshevik majority and passed two important decrees (one concerning the need for an immediate peace and the other dealing with land tenure), set up *Sovnarkom*, and elected an All-Russian Central Executive Committee (**CEC**) which was to act in the name of the Congress when the latter was not in session (Carr, 1979: 14). The revolution was proletarian since workers' control was instituted in industry and the working class expected that they would run the economy and be the dominant class in the state. It was a peasant revolution in that it abolished the private ownership of land, and handed over the landlords' estates to the peasants. Land could henceforth be cultivated only by those who worked it themselves; there was to be no buying, selling or leasing of land or hiring of labour. It was also a national revolution because it affected over half the population and promised non-Russians national self-determination. This implied that they could secede from the new Soviet Russian state if they so desired. When the Russian Soviet Republic was set up by the IIIrd All-Russian Congress of Soviets in January 1918 it was proclaimed as a 'free union of free nations, as a federation of Soviet national republics'.

Sovnarkom: The Council of People's Commissars; the government of Soviet Russia and later of the USSR; it was appointed by the IInd Congress of Soviets in October 1917 and was to be subordinate to it but soon proved stronger; it was the dominant body in the state while Lenin was well, but it was superseded by the Politburo in 1922.

CEC: All-Russian Central Executive Committee of the soviets; the body which acted in the name of the Congress of Soviets when that body was not in session; theoretically, it was the supreme organ in the state but it rapidly lost power to *Sovnarkom* after December 1917.

Lenin accepted that Soviet Russia could not exist on its own, nor could it grow into a socialist state on its own. The Bolsheviks hoped that the spark of the October Revolution would ignite the flame of the international socialist revolution. This in turn would set the whole capitalist world ablaze and lead to socialism replacing capitalism as the dominant force on the stage of history.

However, Soviet Russia had inherited an unwanted legacy – war against imperial Germany and its allies. Soviet Russian sought desperately to end the war but its appeals to the belligerent nations went unheeded. The western Allies were appalled by the Soviet desire for a unilateral peace in the east, by the government's repudiation of Tsarist debts and by the call for worldwide revolution. Germany would only conclude peace on its terms. The issue of war or peace split the Central Committee (**CC**) of the Communist Party in three factions. Lenin, ever the realist, wanted peace at any price. He was well aware that the Reds had no army; the old army had disintegrated as the soldiers left the front to claim their share of the land. The **left communists**, led by **Bukharin**, wanted revolutionary war. To them appeals to the western Allies for aid or for the conclusion of a peace treaty with Germany were tantamount to the betrayal of the international working-class movement. The left communists believed that a revolutionary war would fire workers and peasants for the cause and so lead to the formation of a new army. Trotsky hit on a third solution, neither war nor peace. He thought that the German army was not capable of launching a new offensive, hence all that Soviet Russia had to do was to sit it out until the socialist revolution in Germany swept away the Kaiser. Unfortunately, Trotsky's assessment of German military might was totally incorrect and the German forces moved forward at will – indeed they could have occupied the whole of the country had they so desired. However, the German government calculated that it stood to gain more by reaching a negotiated settlement and since Lenin's faction had gained a majority in the CC a peace treaty was signed at **Brest-Litovsk** on 3 March 1918. The left communists' conviction that such a move was a mistake was mirrored by some officials in the German foreign ministry who would have preferred Germany not to have recognised Soviet Russia. This would have given Germany a free hand, since as far as Berlin was concerned Soviet Russia did not exist in international law.

Peace with Germany did not mean that the danger of an armed overthrow of Bolshevik power had disappeared. On 23 February 1918 – even before Brest-Litovsk – the Red Army was founded, not to carry revolution beyond the frontiers of Soviet Russia, but to defend the gains of the revolution at home. Its moving spirit was Trotsky and he was to fashion it into a very competent fighting force. A threat to Bolshevik power materialised in the north, where the British occupied the port of Murmansk in June 1918 to ensure that

CC: Central Committee of the Communist Party; this organisation acted in the name of the Party Congress when the latter was not in session; it contained all the important party officials, government ministers, leading army and naval personnel, key ambassadors, etc.

Left communists: Bukharin was the leader of this group on the Central Committee (October 1917–18); they favoured the immediate introduction of socialism and a revolutionary war against imperial Germany. Lenin wanted a slow march to socialism and peace with Berlin; he eventually won over a majority of the Central Committee.

Bukharin, Nikolai Ivanovich: In Lenin's phrase, the 'darling of the party', Bukharin was a sophisticated, urban intellectual who was a major economic theorist but, politically, was no match for Stalin. He was associated with the right and a slow transition to socialism. Victim of a Show Trial.

Brest-Litovsk: Brest-Litovsk Treaty with Germany, March 1918, recognised Soviet Russia in international law; fulfilled the Bolshevik pledge to bring peace; revealed how split the Bolshevik leadership could be on a major issue.

the munitions there did not fall into German hands. Soon Italian, American and Serbian troops arrived as well. In the east the Czech Legion, formed of ex-prisoners of war on their way to Vladivostok to be shipped to France, seized part of the Trans-Siberian Railway. In the south there were various 'White' armies forming and Ukraine was still under German control.

The collapse of imperial Germany, the armistice of 11 November 1918, the seizure of power by revolutionaries in Bavaria and Hungary, and the prospect of the whole of Germany going socialist fired the enthusiasm of the Bolsheviks and nourished their belief that the current of history was flowing in their direction. However, the capitalist powers resolved to dam it and this led to their intervention on the side of the Whites during the Civil War. Yet such was the war-weariness and home-sickness of the Interventionist forces that they rarely fired a shot in anger at the Bolsheviks, though considerable war material and diplomatic support was extended to the Whites. By the end of 1919 all foreign troops, except some American and Japanese units in Vladivostok and some British in Crimea, had departed for home. The Americans were later to force the Japanese to abandon their position, thus facilitating Soviet control over the Far East.

Therefore 1919 was the turning point. At one time during that year it appeared that with White troops under Admiral Kolchak moving westwards from Siberia, others commanded by General Denikin moving up from Ukraine and penetrating to Orel (about 300 kilometres south-west of Moscow, the new capital), and General Yudenich poised outside Petrograd, the tables were about to be turned on the Reds. Nevertheless the Whites failed to score a decisive victory and disintegrated quickly thereafter.

To Lenin, Europe in 1919 was pregnant with revolution. In his 'April Theses', proclaimed on his return to Petrograd from exile in Switzerland in 1917, he had proposed the foundation of a new International. This was to replace the Second International which he regarded as having betrayed the working class by supporting war in 1914. The founding meeting of the Communist International (**Comintern**) took place in Moscow in March 1919 but could only muster 52 delegates, many of them resident in Soviet Russia. It was the second Congress, convened in Petrograd on 19 July 1920 and later moved to Moscow, which was decisive. Over 200 delegates were present and they passed the 21 conditions of membership drafted by Lenin. All parties wishing to join the Comintern had to be called communist parties and break with social democracy. Democratic centralism was to be practised. Their first loyalty was to be to Soviet Russia and they were to give uncondi-tional aid to any Soviet republic. All resolutions of the Executive Committee of the Communist International were to be binding. On the face of it an international organisation had come into being, the goal of which was to promote world socialist revolution. In reality, the true beneficiary was the

Comintern: Communist International; interna-tional communist organ-isation established in 1919 and disbanded in 1943.

All-Russian Communist Party (**RCP**). The failure of socialists elsewhere to seize and hold power and the fact that the second Congress met at a time when the Red Army was routing the Poles, who had invaded Ukraine in April 1920, reinforced the dominance of the RCP. Whereas at the first Congress the Bolsheviks expected Berlin to become the socialist capital of Europe, in 1920 Moscow was beginning to take on this role.

The victorious Reds faced a dilemma when they reached the Polish frontier: should they stop and sign an armistice or should they continue and carry revolution to the centre of Europe? Lenin had no doubts, but Trotsky did not share his optimism. The Polish leader Pilsudski called for a national uprising and the workers rallied to the defence of their fatherland. They shared their compatriots' view of the invading army as the Russian bear, hungry once again for Polish territory, and not as the liberating arm of the Third International. The 'miracle of the Vistula' (the Polish victory) was due mostly to Polish resistance but a contributory factor was the lack of coordination in Red Army ranks, for which Stalin must take some of the blame. An armistice was signed on 12 October 1920, shifting the frontier considerably further to the east of the old one, the Curzon line. The peace treaty was concluded at Riga on 18 March 1921.

After their defeat at Warsaw, the communists changed some of their attitudes. There was plainly not going to be a revolution in the west and the lack of enthusiasm displayed by the Polish workers towards the extension of Soviet power was probably shared by the rest of the European working class. Until August 1920 the Bolsheviks had paid little attention to frontiers: theirs was a state in constant flux. Now it was of paramount importance to stake out the frontiers of the new order. The People's Commissariat of Foreign Affairs suddenly became important as the communists sought to conclude treaties with all contiguous states. National self-determination had resulted in Finland, Latvia, Lithuania, Estonia and Poland slipping away. Lenin was taken aback by the number of nationalities which were trying to leave, first and foremost Ukraine and Georgia. Did national self-determination mean that the entire population of a territory had the right to decide whether to remain an integral part of Soviet Russia? Many Bolsheviks heartily disagreed with the whole policy and wanted to restrict the decision to workers. 'No', said Lenin, 'this would mean workers' self-determination and not national self-determination.' However, Lenin postulated three stages. As long as the state was at the pre-bourgeois stage of development the whole population could decide and the nation could secede. After the bourgeois revolution a socialist republic would be set up by the workers in the part of the country they dominated. Finally, when its Communist Party felt strong enough, the socialist republic could apply for admission to the Soviet Russian federal state. This was the theory, but in practice the interests of the Soviet state took

RCP: All-Russian Communist Party (Bolsheviks) 1918–25; formerly All-Russian Social Democratic Labour Party (RSDRP) 1898–1918; renamed All-Union Communist Party (Bolsheviks) 1925–52; renamed Communist Party of the Soviet Union (CPSU) 1952–91.

precedence. Moscow needed the industrial and agrarian riches of Ukraine, it could not tolerate a Menshevik-ruled Georgia, and if other nationalities were permitted to secede they might join the camp of the adversary.

Did Soviet Russia see itself as a revolutionary base or as a state? Liberal attitudes towards the question of national self-determination prevailed as long as the former assumption held sway, but by late 1920 it was apparent that the latter view had taken over.

STATE CAPITALISM AND WAR COMMUNISM

Sovnarkom, headed by Lenin, was subordinate to the CEC. All significant decrees were to be submitted to the CEC for its approval. However, whereas *Sovnarkom* met daily and sometimes twice a day, the CEC met only five times during the first ten days of its existence and then less frequently. This led to more and more legislation bypassing the CEC. During the first year of Soviet power only 68 decrees out of a total of 480 were placed before the CEC. The key role in this process was played by Yakov Sverdlov. A close confidant of Lenin, he became chairman of the CEC on 21 November 1917. As the **Presidium** (the ruling group) of the CEC became more powerful, Sverdlov was able to restrict debate in the full CEC. He was instrumental in getting the CEC to accept the terms of the Brest-Litovsk Treaty. This decision led to the left Socialist Revolutionaries (SRs) breaking with the Bolsheviks. They also abandoned their government posts (which they had held since December 1917) and joined the opposition. Blyumkin, a left SR, assassinated von Mirbach, the German ambassador, in an attempt to rekindle the fires of war with imperial Germany.

The Bolsheviks were now on their own and Sverdlov needed all his skill to dam the flood of opposition. The Presidium increasingly dictated to the CEC and critics were simply not given the floor. In June 1918 Mensheviks and most SRs (moderate socialists) were accused of counter-revolutionary activities and removed from the CEC and provincial soviets. Hence by the summer of 1918 the Bolsheviks held full sway in the supreme Soviet organisation.

The soviets and not the Communist Party were the key institution until the summer of 1918. This was due to the fact that the Bolsheviks were ill-prepared for local government, and there was practically no Communist Party network in the countryside. The best party men went to work in the soviets, since that was where power lay. Yet the sheer profusion of soviets was their undoing. They could hardly resist Bolshevik efforts to amalgamate them

Presidium: Inner council or cabinet, hence supreme body; the Politburo of the Communist Party was also known as the Presidium between 1952 and 1966.

– workers', peasants' and soldiers' soviets were fused into single units. When Bolshevik behaviour became blatantly partisan, Mensheviks and SR deputies would walk out, thus permitting the communists to replace the moderates with their own nominees. By the time the moderate socialists realised that this tactic was self-defeating it was too late to remedy the situation. The Bolsheviks' aim was to centralise decision making in the soviets and by the summer of 1918 they were not far from their goal, thanks to the activities of Yakov Sverdlov in Moscow and communists at the local level. The CC of the Communist Party was undecided about what economic policy to adopt after October. Lenin was well aware that Russian industrial development was in its infancy and that there were only pockets of advanced technology. The banking and financial services sector had been quite advanced in 1914 but was hampered by the backwardness of society. The egalitarian tradition of the countryside did not take easily to active money and credit. When the Bolsheviks took over, the economy was heading for collapse and inflation had ravaged the rouble. Lenin, like Trotsky, knew that workers were quite incapable of running the economy and wanted to keep industry going under its own management. The workers could be limited to supervising production. On the other hand, Bukharin and Preobrazhensky, the leading left communists, wanted the march to socialism to begin immediately. In many cases the decision was made by workers who simply took over the factories when they could and demanded that the CC nationalise them. This move was often successful on the periphery but the CC could frustrate it in the industrial heartland. However, on 28 June 1918, wholesale nationalisation was decreed. This was partly in response to these wildcat moves, but also to the approaching Civil War and to the risk that the factories might be acquired by foreign, especially German, interests. The Supreme Council of the National Economy (**VSNKh**), set up in December 1917, now had a real task on its hands. The nationalisation decree can be seen as the end of the phase of **state capitalism** and the beginning of **war communism**.

Workers' control, official Bolshevik policy as of 27 November 1917, was effected through factory committees. As the proletariat was further to the left than Lenin there were constant clashes on what workers' control actually meant. The main weakness of the factory committee was that it was restricted to one factory, but there was an All-Russian Council of Factory Committees; it in turn, however, recognised the trade unions as superior organs.

By early 1918 the Bolsheviks were in a leading position in the main industrial trade unions after successfully outmanoeuvring the Mensheviks. The latter had found themselves heading key trade unions in October 1917 – the union controlling the railways and the telegraph for instance – but their authority was gradually undermined by such tactics as the setting up of an alternative trade union which was immediately recognised by the government.

VSNKh (*Vesenkha*): Supreme Council of the National Economy; founded December 1917 and responsible for the whole economy and state finances; as of June 1918 it became in effect the commissariat of nationalised industry; in 1924 a VSNKh was created in each republic and made responsible for industry there.

State capitalism: The economic order in existence between October 1917 and June 1918.

War communism: The economic order in existence between June 1918 and March 1921.

With food desperately short, ration cards were handed out only to members of the approved union.

Even with trade unions controlled on paper by the Bolsheviks, it did not follow that they would carry out Lenin's directives. A.G. Shlyapnikov, the first Bolshevik Commissar for Labour, felt strongly that the unions should run the economy, and indeed this found its way into party resolutions. However, the CC and *Sovnarkom* thought that running the economy was one of their duties. Under state capitalism trade unions just about held their own, but the rigours of war communism were such that they changed from organs representing labour to organs representing management. Their chief task was to instil discipline and raise labour productivity. This was a formidable undertaking as cold, hunger and disease disillusioned and decimated the labour force. The cities emptied, Petrograd and Moscow lost half their population, and the best cadres were sent to the front. So desperate was the situation that the IXth Party Congress decided in April 1920 that non-communist specialists were to be employed, one-man management at the factory level was to take over, and party and trade union committees were to be nominated from above and not elected from below. Things were bleak indeed.

A major reason for the débâcle was that the Bolsheviks did not control the most essential strategic product, food. The peasants were very gratified that the Bolsheviks had enacted the land decree (which had been SR policy) on the morrow of the revolution. The peasant land committees thereupon parcelled out among their members estates previously belonging to the crown, the church, the monasteries and private non-peasant owners. This led to the disappearance of the big farms which had produced food for the market.

Lenin had envisaged model or state farms being set up on the confiscated estates, with soviets of poor peasants as the natural allies of the Bolsheviks in the rural areas, but in practice neither the model farms nor the soviets of poor peasants came into being.

The land decree had been a tactical move to keep the countryside quiet while the Bolsheviks consolidated their position in the cities. It achieved this in the short run, but by the summer of 1918 the peasant had very little incentive to sell his surplus production to the state organs since the rouble, at home and abroad, was worth little more than the paper it was printed on. In order to feed the cities and the Red Army the Bolsheviks therefore set up committees of poor peasants, **kombedy**, on 11 June 1918, with orders to 'extract grain surpluses from **kulaks** and rich people'. It was intended that most of the surplus would go to the state, and the peasants were promised 'goods of prime necessity and agricultural implements'. This system did not work: the peasants were primarily concerned with looking after their own interests and still harboured a deep suspicion of central authority. This led to

Kombedy: Committees of poor peasants; established by the Soviet government in June 1918 to seize grain from richer peasants who held surpluses; the state was to get most of grain (to feed cities) but in fact received little. In November 1918 there were 122,000 *kombedy* but in the same month all were disbanded.

Kulak: Peasants were divided into poor, middle and rich by the Bolsheviks; the poor peasant did not have enough land to live off, the middle peasant did, and the rich peasant had enough to produce a surplus; in west-European terms the *kulak* would have been classified as a modestly well-off farmer.

the formation of **workers' detachments**, composed of urban workers who did bring in the grain, the main reason being that they had machine guns to underline their authority.

The policy of favouring the poor peasant against the middle and rich peasants or *kulaks* was abandoned in December 1918, when the state sided with the middle peasant against the *kulak*, but it was all to no avail. The peasants sowed less and consumed more; villages denied the Red Army entrance, soviets voted themselves out of Soviet Russia and others killed their communist members. The honeymoon with the Bolsheviks was over; the peasants had turned their backs on Marxism.

Sovnarkom quickly established itself as the key decision-making body after the revolution. However by 1921–22 the **Politburo** of the CC of the Communist Party had taken over. This was a development which Lenin viewed with some dismay, and both he and Trotsky favoured the top party organ divesting itself of some of its administrative duties. This never came about, however, mainly due to Lenin's ill-health and to the inept tactics adopted by Trotsky.

Lenin was fascinated by administrative detail and devoted more attention to government than to party affairs. The Bolshevik leader, on becoming prime minister, took over the existing structure of government, and the areas of competence assigned to the various **commissars** he appointed were quite traditional. This inevitably led to many practices of the old society being adopted by the new. As a Marxist, Lenin regarded control of the institutions as of paramount importance, not their structure. The demarcation line between the government, composed of Bolsheviks, and the party was always fuzzy. Matters were made worse by the right of every commissar to appeal to the CC. Stalin took a radically different view from Lenin and Trotsky about the role of *Sovnarkom* and, although he was himself a commissar, he gave the party primacy over the governmental bureaucracy. One of the contributory factors in the rise of the party bureaucracy was its power to make appointments not only within the party but also in government, trade unions and soviets. Such was the pressure of work that the practice developed of commissars delegating some of their functions to deputies. This inevitably affected the standing of *Sovnarkom*: it never developed into a cabinet. When Lenin fell ill his deputies waited for him to recover or passed matters on to the Politburo. It was clear that it was only Lenin who invested *Sovnarkom* with its authority.

The destruction of the previous ruling strata produced a void between the state and the workers and peasants. Lenin's daring in taking on the task of promoting socialism from above, in an economically and educationally backward state, meant that there was grave danger of inertia, anarchy and counter-revolution surfacing. The Bolsheviks were wholly unprepared for

Workers' or food requisition detachments: Established in August 1918; they were highly successful in requisitioning grain since they were composed of workers who desperately needed the food for their urban families and the army and because they had machine guns. Forced requisitioning lasted until March 1921.

Politburo: Political Bureau of the CC; key decision-making body of the Communist Party; established in 1919; prior to that the Central Committee was the most significant body; called the Presidium between 1952 and 1966.

Commissar: (a) Government minister; (b) official representing party, government or soviet.

their task and lacked the experience and technical expertise to function effectively. The Communist Party inevitably found itself assuming the management of the state, since government and local soviet agencies had their own ideas about what policies should be implemented. The peasantry, the real winners in 1917, were satisfied and wanted room to develop their own rural culture. This collided head on with the goal of the Bolsheviks, to build socialism. The Bolsheviks were very astute at accumulating authority, the right to take decisions, but they discovered that their power, the ability to implement their policies, was constrained. It was almost inevitable that they would resort to authoritarianism and physical coercion if they wished to retain control of Russia.

It was the Civil War which concentrated power in the hands of the party: the desperate political, economic and military situation meant that all resources had to be brought under central control. Democracy was the first casualty as iron discipline descended on the home front. Military methods became legitimate if they achieved results. Such was the dearth of potential officials that local leaders called on Moscow to send them reliable men. The person in the party **Secretariat** who was responsible for finding and dispatching them was Stalin; he knew more than anyone else about party cadres and he was keenly aware of the significance of this information. He built up a file which was locked away and to which even his secretary did not have automatic access.

Secretariat: The administrative centre of the Communist Party; its key officials were called secretaries and the leading one Secretary-General (1922–53, 1966–) or First Secretary (1953–66); only from 1929 was the Secretary-General the leader of the Soviet Union.

Dissent was endemic in the CC and the Politburo. The latter contained men of great ability and education, such as Lenin, Trotsky and Bukharin, but they split on practically every major question. One issue which almost tore the party asunder was Trotsky's plan to impose military discipline on workers in order to hasten reconstruction. This was eloquent testimony to the gulf which existed between the Bolsheviks and the proletariat. After all, the Bolsheviks claimed to be the avant-garde of the working class. It became a burning question in late 1920 when the Civil War had been won; it was only resolved at the Xth Party Congress in March 1921, when war communism was abandoned and the New Economic Policy (NEP) was adopted. The main reason for the adoption of NEP was the revolt of the countryside against requisitioning. In Samara the SRs set up their own republic. Unless concessions were made there was a risk that the cities would go hungry. The Congress was a fateful one. During it the unthinkable occurred: sailors at Kronstadt, the reddest of the red, revolted and demanded, among other things, free elections to the soviet; the uprising was suppressed in rivers of blood and the chastened delegates turned inwards on themselves. Two opposition groups – the Workers' Opposition, led by Shlyapnikov, which wanted to return to the goals of October, with the trade unions running industry; and the Democratic Centralists, who wanted more democracy in the party – were swept aside. Factionalism was banned; only the whole party could discuss an issue, not groups or platforms; once a party decision had been taken absolute obedience to it had to be observed. Expulsion from the party could be the punishment for infringing this rule and this applied even to members of the CC (although this was kept secret until 1924).

This momentous move, seen by Lenin as temporary until the situation stabilised, introduced Politburo infallibility. Only by adopting such measures, thought Lenin, would the party be prevailed upon to accept NEP.

NEP

NEP was a step backwards for the party. Although the leadership came to like the new policy, the rank and file never came to terms with it. Large-scale industry and public services remained nationalised and all foreign trade was still conducted by the state. It was mainly light industry which passed into the hands of the NEP men. Soviet Russia desperately needed foreign capital and was fully aware of its technological backwardness. The terrible famine of 1921–22 was the legacy of war communism, but afterwards agriculture quickly found its feet again as the peasant was allowed to sell to whomever he chose. The tax in kind, payment in grain, was introduced in March 1921, but this gave way to money taxes as the rouble stabilised and the market reasserted itself.

The Bolsheviks found themselves in the extraordinary position of having to rely on the countryside for survival. Lenin declared that only the 'link with the peasants' could 'save the socialist revolution in Russia until revolution had occurred in other countries'. Agricultural products were in great demand in 1922 and this pushed prices up, but the peasant was not satisfied with the range of industrial goods on offer and refused to buy. Workers lost their jobs; soon over a million were unemployed. In order to survive, the industrial trusts (groups of enterprises producing similar products) resorted to price-fixing and so successful were they that by October 1923 the situation had been reversed with a vengeance. Trotsky dubbed it the 'scissors' crisis' – the blades of agricultural and industrial prices looked like scissors – and the party became alarmed at the enormous fluctuations in prices. Before it could speak on the subject, however, Trotsky launched a scathing attack on economic policy. This was followed by a letter signed by 46 communists – the 'platform of the 46' – mainly supporters of Trotsky, talking of a serious economic crisis occasioned by the incompetence of the CC. This was acutely embarrassing at a time when official party policy was to encourage all peasants to expand production and afford the market economy free rein.

Fortunately, a good harvest in 1923 stabilised the situation and low industrial prices increased demand. Heavy industry did not fare as well but the party was determined to invest more. By 1924 the price relationship between industrial and agricultural goods was more or less back to its 1913 level; exports rose, mostly grain, and NEP appeared to be vindicating the trust placed in it.

In May 1922 Lenin suffered his first stroke, but he appeared to be his old self again during the autumn. Another, but more severe, stroke afflicted him in December 1922. It paralysed his right side but did not affect the brain. He lost his ability to speak as a result of his third stroke, in March 1923, and thereafter vegetated until he died on 21 January 1924. After the third stroke had ended all hope of a recovery the Politburo needed to find a successor. There could never be another Lenin. Although he held no formal office, he had led the party by the power of his intellect and his personality. Nevertheless he died an anxious and saddened man.

All was not right with the party and the leader was plainly unhappy with the changes which had transformed it from a conspiratorial élitist party – there had only been about 24,000 members in February 1917 – into a mass party which contained 733,000 members in March 1921 (McCauley, 1993: 35). The vast majority of these members had only a nodding acquaintance with Marxism and were quite incapable of following the subtleties of the debates among the élite. They all knew what they wanted, namely socialism, which promised to bring them everything they longed for; but how was it to be realised? Despite its numbers the party was weak. It was not in command of the country; its membership was predominantly urban, while about four persons in five lived in the countryside. No wonder Lenin was worried. He was appalled by the low level of culture in Soviet Russia, by which he meant basic literacy.

In an effort to improve the efficiency of the Secretariat, Stalin was appointed Secretary-General in April 1922, with Molotov and Kuibyshev becoming secretaries. This did not make Stalin nominal head of the party, since the Secretariat did not then possess the power it was later to acquire; in 1922 the Politburo was still the key decision-making body. Lenin, Trotsky, **Zinoviev**, **Kamenev** and Bukharin all appeared to be senior to Stalin.

Two incidents sowed the seeds of doubt in Lenin's mind about the fitness of Stalin to hold high office in the party. On the issue of the foreign trade monopoly Stalin flippantly disregarded his leader's passionately held view that the monopoly had to stay. Lenin had his way in the end, overturning a CC decision by personal fiat. Since Lenin had been too ill to fight his own battles he had spoken through Trotsky, thus making it plain whom he considered to be his closest associate.

The other issue over which there was acrimonious debate concerned Stalin's home republic, Georgia. Lenin was especially concerned about the

Zinoviev, Grigory Evseevich: Stalin drew him into a tactical alliance against Trotsky after Lenin's death but after Trotsky's defeat Stalin turned on Zinoviev. In 1926, he lost his place on the Politburo and his Comintern post, and was expelled from the party in November 1927. In April 1936, he was the main accused in the first great Show Trial.

Kamenev, Lev Borisovich: The eternal moderate of the Bolshevik party. He was Lenin's deputy as Prime Minister and sided with Stalin against Trotsky. Later he sided with Trotsky and Zinoviev against Stalin. He was sacked from the Politburo and became Soviet ambassador to Italy, 1926–27. He was a victim of the first Show Trial in Moscow.

Transcaucasian republic which had been dragged back into Soviet Russia by military force in 1921. Stalin wanted Georgia to become an autonomous republic (**ASSR**) in the new Soviet state called the Union of Soviet Socialist Republics (USSR) which came into being in December 1922. The Georgians rejected this notion since, as an ASSR, they would have become part of the Russian Soviet Federated Socialist Republic (**RSFSR**), directly ruled from Moscow. They wanted to become a full Soviet republic and in that way retain some of their independence. Stalin did not wish for a compromise but was determined to dictate to his compatriots. As Commissar for Nationalities he was responsible for relations with all non-Russians, about half the total population of the USSR. Lenin intervened in the furore which resulted and sided with the 'injured party', the Georgians (McCauley, 1993: 53). Eventually Georgia, Armenia and Azerbaidzhan were lumped together and entered the Soviet Union as the Transcaucasian Soviet Socialist Republic. Georgia became a Soviet republic in 1936.

On 24–25 December 1922, shortly after his second stroke, Lenin was able to dictate a Letter to the Congress, known as his 'Testament'. He saw the danger of a split between Stalin and Trotsky. Stalin had concentrated 'unlimited authority' in his hands and Lenin was not sure whether he would 'always be capable of using that authority with sufficient caution'. Lenin regarded Trotsky as the ablest man in the CC but feared that he revealed 'excessive self-assurance and [had] shown excessive preoccupation with the purely administrative side of the work'. So far as Kamenev and Zinoviev were concerned, Lenin thought they were not to be blamed personally for opposing the October Revolution and he referred to Bukharin and **Pyatakov** as the 'most outstanding representatives' of the younger generation, although he thought that Bukharin had never fully understood the motive forces of history. 'There is something scholastic in him', wrote Lenin, but he admitted that Bukharin was considered the 'darling of the whole party'. The Georgian affair excited Lenin to write an addendum to his Testament on 4 January 1923, stating that the Secretary-General was 'too rude' and that the comrades should 'think of a way of removing Stalin from that post'. In March Lenin discovered that his wife, **Nadezhda Krupskaya**, had been insulted by Stalin and he immediately dictated a letter to him warning him that he would break off relations if he did not apologise.

The Testament should have been read to the XIIth Party Congress in 1923, but Lenin's illness, the difficult position of the party, and the criticisms of major personalities the Testament contained, led to its being kept back until the following Congress in 1924.

Another problem which exercised Lenin's mind was bureaucratism. He had a low opinion of the typical Russian bureaucrat, a 'Great Russian chauvinist . . . a rascal and a tyrant', as he graphically put it. Lenin was aware

ASSR: Autonomous Soviet Socialist Republic; an administrative unit of a republic which is populated by a nationality other than the titular nationality: e.g. the Tatars made up the Tatar ASSR in the RSFSR. Although they had their own government, they were ruled from the titular nationality's capital. Hence 'autonomous' here does not mean independent.

RSFSR: Russian Soviet Federated Socialist Republic; when the USSR was formed in December 1922 the RSFSR became the largest republic; between June 1918 and December 1922 the RSFSR concluded treaties with Belorussia, Ukraine, Georgia, Armenia, Azerbaidzhan and Central Asia, together forming the Soviet state.

Pyatakov, Georgy Leonidovich: He was always on the left of the party (his father was a sugar merchant) and he supported Trotsky against Stalin. He was Deputy Commissar for Heavy Industry (under Ordzhonikidze) 1932–36. He was the chief accused at the second great Moscow Show Trial in 1937. He was found guilty and shot.

Krupskaya, Nadezhda Konstantinovna: Lenin's wife but not his great love. She was browbeaten by Stalin who warned her that if she were not careful the party would appoint someone else as Lenin's widow.

that traditional Tsarist practices were becoming standard procedure in Soviet Russia and he believed that Stalin was as responsible as anyone for this.

Why did Stalin clash head on with his leader in 1922–23? Would he not have been better advised to act the obedient cohort and wait for the wounded lion to die before challenging some of his views? Not enough is known to explain Stalin's behaviour satisfactorily. His conduct does reveal that he was not the 'grey blur' of Trotsky's imagination. He had views of his own and was prepared to take considerable political risks. It may be that Stalin was so fearful that Trotsky or Zinoviev or Kamenev would steal Lenin's mantle that he lost control of himself on occasions. An unofficial triumvirate, consisting of Zinoviev, Kamenev and Stalin, had come into existence in 1922 with the express purpose of blocking Trotsky, but its members do not seem to have trusted one another very much. Stalin already controlled the party machine but the Politburo decided policy.

Trotsky, as full of eloquence as he was empty of political ability, played into the hands of the triumvirate by launching, in October 1923, a vitriolic attack on the way the party was being run. He wanted a return to 'party democracy' and an end to the bureaucratic power of the Secretariat. This was instructive, coming from a politician who had favoured the militarisation of labour and had been as dictatorial as the next man when afforded the opportunity. The CC gave him a dressing down and held him indirectly responsible for the appearance of the 'platform of the 46'. Trotsky was not at the CC meeting to defend himself since he was convalescing with his wife in the Causasus. Henceforth illness was to overtake him at vital moments just when his political career demanded that he should be on his mettle. His bouts of ill-health may have been of psychosomatic origin. When Lenin died, Trotsky was still in the Caucasus and missed the funeral; his rather lame excuse was that Stalin had misinformed him about the date.

Lenin, personally a modest man, had always resisted adulation of his person. When he encountered the term Leninism he rejected it, since he held himself to be a Marxist. Nevertheless the level of culture of party members was low and they needed to be disciplined and trained. There was a vast gulf between the culture of the party leaders and the rank and file. Since Lenin was aware that the party committed errors from time to time there could be no talk of party infallibility. If the leadership made a mistake and this was realised by the rank and file, how was the party to be put back on the rails? Lenin never discovered an answer to this vital problem. The whole weight of the party apparatus was geared to suppressing dissent and stifling discussion. This was because the party felt itself to be weak; a strong, self-confident party would have tolerated the differences of opinion.

Stalin had a finely developed sense of what party members were looking for. On the eve of Lenin's funeral, 26 January 1924, Stalin delivered a remarkable speech. The mood was sombre and many feared the future without Lenin. 'We communists are people of a special mould. We are made of special stuff', declared Stalin, and he added that there was nothing higher than the calling of a member of a party whose founder and leader was comrade Lenin. How hearts must have jumped at these words! The Secretary-General first praised party members, then he set out their duties in a Lenin litany. Members swore to be exemplary communists, to preserve the unity of the party and so on. Lenin was not buried in a grave but placed in a mausoleum where the eyes of the people could gaze upon him. The slogan 'Lenin is always with us' was born. The next move was to define Leninism in terms which were accessible to everyone. This Stalin did in the course of six lectures at Sverdlov University in Moscow and they were published in *Pravda* as 'The Foundations of Leninism'. According to Stalin, the essence of Leninism consisted of stressing revolutionary will and political activism and rejecting the views of those Marxists who emphasised the dependence of political change on the development of economic and social conditions. Leninism also meant displaying extreme relativism when assessing social forces and values: if they served the revolution they were good; otherwise they were bad. The same relativism was also to be applied to social reforms, culture, democracy, foreign affairs, etc. The party was declared to be the main motive force of the revolution [**Doc. 1, p. 106**]. The inchoate, spontaneous desires of the workers had to be subordinated to the grinding will of a rigidly disciplined and centralised party, otherwise the revolution could not be saved or socialism built.

Stalin was not the only one who sought to define Leninism. Zinoviev provided his version and Trotsky missed the boat again by opposing the whole venture, arguing that Lenin's utterances could not be dissected in such a way. Another opponent was Krupskaya, Lenin's widow, and she could show how contrary it was to Lenin's wishes. However, the mood of the times was one of veneration. Petrograd, for instance, was renamed Leningrad by the party.

Zinoviev and Stalin approached the task of defining Lenin's legacy differently. Whereas the former placed himself on a par with Lenin, Stalin projected himself as the humble apostle and devoted follower. There were many in the Soviet Union who wanted to play the same role. Bukharin and Stalin accused Trotsky of factionalism and organising a bloc together with former Democratic Centralists and left communists, while Zinoviev came up with the formulation of 'Trotskyism' as a 'definite tendency in the Russian workers' movement'.

By the beginning of 1924 the party had slimmed down to about 350,000 members, but a recruitment campaign, the 'Lenin enrolment', which was to add about 240,000 new members, was launched after Lenin's death. The most sought-after recruits were 'workers at the bench'. Since the enrolment was the responsibility of Stalin, it can be safely assumed that it was impressed on new members that absolute obedience to party directives was demanded; also their political education was in the hands of men appointed by Stalin and his associates. At the XIIIth Party Congress, in May 1924, Zinoviev repeated his charge of factionalism and called on Trotsky to 'recant'. Trotsky was only just re-elected to an enlarged CC, and was isolated in the new Politburo. During the summer Trotsky and his ally, Karl Radek, lost their places on the Comintern central committee.

The political temperature was raised by Trotsky in October 1924 when he published his *Lessons of October*. This book contained vitriolic attacks on Zinoviev and Kamenev and other 'old' Bolsheviks for their criticism of Lenin in 1917. Since Trotsky himself had only become a Bolshevik in June 1917 and had had a long record of disagreements with Lenin, he was stirring up a hornet's nest. Kamenev riposted by writing *Lenin or Trotsky*, in which he accused Trotsky of Menshevism. He found it easy to lay bare Trotsky's record of past altercations with Lenin. A veritable flood of abuse descended on the hapless Trotsky as no communist wished his own Leninist probity to be placed in doubt. The creator of the Red Army gave up his last great government office, that of Commissar for Military and Naval Affairs, and went into the political wilderness.

The controversy over *Lessons of October* gave birth to another dispute, that about socialism in one country. Stalin seized on an article by Bukharin attacking Trotsky's theory of permanent revolution and developed the argument that Trotsky's beliefs contradicted Lenin's doctrine of proletarian revolution. Lenin, according to Stalin, had held the view that the Soviet Union by itself could build socialism, but that the final victory of socialism would have to wait for revolution in several of the advanced capitalist countries. This overturned existing party assumptions that socialism in the USSR could only be built after the socialist revolution had triumphed abroad. Stalin neatly reversed the situation. Now the Soviet Union could become the pace-setter and not have to wait for world events. It was a great psychological shot in the arm for the party and the nation.

Although the 1924 harvest was a fair one, the grain did not flow into the cities. This unexpected development led to price rises, and the terms of trade turned to the advantage of the peasant. As it happened, official policy was also in favour of the peasant and in April 1925 the party announced new concessions. There were clouds on the horizon, however. In July 1924 Evgeny Preobrazhensky, a leading party economist, had argued that 'primitive socialist accumulation' – in plain language the squeezing of the peasant – was the only source of the much needed capital for industrialisation. Bukharin, however, came out with a sturdy defence of official policy and in

April 1925 went even further and encouraged the peasants to enrich themselves, stating that they had nothing to fear from the authorities.

The situation after the excellent 1925 harvest added fuel to the flames. Again prices rose as the producers kept back grain, for they had little incentive to convert stocks into mounds of paper money which might depreciate. The agricultural tax had been reduced and this relieved the pressure of taxation. Anyway there were few quality goods to buy.

Zinoviev and Kamenev now abandoned their previous position and came out against the peasant. One of their targets was Bukharin, but Zinoviev also produced a stinging condemnation of the concept of socialism in one country. Zinoviev, as head of the Leningrad organisation, and Kamenev, as head of the Moscow party, presided over the two most important industrial cities in the country. Favouring the worker and industrialisation and opposing the peasant was natural there. However, there was more to it than this. Zinoviev, who had always regarded himself as the chief member of the triumvirate, was making his bid for leadership now that the bogey of Trotsky had been dispelled. Stalin, in turn, used his command of the party machine to telling effect at the XIVth Congress in December 1925. The Leningrad delegation was isolated as the official line was endorsed by 559 votes to 65. Zinoviev was replaced in Leningrad by **Sergei Kirov**. The defeat of Zinoviev also meant the political demise of Kamenev. Which direction would the victorious Stalin now take?

There were now a number of leading Bolsheviks who harboured a grudge against the leadership. In July 1926 Trotsky, Kamenev, Zinoviev, Krupskaya and nine others combined to pen the 'Declaration of the 13', a condemnation of 'rightist' economic policy and the elimination of free debate which, to the signatories, foreshadowed the degeneration of the revolution. The CC thereupon removed Zinoviev from the Politburo and Kamenev from his remaining governmental post. The **United Opposition** then attempted to take their case to the factories. At a stormy Politburo meeting in late October 1926, Trotsky depicted Stalin as the gravedigger of the revolution. This meant a parting of the ways as everyone understood that the breach was final. At the XVth Party **Conference** in October–November Stalin and Bukharin poured vitriol on the United Opposition. Trotsky made his last speech to the party and was heard in silence. Kamenev was repeatedly interrupted and Zinoviev mercilessly heckled. Soon afterwards Bukharin replaced Zinoviev as chairman of the Comintern.

Foreign affairs, however, provided a stick with which to continue beating the leadership. In China, disaster overtook the Comintern policy of entering into a tactical alliance with Chiang Kai-shek's Kuomintang, for in April 1927 Chiang turned his forces against the communists in Shanghai and massacred them. Then the Soviet Embassy was raided and diplomatic relations were

Kirov, Sergei Mironovich: His assassination in December 1934 was seized upon by Stalin to begin what later became known as the purges. He had been approached by some delegates at the party congress in 1934 to stand against Stalin as party leader. This may have sealed his fate.

United Opposition: Trotsky, Zinoviev, Kamenev and their supporters combined in the summer of 1926 to form the United Opposition – to oppose socialism in one country and the policy of allowing *kulaks* free rein; this opposition was directed essentially against Bukharin and Stalin.

Conference: Differed from a Party Congress in that not all organisations were represented (an exception was the XIXth Party Conference in 1988). In the early years the problems of logistics were such as to make it difficult to call a Congress at short notice. A Conference did not have the right to elect members to the Central Committee and Politburo.

broken off. Across the world in London, Arcos, the All-Russian Co-operative Society, was raided by the British police, and this too led to diplomatic relations being severed (McCauley, 1993: 68). There were rumours of impending war. With the leadership reeling from these setbacks, a document known as the 'Declaration of the 83', chiefly drafted by Trotsky, was launched. It pulled no punches. But the leadership turned the tables on Trotsky by accusing him of treason after he had been manoeuvred into stating that unless certain changes were made he was not prepared to commit himself completely to the defence of the country. During the summer the United Opposition was pilloried in increasingly violent language but there was no legal way in which it could answer its critics, for the main organs of information were controlled by the party machine. When the opposition leaders presented a memorandum to the CC and demanded that it should be printed in preparation for the XVth Party Congress in December 1927, the request was brushed aside. They tried to print it illegally, but the political police located it and all those involved were expelled from the party. In desperation Trotsky and Zinoviev took to the streets of Moscow and Leningrad on the tenth anniversary of the revolution to proclaim their opposition. The CC responded by expelling Trotsky and Zinoviev from the party while Kamenev and some others were deprived of their seats on the CC. At the XVth Congress there was another purge. Trotsky and his closest supporters were dispatched to Alma Ata, on the Chinese frontier – in those days the back of beyond – yet even there he carried on a lively correspondence with oppositionists, so eventually, in 1929, he was deported to Turkey.

The 1927 harvest was satisfactory but the grain did not flow into the cities as expected; the better-off peasants preferred to build up stocks. The grain crisis predicted by the United Opposition came to pass but it was a year too late from their point of view. The Communist Party thereupon went over to the offensive and between January and March 1928 large quantities of grain were forcibly requisitioned. This led to Bukharin, **Rykov** and Tomsky forming the core of a new opposition group, the **Right Opposition**. They wanted an end to the use of force, a better deal for the peasants and a less headlong rush into industrialisation. The government began to pay more for grain but the private market price was still higher, and the winter of 1928–29 saw frequent bread shortages in Moscow and Leningrad.

The defeat of the United Opposition removed any inhibitions Stalin and his supporters may have had about stepping up industrialisation. With Trotsky out of the way, the party could engage in a U-turn away from the peasant. The new course came as a surprise to Trotsky, who had predicted a veering to the right in 1928. Many former oppositionists were favourably impressed, for Stalin was now doing what they had previously advocated. The rapid industrialisers had the wind in their sails, and the annual wrangle

Rykov, Aleksei Ivanovich: Stalin's ally in the battle against Trotsky after Lenin's death, Rykov reaped the whirlwind later. He became a leading member of the right opposition, against Stalin's policies. In 1930 he was sacked from all his posts and from the Politburo, tried for treason in the third great Show Trial in 1938 and executed.

Right Opposition: Bukharin, Rykov, Tomsky and their supporters came together in the summer of 1928 to oppose the headlong rush towards industrialisation which was then beginning to gain momentum; they favoured voluntary collectivisation which meant in practice very slow collectivisation; by early 1929 they had been defeated by Stalin.

over grain requisitions strengthened their resolve to deal with the *kulaks* once and for all. Stalin deliberately exaggerated the danger from the right [**Doc. 2, p. 107**] and went so far as to claim that Bukharin and his supporters were betraying the working class and the revolution. If anyone refused to fight the right then he too, declared Stalin, was a traitor. Bukharin desperately tried to link up with Kamenev, but the latter was a spent force. He expressed his views in *Notes of an Economist* in September 1928, but this merely provided raw material for the Stalinist propaganda machine to devour. Stalin's victory was confirmed in January 1929 when Bukharin, Rykov and Tomsky resigned from the Politburo and forfeited their state offices as well.

The first Five-Year Plan (**FYP**) was adopted at a party conference in April 1929. It had been drafted in two variants, the basic and the optimum. The latter was approved, even though it was wildly optimistic and reflected the prevailing euphoria that the sky was the limit as far as industry was concerned. It now became the fulcrum of Soviet activity and all other aspects of life were linked to it.

The plan set the relatively modest target of bringing 20 per cent of the sown area under the control of collectives within five years. Entry to these collective farms, or *kolkhozes*, was to be voluntary. At the same time state farms, or **sovkhozes**, were to be expanded, particularly in areas of virgin land, where they were to be very large.

The cult of Stalin's personality dates from 21 December 1929 when his fiftieth birthday was celebrated amid mountains of effusive prose. The leader had at last emerged openly on to the stage. Nevertheless he still did not have the authority over other persons' lives which he was to acquire in the course of the 1930s. Some of his cohorts did not regard themselves as eternal second-rank figures. It was only in 1936 that he became politically unassailable.

The party machine was Stalin's power base. The great majority of lower and middle-ranking officials were Stalin nominees. Areas outside his control were incorporated one by one: the youth organisation (the **Komsomol**), then Leningrad, then Moscow. As the state became stronger so it became the prerogative of the centre to fill more and more posts. A nomenclature system developed which gave the party the final say in every important appointment. Lacking skill and experience the Stalinist appointees became more and more abrasive. Bluster and abuse were their only answer to criticism. The rough and often violent treatment of the peasants during the grain requisitioning of 1928 and 1929 paved the way for what was to come later. The campaigns against Trotsky, the United Opposition and the Right Opposition afforded full scope to ambitious men to demonstrate their loyalty to the party leadership. An additional spur was that if the oppositionists were defeated there would be more plum jobs to fill. Since life was often hard, the privileges and perquisites of office were eagerly sought. This form of behaviour

FYP: Five-Year Plan; first FYP ran from October 1928 to December 1932; second from January 1933 to December 1937; third from January 1938 to June 1941; fourth from January 1946 to December 1950; fifth from January 1951 to December 1955.

Sovkhoz: State farm; run like a factory with guaranteed minimum wages higher than those of *kolkhozniks*; operatives were classified as workers and enjoyed their social benefits.

Komsomol: Communist youth movement for those between ages 14 and 28.

was not restricted to party and state affairs, but extended to other facets of life, including culture. In this field battles were waged throughout the 1920s between those who believed that writers and artists should devote their talents to furthering the proletarian cause and those who regarded art as being above party politics. The All-Russian Association of Proletarian Writers (RAPP), formed in 1928, actively invited party intervention in literature, believing it could only help their members. They discovered too late that their goals were not those of the party leadership.

Stalin was not the ostensible leader of any faction. He always played the role of the moderate and this lulled many into misjudging him. He has frequently been accused of having no ideas of his own, of being a parasite who needed a host on whom to live. At Politburo meetings during the early 1920s he often spoke last and then it was to chart a *via media* between the extremes of his more eloquent colleagues. He was instinctively on the left but could not adopt this position until Trotsky and the United Opposition had been rendered impotent. He was a very skilful politician who had a superb grasp of tactics, could predict behaviour extremely well and had an unerring eye for personal weaknesses. He floated into and out of alliances, since he had no sense of personal loyalty to any of his colleagues, and would turn on anyone if he judged it politically opportune. This personal ruthlessness served him well.

Stalin's attitude to ideas was utilitarian. If they served to make the Soviet Union stronger they were welcome. His incursion into ideology after Lenin's death served two purposes: to provide a simple, accessible exegesis of Marxism-Leninism, and to outmanoeuvre his opponents. All the issues taken up by Stalin served a practical purpose, for he was not interested in ideology as such. Industrialisation and **collectivisation**, said Stalin, amounted to the revolution from above. It did not concern him that orthodox Marxism required the working class to be the agent of revolution, and that it should therefore have come from below.

Collectivisation: Establishment of *kolkhozes* and *sovkhozes*, which meant the end of private farming. Collectivisation began in 1917 but had made little impact by 1929 when it really got under way; was completed by 1937.

Stalin was greatly assisted by the inept tactics of his opponents. Trotsky, the most formidable intellectually, was a broken reed after Lenin's death. His attacks on the party and state bureaucracy merely served to weld these groups more closely around Stalin in defence of their own positions at a time when alternative employment was hard to find. The gulf between the left and the right, in fact, was never wide; it was only Stalin's skilful manoeuvring that made it appear so. All Bolsheviks agreed that socialism entailed industrialisation. The argument between the left and the right was about the pace at which this should go ahead (Nove, 1992: 38). The left wanted rapid growth – by which they simply meant growth rates above those being achieved at the time – while the right would have been satisfied with moderate growth. The left was ready to subordinate everything to the achievement of a predetermined target, say 10 per cent annual industrial growth. The money for this would have been found by squeezing the peasants through heavy taxation, and anything which aided the fulfilment of the plan was regarded as legitimate. The right, on the other hand, looked at the economy as something that should grow organically, with industry and agriculture in tandem. Both factions regarded socialist or cooperative agriculture as the goal, but whereas the left was unwilling to allow the peasant to dictate the speed of economic growth (four out of five persons lived in the countryside) the right thought that coercion would force the peasant into resistance and would be economically disastrous. Bukharin, the main economic theorist on the right, hoped that the peasants would gradually come to see that cooperative agriculture was in their best interests. In prospering they would buy more industrial goods, thus stimulating industrial expansion. Neither Trotsky nor Preobrazhensky, the main economic thinker on the left, envisaged forced collectivisation. Stalin's recourse to this was closely linked to his drive for industrialisation. He and his supporters adopted growth rates which far surpassed the demands of the left. This meant extra labour for industry and guaranteed food supplies at the expense of the countryside. So miserable were living standards in the rural areas after 1930 that peasants abandoned the land in droves to become industrial workers. Most of the food produced by the collectives was simply requisitioned by the state.

Some of the blame for the débâcle of the right must be pinned on Bukharin. Although an able economist, he never produced a convincing plan to counter the dreams of the super-industrialisers.

The very weakness of the party required the Politburo to show a united face to the public. The leadership could not afford to be seen engaging in infighting and factionalism. Controversies did burst into print, but Stalin's creeping control of the media dictated how the debate was conducted. The press gradually became a vehicle of the ruling faction, in which defeated political opponents were pilloried mercilessly without any right of reply. By 1929 all non-party journals had been closed down and there were no private publishing houses left.

Stalin also enjoyed his fair share of luck. Had Yakov Sverdlov not died in 1919 he would have been the natural candidate for the post of Secretary-General. Also Lenin's death saved Stalin from almost certain demotion. Dzerzhinsky, head of the political police – the **Cheka**, renamed the OGPU (United State Political Administration) in 1922 – and on the left, died in July 1926. He had also been head of VSNKh, a key economic institution. His death opened the way to the appointment of Kuibyshev, an ally of Stalin and an advocate of forced industrialisation.

Cheka: All-Russian Extraordinary Commission to Fight Counter Revolution, Sabotage and Speculation; established December 1917; renamed OGPU in 1922; later KGB.

Part 2

ANALYSIS

3

The Thirties

POLITICS AND THE ECONOMY

After the war scare of 1927 came the fear of foreign economic intervention. Wrecking was taking place in several industries and crises had occurred in others – or so Stalin claimed in April 1928. The following month he put the nation's youth on the alert: 'Comrades, our class enemies do exist. They not only exist but are growing and trying to act against Soviet power.' Then it was announced that a large-scale conspiracy involving engineers in the Shakhty areas of the Donbass had been uncovered. Stalin skilfully used the perceived threats to Soviet power to create an atmosphere of tension and apprehension. The coiled-up energy of the population could thereby be released and directed towards the achievement of specific targets. The first Five-Year Plan (FYP) set these goals. In December 1929 it was decided that the plan could be achieved in four years and in the end it ran from 1 October 1928 to 31 December 1932. Plan goals were continually increased irrespective of economic rationality, as human will overruled mathematical calculations. As one planner stated: 'There are no fortresses which we Bolsheviks cannot storm.' The Great Depression, which began in 1929 in the advanced industrial states, added fuel to the conviction that the Bolsheviks were on the highway to success.

The Soviet leadership appears to have been surprised how easy it was to speed up collectivisation. Party officials in several selected areas competed with one another and when they proved successful Stalin and the key officials concerned with collectivisation, Molotov and **Kaganovich**, knew that they could outstrip the modest aim of collectivising 20 per cent of the sown area laid down for 1932.

The number of peasants in collective farms of all types doubled between June and October 1929, and Stalin declared on 7 November 1929 that the great movement towards collectivisation was under way. The Politburo stated on 5 January 1930 that large-scale *kulak* production was to be replaced by

Kaganovich, Lev Moiseevich: True to Stalin to the end; he even denied he was a Jew. He was party leader in Moscow in 1930 and helped Khrushchev's career. Jews complained of his anti-Semitism. Stalin told him to shave off his beard because he did not want a rabbi near him.

large-scale *kolkhoz* production. Ominously, for the better-off farmers it also proclaimed the 'liquidation of the *kulaks* as a class'.

It was hoped that the collectivisation of the key grain-growing areas, the North Caucasus and the Volga region, would be completed by the spring of 1931 at the latest and the other grain-growing areas by the spring of 1932. A vital role in rapid collectivisation was played by the 25,000 workers who descended on the countryside to aid the 'voluntary' process. The 'twenty-five thousanders', as they were called, brooked no opposition. They were all vying with one another for the approbation of the party. Officially, force was only permissible against *kulaks*, but the middle and poor peasants were soon sucked into the maelstrom of violence. *Kulaks* were expelled from their holdings and their stock and implements handed over to the *kolkhoz*. What was to become of them? Stalin was brutally frank: 'It is ridiculous and foolish to talk at length about dekulakisation. . . . When the head is off, one does not grieve for the hair. There is another question no less ridiculous: whether *kulaks* should be allowed to join the collective farms? Of course not, for they are the sworn enemies of the collective farm movement.' *Kulaks* were divided into three classes. The first consisted of about 63,000 'counter-revolutionary' families who were to be executed or exiled and have their property confiscated. Group two was made up of 150,000 households labelled 'exploiters' or 'active opponents' of collectivisation. These were to be deported to the remote regions of the east and north, but permitted to retain some possessions. Another group was composed of between 396,000 and 852,000 households who were to be allowed to remain in their home region but on land outside the collectives. (This meant, in fact, on land which was at that time not arable.) If one assumes a modest five members per household, the first two groups amounted to over one million persons. No one in the Politburo cared whether they survived or not. Others abandoned their home villages and made for the towns, desperately trying to beg enough for survival. *Kulak* children were sometimes left to die, since their deported fathers belonged to the 'wrong class'.

Sufficient sporadic peasant violence met the 'twenty-five thousanders' and their cohorts to make the leadership nervous. Thereupon Stalin changed course and launched an attack on all those officials who had herded peasants into collectives against their will. His article in *Pravda* on 2 March 1930 was entitled 'Dizzy with Success' [**Doc. 3, p. 108**]. In it he pilloried the wayward officials, but this was mere double-talk. It was he, in fact, who had driven them on! *Pravda* became a best-seller in the countryside as desperate officials attempted to restrict circulation. There was a stampede to leave the *kolkhozes*, and only 23 per cent of the peasants were left in collective farms by 1 June 1930. Stalin had not lost his nerve; he merely wished to ensure that the spring sowing was completed. Afterwards the collectivisation offensive was resumed, and the beaten peasants took to slaughtering their livestock and breaking their implements rather than see them collectivised. Mikhail Sholokhov, the Nobel Prize-winning Soviet novelist, catches the atmosphere in *Virgin Soil Upturned*. ' "Slaughter! You won't get meat in the *kolkhoz*", crept the insidious rumours. And they slaughtered. They ate until they could eat no more. Young and old suffered from indigestion. At dinner time tables groaned under boiled or roast meat. Everyone had a greasy mouth, everyone hiccoughed as if at a wake. Everyone blinked like an owl, as if inebriated from eating' (McCauley, 1993: 162).

Livestock numbers in 1932 were less than half those of 1928. To the government the tractor was the symbol of the mechanisation and modernisation of agriculture and the trump card of the new *kolkhozes* and state farms, *sovkhozes*. It penetrated the countryside more rapidly than expected. Since so many draught animals had been slaughtered, scarce resources had to be diverted to the production of even more tractors. The shortage of cattle and sheep meant less leather and wool for consumer goods.

Timid voices were raised about the breakneck speed of industrialisation. Could the pace not be slowed down a little? Stalin firmly rejected such thinking [**Doc. 5, p. 110**]. He even wanted the economy to expand more rapidly, on the grounds that with imperialist vultures circling overhead the Soviet Union had to become strong enough to keep them at bay. 'Specialist baiting' was a popular sport during the early years of the first FYP. After the Shakhty trial in 1928 came the 'industrial party' trial in November–December 1930, when industrial experts confessed to wrecking and other heinous crimes. The Shakhty trial was followed by the arrest of thousands of 'bourgeois' or non-party engineers. By 1931 half of the engineers and technical workers in the Donbass, a key industrial region, had been arrested. What did the charge of wrecking amount to? If a machine broke down – as happened quite often, due to the fact that the peasant turned worker had to learn on the job – someone higher up was to blame. If imported machinery was not adequately used it could be construed as wrecking. It may seem paradoxical that, at a time when their skills were desperately needed, 'bourgeois' and foreign engineers were being held behind bars. However, there was a rationale behind the arrests: the leadership was desperately anxious to break down all resistance to central directives. The 'bourgeois' engineer could see the orders were not feasible and said so. Moscow wanted engineers who would attempt to do the impossible.

A declared opponent of the campaign against 'bourgeois' engineers was **Sergo Ordzhonikidze**, who became head of the Supreme Council of the National Economy (VSNKh) at the end of 1930 and thereby the *de facto* leader of the drive for industrialisation. He appears to have influenced Stalin's decision to call a halt to the campaign. On 23 June 1931 the

Ordzhonikidze, Grigory Konstantinovich (Sergo): A prominent Georgian revolutionary who was influential in the 1930s during industrialisation. He was a supporter of Stalin and in 1926 became chair of the Central Control Commission and Rabkrin. In 1930 he became chair of VSNKh and a full member of the Politburo, and in 1932 Commissar for Heavy Industry.

Secretary-General declared that the policy of considering every specialist an 'undetected criminal and wrecker' should be dropped. Show trials of engineers did not completely cease, however, as the case against the Metro-Vickers engineers in 1933 demonstrated.

The change of heart towards the experts was accompanied by a dramatic change in the fortunes of labour. The years 1928–31 saw workers exercise an influence over production never again to be equalled. Shock workers and shock brigades showed the workers the way, and there was a great deal of worker initiative as hierarchy was played down. This happened at a time when the planners could not accurately plot the way ahead. Some members of the leadership, working on the assumption that socialism meant a money-less economy, believed that the exchange of products would replace money as NEP was phased out. Indeed, many of them in 1930 thought that this stage was fast approaching. It was also widely assumed that society could be transformed very rapidly and that workers would be motivated by enthusiasm, so that an end could be made to payment by result. In July 1931, however, Stalin changed his approach. He attacked the prevalent egalitarianism and proposed wage differentials which reflected skill and responsibility. The ideas of the American time and motion expert, F.W. Taylor, found favour, and engineers were given the task of setting scientifically based norms. Authority was reinvested in specialists and engineers.

The first FYP was a period of genuine enthusiasm, and prodigious achievements were recorded in production. The 'impossible' targets galvanised people into action, and more was achieved than would have been the case had orthodox advice been followed. New cities, such as Magnitogorsk in the Urals, rose from the ground. According to official statistics the first FYP in industry was fulfilled [Doc. 7, no. 5, p. 113] with the plan for producers' goods – the production of the means of production (heavy industry) – being over-fulfilled [Doc. 7, no. 9, p. 113]. Consumption goods (light industry), on the other hand, fell short of the target [Doc. 7, no. 10, p. 113]. These figures are open to criticism, however. They are expressed in 1926–27 prices, but many of the goods produced during the plan were not made in 1926–27. Money values in roubles were used instead, and these certainly erred on the high side. Various western economists have recomputed the results and their estimates range from 59.7 to 69.9 per cent fulfilment [Doc. 7, nos. 6–8, p. 113].

Whatever the figures, a great engineering industry was in the making and the rise in the output of machinery, machine tools, turbines and tractors was very impressive. Ukraine, the Volga, the Urals and the Kuzbass (south-west Siberia) saw most expansion. Engineering enterprises in the Leningrad and Moscow regions were modernised and expanded. Industry also penetrated the less well developed republics, especially Kazakhstan and Central Asia. Power for expanding Ukrainian industry flowed from the huge Dnieper dam which was completed during these years. The plan for railway expansion was less than half achieved but canals increased rapidly, often using forced labour, as in the case of the Volga–White Sea canal.

Not surprisingly, the agricultural performance was abysmal [**Doc. 7, no. 11, p. 113**]. The rush out of the countryside led to the over-fulfilment of the labour plan [**Doc. 7, no. 16, p. 113**] and unemployment in the cities had disappeared by 1932. Industry took on many more workers than planned [**Doc. 7, no. 17, p. 113**]. All this meant that money wages were far in excess of the plan [**Doc. 7, no. 18, p. 114**]. Thus there was even more money than expected chasing the few consumer goods on offer. Living standards were miserably low, and if they were low in the towns they were even worse in the countryside.

Despite the over-fulfilment of the labour plan, industrial production was officially only a fraction over the plan [**Doc. 7, no. 5, p. 113**]. This meant that labour productivity was very low, and came as a great disappointment to the planners. Determined efforts were made to increase labour discipline during the FYP. The first legislation involving prison sentences for those who violated labour discipline was passed in January 1931. Work books were introduced for all industrial and transport workers in February 1931, and the death sentence could be applied for the theft of state or collective farm property as from August 1932. Missing a day's work could mean instant dismissal after November 1932, and the internal passport (not issued to **kolkhozniks**) was introduced on 27 December 1932 to restrict movement and increase control. Such draconian measures bear eloquent testimony to the difficulty of transforming the peasant into a worker.

The industrial achievements of the first FYP were mainly the result of util-ising the available capacity more fully, including the extra plant which came on stream as a consequence of pre-1928 investment. Plant started during the first FYP was completed, in the main, in 1934–36, and the investment plan was only half fulfilled [**Doc. 7, no. 26, p. 114**].

However, not everyone was willing to put up with low living standards indefinitely. Stalin, speaking at a CC plenum in January 1933, had a message for all the grumblers: 'We have without doubt achieved a situation in which the material conditions of workers and peasants are improving year by year. The only people who doubt this are the sworn enemies of Soviet power.'

The mayhem of collectivisation and low yields of 1932 led to a famine in 1933. It was made even worse by the need to seize seed grain from the farms to build up stocks to feed the Red Army if a conflict with Japan occurred in the Far East. The number of deaths from starvation was 7.2–8.1 million (Ellmann, 1991: 379) but these were not mentioned in the Soviet press.

Thus the second FYP (1933–37) got off to a very inauspicious start and the XVIIth Party Congress in January–February 1934 redrafted it. The new version revealed that Soviet planning had become more realistic, for this time

Kolkhoznik: Collective farm peasant; between 1929 and 1966 there was no guaranteed basic wage; wages were paid out at end of harvest according to the profit-ability of the farm; the private plot kept the *kolkhoznik* and his family alive until the 1950s.

the targets set did not belong to cloud cuckoo land. Agriculture was in a parlous state in 1933 but improved rapidly afterwards. Although there were still about nine million peasants outside the collective farm sector in 1934, by 1937 they had practically all been collectivised. High taxes and compulsory deliveries were levied on the peasant, and when he could not meet his obligations all his goods and belongings were sold to meet the deficit.

Livestock numbers recovered rapidly after the depredations of the early 1930s. This was due in large part to the state's willingness to permit farmers to own their own animals – within strict limits, of course. Each household was also allowed a private plot. Surplus produce could be sold legally in towns in the *kolkhoz* market, though only by the producers themselves. No middlemen were permitted to reappear.

A Congress was convened in 1935 to draft a model charter for the *kolkhozes*, which was to stay on the statute book until the early 1970s. The *kolkhoz* was defined as a voluntary cooperative working land provided by the state rent-free in perpetuity. The chairman was to be elected by the members, but in practice the *kolkhoz* enjoyed little autonomy since its goals were set by the party and the government. The mechanical work was done under contract by machine tractor stations. Thus the available machinery was spread around as much as possible. The farms paid for such services in kind. Unlike state farms or *sovkhozes*, collective farms did not offer their members a guaranteed wage before 1966. If the farm did well, the profits were shared out at the end of the year. If results were poor, little or nothing was paid out. Hence it was possible for a *kolkhoznik* to work assiduously and to receive little or no reward for his labours. Not surprisingly he quickly came to realise that the private plot was his staff of life and that his cow was especially valuable. He therefore devoted his energies to his private plot and merely went through the motions on the collective farm. The girls often opted out of agriculture altogether by moving to the towns, and the more ambitious young men followed them.

The second FYP was over-fulfilled, in general, by 3 per cent [**Doc. 7, no. 5, p. 113**]. The engineering industry again expanded rapidly. The output of steel almost trebled, the main reason for this being that the great plants begun during the first FYP entered production. Magnitogorsk, Kuznetsk and Zaporozhe, for example, became great industrial centres. Karaganda (Kazakhstan), the Kuzbass and the Urals saw a great expansion of coal production; the generation of electricity grew but oil output was disappointing as Baku and the Urals–Volga fields failed to cope with their technical problems. Industry was spread around the country, even to the non-Slav republics where the return on investment was lower that in 'older' industrial areas.

The pious hopes about according consumer goods greater emphasis bore no fruit [**Doc. 7, no. 10, p. 113**]. One of the reasons for this was the increasing share of industrial production being devoted to defence – officially only 3.4 per cent of total budget expenditure in 1933 but 16.5 per cent in 1937. (Real defence expenditure in 1933 appears to have been about 12 per cent.) Agriculture flopped again [Doc. 7, no. 11, p. 113]; indeed no FYP for agriculture ever achieved its targets in the Soviet Union.

The number of workers in the economy as a whole, and especially in industry, fell below the levels projected by the FYP [Doc. 7, no. 16, p. 113], but as output had exceeded the targets this meant that labour productivity was rising faster than expected. One of the contributory factors to this was the impact of the Stakhanovite movement, named after Aleksei Stakhanov, who on 30–31 August 1935 had shown just what *could* be done by mining 102 tonnes of coal in 5 hours and 45 minutes (the equivalent of 14 norms). Doing the work of 14 men is an astonishing feat, but Stakhanov's achievement was also eloquent testimony to the low productivity of Soviet miners. Needless to say Stakhanov did not achieve the feat on his own: he had all the help he needed and all the machinery was in working order. For instance, he did not stop and put in props to keep the ceiling from collapsing on him. Someone else did that. Stakhanov, in his personal account, maintains that his record was bettered the following day by another miner. He allegedly mined 115 tonnes. Then someone else achieved 119 tonnes. This world of make-believe ended with a superman mining 536 tonnes! Needless to say it could not have been done without the inspiration provided by the thoughts of comrade Stalin. These heroes of labour were showered with material rewards. This bred resentment and many comrades would cheerfully have wrung their necks, had they thought they could get away with it.

Real wages increased greatly during the second FYP but were still lower in 1937 than in 1928 and in that year were little better than in 1913. Rationing was gradually phased out in 1935, but even with a ration card (only issued to workers and state employees or about 20 per cent of the population – the other 80 per cent had to fend for themselves) there was no guarantee that the desired goods would be available. Free market prices were very high, reflecting especially the shortage of bread, a staple food.

There was a special provisioning system for all those deemed of importance in building socialism. They obtained special norms (managers were awarded 9 kg of meat and workers 6 kg monthly, in 1932) and they paid lower prices for consumer goods. The Politburo, in 1931, invited 10,000 foreign specialists to work in the Soviet Union and they lived very well. One of their perks was that they could import goods duty free whereas a Soviet citizen had to pay prohibitive duties (three weeks' wages to bring in a few bars of soap!). Academics lobbied to be afforded privileges. A complicated system came into being in which benefits multiplied as the academic climbed the ladder. The quickest route to success was to obtain a party card. Professors were very well looked after and were provided with housing, food, transport, travel and so on. No wonder women would kill to become the wife of a professor. Professors were better off than in the west. They did not retire at 65 years of age and kept their salaries and perks until they died. Stalin, when it came to sex, was a puritan. He did not trust a comrade who divorced his wife. All this was forgotten under Khrushchev when a professor could change his wife annually for a new model. After all he could afford it!

The third FYP (1938–41) was adopted at the XVIIIth Party Congress in 1939, but was cut short after three and a half years by the German invasion. It reaffirmed the emphasis placed on heavy industry, but it also increased defence expenditure to 18 per cent of GDP in 1940. As a consequence the living standards of workers and employees stagnated and may even have fallen slightly by 1941.

Forced labour, supervised by the People's Commissariat of Internal Affairs (NKVD), made a significant contribution to the fulfilment of the plan. Western estimates of the number of prisoners in 1941 range from 3.5 million to 15 million. Recent Soviet research has produced a figure of 1.9 million in 1941 rising to 2.5 million in 1952. It would appear that the Soviet figures only include part of those doing compulsory labour.

Government attitudes towards the workers became noticeably harsher in 1939 and 1940. Hitherto workers had been able to choose their place of work, and this produced a high labour turnover as they sought to improve their lot. In 1940, however, the state decreed that the free labour market was to end. No worker could change their job without permission, and skilled workers and specialists could be directed anywhere. Absenteeism, which could mean being 20 minutes late for work, became a criminal offence and one woman was actually convicted of the crime while she was in a maternity ward. The legislation stayed on the statute book until 1956, and if judges were soft on offenders they were put in the dock themselves. Theft was severely dealt with. One man who worked in a flour mill brought home a handful of grain for his hungry family, and was sentenced to five years' imprisonment. Social benefits for most workers were cut and fees were introduced for students in institutions of higher learning and for senior pupils in secondary schools. The population must have been frightened.

CULTURE

Education changed dramatically as the entire pedagogical system was transformed. Schools were handed over to collective farms or enterprises, pupils and teachers abandoned formal learning and sought to learn through 'productive labour' or were mobilised to fulfil the plan. There was even talk of the 'withering away of the school' altogether. Universities were transferred to Vesenkha (VSNKh) or the major economic commissariats. The majority were restructured along functional lines, involving narrow specialisms. 'Bourgeois' academics were, like school teachers, hounded out. However, by 1932 literacy was back in fashion. The socialist substitute, the *rabfak*, had produced high drop-out rates and little technical expertise. (One of those who dropped out was Nikita Khrushchev.) Selection reappeared and by the end of 1936 non-proletarians could again enter higher education. Russian nationalism was promoted and all other nations were referred to as 'younger brothers'. Tuition fees had to be paid for the final three forms of secondary education. Compulsory uniforms were introduced (including pigtails for girls) and these remained until the end of the Soviet era. Out of experimentation developed a fine educational system with a particularly good record in the pure sciences.

The party did not attempt to control all aspects of culture during the 1920s, and a 1925 decree made this clear. The defeat of the right, however, had serious repercussions, since several key writers were linked to Bukharin. The All-Russian Association of Proletarian Writers (RAPP) was in the ascendant in 1928 and propagated the hegemony of working-class values in fiction. There was only one fly in the ointment as far as RAPP was concerned, namely the All-Russian Union of Writers (AUW). The latter tried to keep politics out of their fiction but, although RAPP disapproved strongly of this attitude, most of the leading Russian writers were members of the AUW. Undeterred, RAPP launched a campaign against Evgeny Zamyatin, the AUW chairman, and Boris Pilnyak, head of the Leningrad branch, accusing them of publishing anti-Soviet works abroad. They were found guilty, and the AUW was dissolved and replaced by the All-Russian Union of Soviet Writers (AUSW). About half of the former AUW members were denied admission to the new organisation and, since they could not legally publish unless they were members, they faced a stark choice: recant and seek admission, or give up hope of publishing in the Soviet Union. RAPP was jubilant. However, in 1930 Stalin wrote an article for the party journal *Bolshevik*, in which he argued that nothing should be published which was contrary to the official point of view. This should have warned RAPP (which believed that literature should tell the truth, warts and all) that party goals might not always be identical with its own. In fact, the party disbanded both RAPP and AUSW in 1932 and set up a single organisation, the Union of Soviet Writers.

The end of RAPP was the end of an era in Russian literature. Writing during the years 1928–31 saw the glorification of the small man, as everyone pulled together to build the new USSR. Plots displayed an absence of hierarchy and experts and managers faded into the background. The machine was worshipped; indeed only a country as backward as the Soviet

Union could have placed so much faith in technology as the answer to man's problems. The rest of Europe had had the myth of the good machine exploded during the First World War, but for post-war Russia noise was still a sign of progress, and the smoke belching out of factory chimneys a symbol of a brighter future.

After 1931 the literary hero changes. The manager, the expert, the party official, in other words the decision-makers, take over. The writer had also to be a skilled craftsman, the 'engineer of the soul', as Stalin graphically put it. His frame of reference was laid down by **Andrei Zhdanov** in April 1934 at the 1st Congress of the Union of Soviet Writers. Socialist realism was to be the guiding light. In essence it meant building the brave new world with the bricks of the present. Literature was to uplift readers so that they would become more efficient constructors of socialism. It was to be deliberately didactic, and optimism was compulsory. Every novel, like a Hollywood picture of the period, had to have a happy ending as the hero or heroine battled against impossible odds to final victory.

The main hero, of course, was Stalin. Another was the Russian nation and its great figures; Peter the Great and Ivan the Terrible walked again. This tide of nationalism boded ill for the other nationalities. Stalin formulated the slogan 'National in form, Socialist in content', to describe what was permissible. In reality this amounted to little more than saying, for example, in Uzbek, what was being said about Stalin and Russia in Russian. The national heroes who had fought against imperial Russian control were banished; the local bards were swept aside and replaced by Russian luminaries. The purges which wiped out the non-Russian élites completed the process.

Zhdanov, Andrei Aleksandrovich: The guardian of Stalinist cultural orthodoxy, from socialist realism to the xenophobia of the late 1940s, known as the Zhdanovshchina, he became a member of the Politburo in 1939. In 1934, he laid down the rules for writers. He led the defence of Leningrad, 1941–44. He died suddenly in 1948, probably naturally.

THE PURGES

All the Show Trials between 1928 and 1934 linked the accused to the economy: the Shakhty engineers, the 'industrial party' trial, the Menshevik trial of 1931, the two secret trials of March 1933 which resulted in 70 state farm and People's Commissariat of Agriculture officials being shot, and the trial of the Metro-Vickers engineers. Other trials led to the passing of the death sentence on food scientists and bacteriologists. The trials all had to be carefully prepared since they had to appear plausible both inside the Soviet Union and outside. The paraphernalia of the great Purge Trials of 1936–38 was already in place: the written confessions, often to the most preposterous crimes, the bullying, sarcastic behaviour of the prosecutor, and the complete absence of any rules of evidence. All the shortcomings of the economy were to be blamed on the unfortunates in the dock.

The only major trial with political overtones which occurred before 1934 was that involving a group around a communist called M.N. Ryutin. They had produced a 200-page indictment of Stalin and his regime from a Bukharinist point of view in late summer 1932, in which the Secretary-General was described as the 'evil genius of the Russian revolution who, motivated by personal desire for power and revenge, had brought the revolution to the brink of destruction'. Since they wanted Stalin removed, he took this to mean that they were going to kill him, and therefore demanded the death penalty. But a majority of the Politburo was opposed to such an extreme measure, and in the event Ryutin and his followers were merely expelled from the party. Since many other party members had seen the offending document and had not reported it, the opportunity was seized to purge the whole organisation. Some 800,000 members were expelled in 1933 and a further 340,000 in 1934. The Ryutin affair rankled with Stalin, and time and again during the Purge Trials reference was made to it.

Stalin was shaken by the suicide of his second wife, **Nadezhda Alliluyeva**, in November 1932. She took her own life as a protest against the brutalities of collectivisation. Stalin never remarried and over time isolated himself more and more from his family. He seems to have lived surrounded by men, and although Khrushchev records that on one occasion he encountered a 'dark Caucasian beauty' in the Kremlin, she scurried away in an instant.

The murder of Sergei Kirov, party secretary in Leningrad, on 1 December 1934 set in motion a train of events which resulted in death for hundreds of thousands of people. Some of the details of the assassination are still not known, but it would appear that Stalin himself was implicated. Kirov was the only credible political alternative to Stalin, for he had been elected a secretary at the XVIIth Party Congress in 1934 at which Stalin had lost his post of Secretary-General. Kirov had been approached by delegates to stand for the post of Secretary-General but declined and reported this to Stalin. It is tempting to regard this episode as sealing Kirov's fate. With Kirov dead, much repressive legislation was introduced. One of the chief targets was the party itself, as inhibitions about spilling Bolshevik blood were cast aside. The XVIIth Congress, described at the time as the 'Congress of Victors', might more appropriately have been called the 'Congress of the Condemned', for 1,108 of its 1,966 delegates were executed and 98 of the 139 members of the CC elected at the Congress were shot in the years following.

The punitive legislation introduced – which included, for example, the death penalty for boys of 12 – was consonant with Stalin's views of the class struggle. Classes would disappear, he said, 'not as a result of the slackening of class conflict but as a result of its intensification'. The state would wither away 'not through the weakening of its power but through it becoming as strong as possible so as to defeat the remnants of the dying classes and to

Alliluyeva, Nadezhda Sergeevna: She married Stalin as his second wife at the age of 17 and was a student at the Industrial Academy where she met Nikita Khrushchev. She committed suicide, mainly because she could not cope with the harsh political reality of the time.

defend itself against capitalist encirclement'. This really was standing Marx on his head and is another example of Stalin's ideological relativism. An orthodox Marxist would expect classes to disappear as class conflict declines and for the state to wither away as the need for it disappears. Marx saw the state as an oppressive instrument used by the minority to oppress the majority.

Paradoxically, at the same time as these punitive measures were being applied, the Stalin constitution of 1936 – the 'most democratic in the world', as Stalin described it – came into effect. This introduced a bicameral legislature, the Soviet of the Union and the Soviet of Nationalities, collectively known as the USSR **Supreme Soviet**. The role of the local soviets now changed. Hitherto they had been seen as both legislative and executive organs, not mere extensions of the central authority, constituting a unified system of equal links of varying sizes. They had also been seen as peculiar to the stage of the dictatorship of the proletariat. The 1936 constitution shattered the unity of the soviets. Local soviets (all those below republican level) were reduced to the status of local authorities. The Supreme Soviets ('the supreme organs of the soviets') became legislative organs; and the government ('the supreme organ of state power') became the executive organ. The Supreme Soviets even began to call themselves parliaments, despite Lenin's contempt for that institution.

The new constitution stated that the foundations of socialism had been laid and that the exploiting classes had ceased to exist. There were now only fraternal classes – the working class and the collective farm peasantry – and they coexisted harmoniously with the intelligentsia, defined as a stratum rather than a class since it owned no property.

Freedom of speech, of the press, of assembly and of religious observance were guaranteed by the 1936 constitution. However, it was pointed out that the party remained the key institution and it was clear to every Soviet citizen that the party's interests would override any personal or group interest. Nevertheless, the Soviet Union appeared to be moving in the right direction and made a refreshing contrast to the rest of Europe where fascism was on the march.

There were three great Show Trials during the years 1936–38. The first took place in August 1936 and involved Kamenev and Zinoviev, along with sundry minor officials. Trotsky was introduced as the arch villain and it was claimed that he had ordered numerous assassinations and wreckings. **Andrei Vyshinsky** Andrei Vyshinsky, who became notorious as a brutal prosecutor, demanded in his closing speech that these mad dogs be shot, every last one of them! They were all shot, but it was Stalin who was the real judge. Vyshinsky epitomised a certain type of official who slavishly served Stalin. As an ex-Menshevik he felt that he had repeatedly to reaffirm his credentials of loyalty to the regime.

Supreme Soviet: Set up by the 1936 constitution; the USSR Supreme Soviet was bicameral: Soviet of the Union and Soviet of Nationalities; each republic and autonomous republic had its own Supreme Soviet but they were unicameral.

Vyshinsky, Andrei Yanuarevich: A venomous, merciless state prosecutor who gained worldwide notoriety for his courtroom behaviour during the great Show Trials. In 1949, he replaced Molotov as Minister of Foreign Affairs and was permanent Soviet representative at the United Nations. He turned his venom on the United States, especially during the Korean War, 1950–53.

The second great Show Trial should have involved Bukharin, Rykov and Tomsky in September 1936, but it was cancelled. Tomsky cheated the executioner by taking his own life and it was possible that neither Bukharin nor Rykov would make the obligatory confession. Also **Yagoda**, the man in charge, lost his position to **Nikolai Ezhov** in September 1936. Yagoda's dismissal may have been connected with his failure to deliver Bukharin and Rykov to the executioner. Everyone who knew Ezhov before he became head of the NKVD commented on how nice a man he was. There was, however, nothing nice about his two years in office (he was replaced by **Lavrenty Beria** in December 1938). They were the most dreadful peacetime years in the history of the Soviet Union. During the *Ezhovshchina*, the Ezhov times, blood flowed in rivers, and the guilt or innocence of the accused was completely immaterial. The political police had their plan targets like everyone else and were certainly not going to underfulfil them. According to a report, dated 11 December 1953, sent to Khrushchev and **Malenkov**, the total number condemned by the political police (*Cheka*, NKVD, etc.) between 1921 and 1953 was 4,060,306. The number shot was 799,455 of which no fewer than 681,692 were executed during 1937 and 1938, the *Ezhovshchina*. Lesser peaks of repression were 1930–33, 1942 and 1945–46. Another remarkable statistic is that over the period 1923–53 over 42 million Soviet citizens were imprisoned (39.1 million in the RSFSR alone). The vast majority of these were sentenced for non-political offences. If one excludes those under 14 and over 60 years of age, then during the course of one generation, 1923–53, every third citizen was sentenced to a term of imprisonment. In comparison, the highest number in prison in the immediate pre-war period was 111,800 in 1912. There were 884,000 children in internal exile (not permitted to live in their home towns but obliged to reside hundreds and sometimes thousands of kilometres away) in 1954. The bloodiest year for the Russian Orthodox Church was 1937 when 85,000 priests were shot. Add to this the fact that 5 million persons starved to death in the man-made famines of the 1930s. Five and a half million families (one can assume on average four members per family) were deported or exiled, half of them dying en route. In all, over the years 1918–53 about 3.5 million people from ethnic groups (the repressed people) were driven from their homes with, perhaps, a third dying en route.

The second great Show Trial turned out to involve Pyatakov, mentioned by Lenin in his 'Testament'; Sokolnikov, a signatory of the Brest-Litovsk Treaty and later a Commissar for Finance who had resisted the wild targets of the first FYP; and various other party functionaries. They were all lumped together as an 'Anti-Soviet Trotskyist Centre'. Pyatakov debased himself but nevertheless was shot. Sokolnikov died in a labour camp in 1939.

Yagoda, Genrikh Grigorevich: One of Stalin's bloodiest police chiefs, he himself fell victim to the executioner's bullet. Stalin made him head of the NKVD, 1934–July 1936. Just to keep him dangling, Stalin appointed him Commissar for Posts and Telegraph, 1936–37, and then had him arrested.

Ezhov, Nikolai Ivanovich: A 'bloody dwarf' and 'iron people's commissar', Ezhov gave his name to the bloodiest period of the purges, the Ezhovshchina. He succeeded Yagoda in September 1936 and, in turn, gave way to Beria in April 1939.

Beria, Lavrenty Pavlovich: A political gangster who was kind to his family. A fellow Georgian, he was Stalin's butcher in the Caucasus and succeeded Ezhov in 1939. He headed the Soviet atomic programme. He lost out to Khrushchev and others after Stalin's death and was executed.

Malenkov, Georgy Maksimilianovich: A skilled administrator, he played a key role during the war as a member of GKO. He was elected to the Politburo in 1946 and was also Deputy Prime Minister. Stalin poked fun at his excess flab.

The turn of the military came in due course. **Marshal Tukhachevsky**, a deputy Commissar for Defence and a leading strategic thinker, and many other top military figures were branded as traitors and shot in June 1937. Then followed a veritable slaughter of the top brass. All 11 deputy Commissars of Defence and 75 of the 80 members of the Supreme Military Council were executed. All eight admirals were shot. In total 35,000, half of the officer corps, were either executed or imprisoned. As Khrushchev was to admit later, it had all been a ghastly mistake since the charges against the officers were baseless (Khrushchev, 1971: 75).

The last great Show Trial opened on 2 March 1938 and involved the pair who had previously slipped the net, Bukharin and Rykov. Others thrown in included Yagoda, getting a taste of his own medicine. Vyshinsky branded them as the 'Bloc of the right wingers and Trotskyites', and the inevitable death sentence followed.

Foreign communists in exile in the Soviet Union were mown down like ripe corn, the NKVD being especially severe on the Germans and Poles. The greatest prize of all, however, eluded them until 20 August 1940, when an agent put an ice pick through Trotsky's skull in Mexico.

After such a catalogue of methodical madness the question must arise: was Stalin himself a victim of the frenzy of the period? Did he lose his sanity for a while? Svetlana Alliluyeva, his daughter, believes that officials such as Beria poisoned his mind and convinced him that the mad accusations were true. This is not so. Stalin himself edited the indictment against Pyatakov, Sokolnikov, Radek and others for the second great Show Trial. All lists of condemned were forwarded to Stalin and during 1938 at least 383 lists, containing 44,000 names of whom 39,000 were executed, were passed on to him. Stalin signed 362 lists, Molotov 373, **Voroshilov** 195, Kaganovich 191

and Zhdanov 177. Stalin's Politburo colleagues were enthusiastic in their support of these repressions. They often wrote comments in the margin encouraging the NKVD to step up the torture: for example, against certain names: 'beat again and again!'. The terror was turned off like a tap in 1939, but the show trials had had a momentum of their own. The NKVD did not have to go and look for suspects; they were inundated with denunciations. Such was the spirit of the times that in order to avoid being denounced one had to denounce everyone else first. There were even targets set for the number of people one had to denounce in a given period.

The heroic work of Aleksandr Yakovlev (Gorbachev's 'Comrade Glasnost') and others have seen over 4 million rehabilitated in the half-century after Stalin's death, a fraction of those who were unjustly sentenced, being quite innocent, but a laudable move to redress the moral balance. Yakovlev continues to be shocked by what he found in the archives. Repression was very wide-ranging. 'Terrorist gangs and groups' were discovered even in the

Kremlin commandant's office and in the government library. In some departments, socialist competitions were held to see which could achieve the highest numbers of people shot and quotas of people proposed for shooting were also the subject of competitions.

An understanding of the period can be gleaned from the fortunes of two persons caught up in the NKVD net, Osip and Nadezhda Mandelstam (Mandelstam, 1971: 304–5). Thousands, perhaps millions, had similar experiences.

Osip Mandelstam was a gifted poet but never became a Bolshevik. Like many other writers his patron was Bukharin. He was arrested in May 1934 for composing a poem which contained an unflattering reference to Stalin [**Doc. 8, p. 114**]: 'All we hear is the Kremlin mountaineer/The murderer and peasant-slayer.' His wife Nadezhda recalls the techniques used to force confessions [**Doc. 9, p. 115**]: lack of sleep, bright lights shining in the eyes, poor food, the deliberate telling of lies to confuse the prisoner and make him more anxious – 'such and such a person had been arrested and had confessed everything' – and physical beatings, although Mandelstam was spared these. This goes a long way towards explaining why innocent men and women confessed to the most outlandish crimes. Broken down they were willing to admit anything providing they could just get some sleep and be left in peace. Of course some did not break down: they were the prisoners who never appeared at the trials. Nadezhda Mandelstam draws a distinction between the type of person who was an interrogator before 1937 and afterwards. Until 1937 the Chekist or NKVD man was often well read in Russian literature, the sort of person who would have been all in favour of RAPP and delighted to display his culture, convinced that his work was helping to build the new Russia. In 1937 a new type took over: men who had little culture and no beliefs, and were only concerned with meeting their quota of confessions. Osip Mandelstam's interrogator, like many of the pre-1937 men, himself became a victim of the purges and was shot.

Denunciations flowed into the NKVD in torrents. Before 1937 they had to have a semblance of truth to be effective; afterwards it did not matter. Denunciations became a convenient way of acquiring something desirable. If one's superior was found guilty, promotion was in prospect. If neighbours were removed, a flat would become vacant. Personal relations became hazardous, for anyone might let something slip which would then be reported to the police. Spontaneous and personal openness became things of the past. Parents could never be completely frank at home, since something they said might be repeated at school with disastrous consequences. If the head of the household was sentenced the whole family fell into disgrace. Wives and children could then be expelled from the cities and obliged to live at least 105 km away. Life for the convicted was relatively easy before 1937, but then things got worse. Wives were interned in camps and small children were confined in special institutions.

Mandelstam was saved from death by the intervention of Bukharin. He was packed off to the Urals, but a further plea resulted in him and his wife being allowed to reside in Voronezh. They spent three years in exile in Voronezh and returned to Moscow in May 1937. Mandelstam had even tried to write an Ode to Stalin in January 1937 in order to rehabilitate himself and his wife but the words would not come. He and his wife were again thrown out of Moscow in June 1937 and told to reside at least 105 km from the capital, since they were 'convicted persons'. They eventually moved to Kalinin, north-west of Moscow. Mandelstam travelled frequently to Moscow and begged the Union of Soviet Writers for work. He and his wife were given accommodation in a rest home east of Moscow, but shortly after their arrival, on 1 May 1938, Mandelstam was arrested and was never seen again. His wife returned to Kalinin and narrowly escaped arrest. She then moved to a small town north-east of Moscow, coming in regularly to the capital in search of information about her husband. She eventually discovered that he had died in a labour camp, probably in December 1938.

FOREIGN POLICY

The rise of fascism was completely misinterpreted in Moscow, where it was assumed to be the most predatory face of finance capital, with only a limited capacity to endure, if it ever came to power. The Comintern, the Russian Communist Party wearing its foreign suit, came to the conclusion that the German National Socialists (**NSDAP**) were claiming to do the impossible. They promised to put German industry back on its feet, which implied that big business would do very well, but at the same time they canvassed the votes of small businessmen, shopkeepers and farmers. They promised the latter they would protect them against unfair competition and secure a bright future for them, yet in order to do this the Nazis would have to restrict the activities of the industrial giants. In other words the Nazis could not satisfy both sides. The Italian fascists were not seen as a threat to the Soviet Union, so why should German fascism be different? The Social Democrats (**SPD**) were regarded as the main enemy and labelled 'social fascists'. In Germany the SPD was the main supporter of the Weimar republic, and it was assumed in Moscow that the destruction of the SPD would topple the republic.

The breath-taking ease with which Hitler and the NSDAP swept the Communist Party of Germany (**KPD**) off the political stage, the pusillanimity of the other political parties and the Führer's ruthlessness in disposing of Ernst Röhm and the SA (*Sturmabteilung* or storm troops) as part of a deal with the German army, the *Reichswehr*, rudely awakened Moscow. The

NSDAP: National Socialist German Workers' Party or Nazi Party.

SPD: Social Democratic Party of Germany; re-founded in 1945 and fused with KPD in Soviet Zone of Germany in April 1946 to form SED.

KPD: Communist Party of Germany; founded in December 1919; re-founded in Soviet Zone of Germany June 1945; fused with Soviet Zone SPD in April 1946 to form Socialist Unity Party of Germany (SED).

Comintern, at its VIIth and final Congress in August 1935, called for the formation of a popular front. Western governments were slow to react. After all, the previous Comintern policy had been to appeal to rank-and-file social democrats over the heads of their leaders, who were publicly vilified.

The Soviet Union set out to repair its fences with the rest of Europe. It joined the League of Nations in 1934 and signed a treaty with France in 1935 which was extended to embrace Czechoslovakia. The 1936 constitution, partly for external consumption, made the USSR more attractive. However, 1936 was a bad year for Moscow. The German remilitarisation of the Rhineland, the signing of the Anti-Comintern Pact by Germany, Italy and Japan, and the onset of the Spanish Civil War, with the Soviet Union as the main ally of the Spanish republic, boded ill for Soviet hopes. In 1936, Hitler launched a four-year plan to prepare for war. The main target was the Soviet Union and Stalin was aware of this. In order to buy time to prepare the country for the forth-coming titanic struggle, Stalin hoped to forge a Soviet–German pact along the lines of the relationship before 1933. Negotiations began in early 1937 to revive Soviet–German trade but they failed because Hitler would not coun-tenance a political dimension. When the Soviet team returned to Moscow, in March 1937, they were imprisoned or shot.

The Munich Agreement of September 1938, from which the Soviet Union was excluded, led Stalin to doubt whether France and Great Britain would ever stand up to Germany. The Soviet Union stated on numerous occasions that it would fight in support of Czechoslovakia, even if the other powers did not. Had Stalin been willing to risk a war with Germany at that time, it would not have been necessary. It is now known that the Czechoslovaks had decided not to fight.

Stalin had at least two alternatives so far as policy towards Germany was concerned. He could enter into an alliance with France and Great Britain and thereby effectively checkmate the Third Reich, which could not face a war on two fronts. However, the Soviet leader could not be absolutely sure that France and Great Britain would remain committed if war with Germany did break out. Stalin's other option was to sign a pact with Hitler and unleash the dogs of war westwards. When he came to the conclusion that war was inevitable his main objective was to keep the USSR out of the conflict. After what he had done to the Red Army and Navy this was the most prudent course. The Soviet Union began negotiating seriously in May 1939, when Litvinov, a Jew, was replaced as Commissar for Foreign Affairs by Molotov. Litvinov was spared imprisonment or death and was sent off to Washington as ambassador. His subordinates were not so lucky. They were demoted, imprisoned or killed. They paid a heavy price for failing to fashion a col-lective security system to keep the Soviet Union out of the coming war (Overy, 1997: 136). The German–Soviet Non-Aggression Pact was signed by Ribbentrop and Molotov in Moscow on 23 August 1939 (Stalin and Hitler never met) and it was consequently only a matter of time before Hitler attacked in the west. Moscow was alarmed by the rapid success of the German *Blitzkrieg* in Poland and by the fact that neither France nor Great Britain made any move to attack Germany. Stalin even began to fear that the *Wehrmacht* (German armed forces) would not stop at the agreed demarcation line in Poland and would carry on to invade the Soviet Union. He therefore ordered the Red Army to enter Poland on 17 September 1939 to secure the USSR's slice of the bargain. France and Great Britain obligingly did not treat this as an act of war against them.

With Finland part of its zone of influence, Moscow pressed the Finns to accept a frontier away from Leningrad. The Soviets also wanted naval bases on Finnish soil, but Helsinki would not countenance this. The Red Army therefore launched an assault against Finland on 30 November 1939, but the Winter War highlighted its deficiencies, and led to the death of some 200,000 of its soldiers. In order to forestall intervention by France and Great Britain, a lenient peace was signed in March 1940. The Finnish debacle ended the 'cult of the Civil War', Stalin's words, in military thinking.

Klimenty Voroshilov was sacked as Commissar for Defence and replaced by **Marshal Timoshenko**. He concentrated on building up rapidly huge tank and aircraft numbers and training many more officers. Over 80 per cent of officers arrested in the purges were reinstated. Timoshenko brought back the old uniforms and promoted over a thousand to the rank of general or admiral. Junior officers could no longer criticise their superiors. The political commissar slipped into the background. Work began on fortifying the new border with Germany.

Hitler regarded a war between Germany and the Soviet Union as inevitable. The world was too small for two such ambitious ideologies as fascism and communism. Stalin considered that a conflict could be avoided. He thought that Hitler could be bought off with concessions and believed that Germany had to defeat Great Britain first. This would give the Soviet Union the breathing space necessary to build up its armed might to such a pitch that the *Wehrmacht* would not invade.

Stalin handled his relations with Hitler very badly. Since the USSR was the weaker power he had to appease the German dictator. When Molotov visited Berlin in November 1940 Hitler proposed that the Soviet Union should join the Tripartite Pact which linked Germany, Italy and Japan with Berlin's east European satellites. The bait was Soviet gains in the Black Sea area and in Central Asia. Molotov astonishingly then produced his own shopping list. Finland and southern Bukovina (Romania) were to fall under Soviet sway; Bulgaria was to form part of a Soviet security zone, as was Sweden; and notice was served that the Soviets had future designs on Hungary, Yugoslavia, Greece and even on part of German-occupied Poland. The Soviets also

Timoshenko, Marshal Semen Konstantinovich: He occupied many top military posts during the Great Fatherland War but it was his friendship with Stalin, going back to the Civil War, which saved him from retribution for failure. He was defeated by the Germans at Kharkov, May 1942. This cost him his command and he was transferred to the north-western front, then moving to *Stavka* for the rest of the war.

wanted military bases in the Dardanelles and a Soviet–Danish condominium over the Baltic. Shortly afterwards Stalin accepted the invitation to join the Tripartite Pact and demanded that the Soviet Union be permitted to expand through Iran to the Persian Gulf. New documents reveal that Stalin's main aim was to agree a new pact defining spheres of influence in eastern Europe. Everything else would be a bonus.

Stalin's demands revealed the weakness of the Soviet Union, and instead of pacifying Hitler they provoked him. Just why did Stalin act so clumsily? Perhaps he thought that if he did not make any demands Hitler would have regarded the Soviet Union as weak and afraid to assert its interests. Stalin remained unaware of his blunder, however, and the German invasion of 22 June 1941 took him completely by surprise, even though he had been forewarned by his own intelligence services. He simply refused to believe the information. The *Wehrmacht* had intended to attack earlier, in May 1941, but had been detained in Greece and Yugoslavia. Stalin thought he was safe in June, since this would be too late for a summer offensive.

If the prime goal of Soviet foreign policy during the 1930s was to keep the country out of a European war, then it was a dismal failure. The rise of fascism was looked on with equanimity; indeed, the NSDAP and the KPD co-operated from time to time and were even known to share the same offices in some places. Stalin thought that the Second World War would be a re-run of the First, with the European powers becoming bogged down. When they had exhausted themselves the USSR would be free to intervene and do as it pleased. Again, this was a disastrous miscalculation. All the USSR succeeded in doing was to make Germany even stronger. A Machiavelli might argue that in the end it all turned out right for the Soviet Union. Not only was Germany defeated but Moscow ended up occupying part of Germany, thereby making the USSR a great power. This, however, is no justification for a policy which unleashed a holocaust which killed over 50 million and maimed millions of others in body and mind. Also, this argument assumes that the Soviet occupation of eastern Europe was a net benefit to Moscow. All the European powers must assume some responsibility for the outbreak of hostilities, but had France, Great Britain and the Soviet Union acted decisively together in 1939, Germany could not have launched a European and eventually a world war.

STALINISM TRIUMPHANT

Stalinism flowered in a responsive soil. Without his army of willing cohorts, Stalin could not have propelled the Soviet Union into breakneck industrialisation and collectivisation and maintained the pace after the initial enthusiasm had ebbed. A corps of state and party officials came into being who were welded to the Stalin chariot. The bloodletting and the violence of collect-ivisation found many wanting, and they passed from the scene and were replaced by those who were not so squeamish. Battle-scarred, ruthless and dedicated, the new men really were people of a special mould. Since their goal was socialism, any measure which advanced the USSR towards that glorious culmination was justified. If mistakes were made they paled into insignificance when placed alongside the triumphs of the period. Since capitalism had been left behind, what was being built in the USSR had to be socialism.

What were Stalin's aims during the 1930s? Simply to make the Soviet Union politically, economically and militarily strong. The greater the indus-trial growth, the stronger the USSR became. The terror was used to produce a pliable, malleable work force, to destroy opposition to central directives, to render everyone insecure, from the top official to the collective farmer, and to shift blame for all the shortcomings of everyday life on to the shoulders of those arrested and sentenced.

The typical Stalinist official was of peasant origin. He eagerly followed the party leadership and quickly accepted the view that all opinions which differed from those of the leadership were treasonous. The XVIIth Party Congress in 1934 can be seen as a watershed. Eighty per cent of the delegates had joined the party before 1920 and hence really belonged to the Leninist élite. At the Congress, however, Stalin secured the abolition of **Rabkrin**, the Workers' and Peasants' Inspectorate, which supervised government officials, and of the Central Control Commission, which was responsible for party officials. This breakthrough, allied to Kirov's murder, opened the floodgates to violence. The purges swept most of the Leninist élite to their doom. They were replaced in turn by the Stalinist élite. Some of the Stalinist cadres were motivated by idealism, some were attracted by the perquisites of office, others by the feeling of power which their position afforded them.

Rabkrin: People's Com-missariat of Workers and Peasants Inspection; founded in 1920 to sup-ervise all government organs; dissolved in 1934 when functions were transferred to Commis-sion of Soviet Control; in 1940 became People's Commissariat of State Control and from 1946 Ministry of State Control.

Stalin liked military metaphors. He referred to the party as the General Staff of the proletariat [**Doc. 1, p. 106**]. At a CC plenum in March 1937 he divided the party into leaders and the led. There were 3,000–4,000 senior leaders, who were the generals; the 30,000–40,000 middle-rank officials made up the officer corps, and the 100,000–150,000 lower-level leaders were the NCOs. This neatly illustrates Stalin's hierarchical way of thinking. No one had any right to an opinion unless his seniority entitled him to one.

The way Stalin projected himself is instructive. During the 1920s he claimed to be the only true apostle of Lenin; others, such as Trotsky and Zinoviev, were anti-Leninists. Gradually, Stalin became the equal of Lenin, and the phrase 'Lenin-Stalin' made its appearance. The slogan 'Stalin is the Lenin of today' marked the next stage, in which Stalin was ahead of Lenin. Stalin was projected as the father of the nation and the epithet 'Stalinist'

Plate 1 Voroshilov, Molotov, Stalin and Yezhov visiting the Moscow–Volga Canal under construction, 22 April 1937

© David King Collection

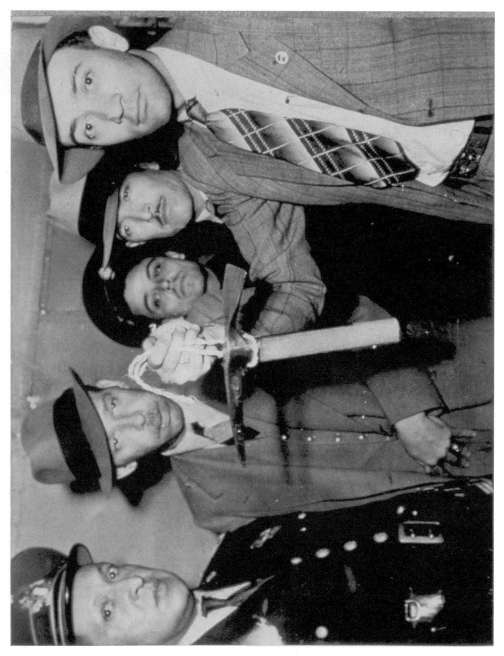

Plate 2 A Mexican policeman shows the ice-pick which killed Trotsky, August 1940
© David King Collection

Plate 3 The siege of Leningrad: the dead are carried away on sledges, 1941
© David King Collection

Plate 4 The dead dictator is laid to rest, March 1953
© David King Collection

guaranteed success. He could work miracles and his intervention produced exaltation and joy [**Doc. 14, p. 125**]. So successful was the projection of this image [**Doc. 15, p. 127**] that many people accepted it and believed that all the injustices of the 1930s were the fault of nasty and incompetent officials. Some went to their deaths convinced that if only comrade Stalin had known what was really going on he would have stepped in to right the injustice.

Stalin's rise meant that the role of the party changed. It was no longer true that the party knew best. Stalin's thought became the fount of all wisdom.

There was an assault on learning after 1928 so as to destroy the influence and power of the 'old' élites. They were replaced by new élites whose attitude to learning was radically different. All intellectual activity was to be channelled into fighting the battle for socialism. Learning was demystified, and anyone with the right attitude, a Stalinist attitude, could become a specialist. Folk heroes appeared in many fields: Makarenko in education, Vilyams in grassland management, Lysenko in agrobiology, Marr in linguistics and Michurin in fruit-farming. The fact that practically everything they preached was dismissed out of hand in the west only strengthened their position. What else could one expect from bourgeois scientists jealous of the successes of socialism?

Hence Stalinism meant modernisation, it meant technology, it meant a bright future, it meant victory. The tide of Russian nationalism also rose as national self-adulation increased. This, as has been mentioned, spelled doom for the non-Russian élites.

How did Stalin's state function? The twin pillars of power were the party and the government. The party acted as a parallel government and checked on the implementation of the plans. The flow of information was restricted. The more important an official, the more he was told. The party watched the government, but the political police watched both. Key decision making was centred in Stalin's own chancellery, presided over by a trusted official, Poskrebyshev. All the threads came together in the chancellery, all the information was pieced together there, the jigsaw was complete. Stalin was the only person in the entire country who saw the whole picture and he skilfully used the information available to him. Stalin's power was not based on control of the government or the party or the political police. It involved exploiting all three. It was vital to Stalin that he should maintain several independent sources of information; in that way he hoped to judge which source was misleading. After 1936 he successfully prevented any body, be it the Politburo or the CC of the party or the government, meeting as a group and taking counsel together independent of him. He preferred to consult individuals or small groups, and here his tactics were based on setting one person against another. This explains why there were only two Party Congresses between 1934 and 1953, for they were frankly unnecessary. Stalin very seldom left Moscow. He disliked mass meetings and was always conscious of his Georgian accent. He restricted the number of people who had direct access to him and in so doing created a mystique around his person.

Why and how did Stalinism function? The destruction of the old ruling strata, the more able farmers, the *kulaks* and the old intelligentsia left a void. It was inevitable that the authoritarian political culture which was just being challenged by civil society (autonomous institutions outside the control of the government) and the new élites (industrialists, lawyers and so on) before 1914 should reassert itself. Lenin changed his views on the state, moving from a weak to a strong state. This fitted the pre-1917 Russian tradition. Autonomous labour organisations, such as factory committees and trade unions, were emasculated because they wished to share in decision making. No independent institutions were permitted to emerge. Hence all the new institutions and organisations were instrumental, to serve Bolshevik, later Stalinist, goals. The Soviet constitution afforded soviets legislative and executive functions but this constitution was at variance with the newly emerging Bolshevik state. The failure of world revolution isolated Soviet Russia and it had to survive on its own. Outside ideas, 'bourgeois' ideas, were by definition counter-revolutionary. The violent internecine strife which illuminated the 1920s encouraged authoritarianism. Utopianism was given its head during the first Five-Year Plan and led to untold misery for millions of peasants and others. Bukharin, perceptively, warned of the 'Leviathan state' which would emanate from the 'military-feudal exploitation of the peasantry'. The Bolsheviks were determined to eliminate the peasant **mir** or community. The **muzhik** had to depart the stage.

Mir: Peasant commune.

Muzhik: Russian peasant.

The type of economic planning adopted shaped the regime. Bolshevik rejection of the market was total and this was in part due to the fact that the market was only just emerging in Russia in 1914. Communist planners declined to base their plans on value and price and concentrated on material balances instead. The former would have afforded enterprises the opportunity, in their own interests, to achieve the plan more effectively by cutting costs. Costs, in fact, were ignored in the early years of the first FYP. Material balances meant that an increasing number of quantitative goals, which could not encapsulate quality and innovation, had to be set, thereby requiring more and more bureaucrats. Stalin, significantly, complained of the difficulty of obtaining objective information about enterprise potential during the 1930s. Planners were reduced to increasing annual targets by a certain amount (the ratchet principle). Stalin was forced to legalise the market, but only the *kolkhoz* market. Illegal markets began to develop to make up for the lacunae which the planners could not or would not cope with.

There appears to have been an inner logic to the course of the terror. Stalin removed Genrikh Yagoda, People's Commissar for Internal Affairs, in

September 1936, and appointed Nikolai Ezhov in his place. Stalin talked about being 'four years behind' in the struggle against Trotsky and other political foes. It seems that he perceived that Yagoda was not up to the task of organising the Show Trials. Ezhov had the ability of sensing what Stalin wanted and of acting on it. He was able to continue and accelerate the collection of material against Bukharin and the right, which Yagoda had begun. In line with the fear of war at the time, Yagoda and his top NKVD aides were branded German spies, among other things. Ezhov recommended the arrest of 2,273 NKVD officers between October 1936 and August 1938. They were all replaced by Ezhov appointees.

In May 1937, Stalin declared that the Red Army Intelligence Directorate and its apparatus had 'fallen into German hands'. He ordered the elimination of the agents' network. According to one estimate about half of the military intelligence officers were executed. Then the professional military was severely dealt with. While this was going on the campaign against former oppositionists, mainly Mensheviks and SRs, continued. In fact it ran from December 1934 to March 1937. After the February–March 1937 CC plenum mass repression against party cadres began. The main targets were rightists and Trotskyists. NKVD regional departments vied with one another to arrest these 'enemies of the people'. In fact a veritable socialist competition developed. It was up to party bureaux and conferences to expel comrades. Then the NKVD arrested them. Hence local party and NKVD organisations had considerable latitude when it came to deciding who should be repressed. However, senior party expulsions were decided by Moscow. Rank-and-file party members were encouraged to denounce their seniors and did so with gusto. One of the consequences was that the June 1937 CC plenum expelled CC members in unprecedented numbers. Stalin spoke of dealing with a universal conspiracy against Soviet power.

War was held to be inevitable and evidence of this was that Stalin failed to take his usual vacation in Sochi, on the Black Sea coast, in 1937. In fact, he did not return to Sochi until 1945. He was concerned about the preparations for war by Germany, Poland and Japan and demanded action against 'fifth columnists' and agents of foreign intelligence services. Arrests of 'national contingents' got under way in July 1937. On Stalin's orders all Germans working in defence industries were arrested. Some of them were to be deported. An NKVD order stated that the Gestapo and German General Staff were using German nationals in leading sectors of industry, especially the defence sector, for espionage and sabotage. Other nationalities were swept up as well. About 68,000 were arrested and 42,000 shot. Only about a third of them were actually German (Jansen and Petrov, 2002: 94). Then in August 1937, Ezhov ordered, with the permission of the Politburo, the liquidation of 'Polish diversionary and espionage groups'. As usual those arrested were divided into two categories: the first were to be shot and the second put in the Gulag. Almost every Pole in the Soviet Union was caught up in this purge. Other 'national operations' were conducted against those who had returned from Harbin after the Chinese Eastern Railway had been sold to the Chinese in 1935: Latvians, Estonians, Romanians, Greeks, Afghans, Iranians and a host of other nationalities. The regional NKVD chiefs were given their heads. One got carried away and proposed that they should all be 'exterminated like mad dogs'. The 'national operations' were completed in November 1938 and involved about 350,000 persons. Of these 247,000 were executed, with the Poles the hardest hit. Of 144,000 Poles arrested, 111,000 were sentenced to death. Almost every Pole in the Comintern was killed.

In July 1936, the NKVD began deporting Germans and Poles living in the Ukrainian-Polish border region to Kazakhstan. About 35,000 Poles and 10,000 Germans were sent east. In July 1937, deportations of those living on the borders with Iran and Afghanistan began. Over a thousand Kurdish families and 2,000 Iranian families were removed in 1937–38 (Jansen and Petrov, 2002: 99). The Japanese invasion of Manchuria alarmed Moscow and, in August 1937, the NKVD began deporting all Koreans from the Far East. In October 1937, almost 172,000 Koreans had been dispatched to Kazakhstan and Uzbekistan. About 11,000 Chinese were also sent west. The logic behind these moves appears to have been Stalin's determination to prevent the emergence of a fifth column in the Soviet Union. While these deportations were going on, wives and children of 'rightists and Trotskyists' were being placed in Siberian camps. This involved over 18,000 wives and 25,000 children.

While the 'national operations' and deportations were in full swing, top party officials such as Kaganovich, Molotov, Zhdanov, Andreev, Malenkov, Khrushchev, Mikoyan, and Ezhov himself fanned out to accelerate the purge of party members and state officials in the republics. In the second half of 1937, about 97,000 party members were expelled.

Another target was the Comintern. In November 1937, Stalin told Georgy Dimitrov, head of the organisation, that Trotskyists should be 'persecuted, shot and destroyed'. They were 'worldwide provocateurs and the most vicious agents of fascism' (Jansen and Petrov, 2002: 101). The purge penetrated Mongolia as well. In April 1938, almost 11,000, including 7,800 lamas, had been arrested. Around 4 per cent of the adult male population was liquidated.

The Soviet constitution of 1936 had declared that the battle to build socialism had been won. There were two classes, workers and collective farm peasants, and a stratum, the intelligentsia. However there were 'other people', such as former *kulaks*, who were superfluous to the further development of socialism. The decision was taken to liquidate them. Order no. 00447 [**Doc. 11, p. 121**], approved by the Politburo, dated 31 July 1937 and entitled 'On Operations Aimed at Repressing Former Kulaks, Criminals and other Anti-Soviet Elements', was lethal. Throughout the country, 268,950 persons were to be arrested of whom 75,950 were to be executed. Each republic and region was given a quota. The Procurator General, Andrei Vyshinsky, set the tone. The 'observance of legal procedures and the preliminary approval of arrests are not necessary.' Needless to say quotas were over-fulfilled so the Politburo simply increased the targets. Eventually, between August 1937 and November 1938, over 767,000 were arrested, of whom almost 387,000 were shot. Sometimes a region exceeded its death quota without the permission of the centre. Stalin personally gave permission for many extra executions. One example was Omsk *oblast* where the death tally was raised from 1,000 to 8,000.

The terror was a colossal undertaking. Order no. 00447 was being executed at the same time as the repression of the 'national contingents', the purges of party and state officials, the weeding out of military intelligence and top military officers and so on. Under Ezhov (he gave way to Lavrenty Beria in December 1938) an estimated 1.5 million were arrested and about 700,000 executed. However, this staggering total may still be an underestimate.

Inevitably mistakes were made but the only ones acknowledged were those involving party members. In January 1938, a CC plenum adopted a resolution on errors committed during the purge of the party. Serious 'errors and perversions' had come to light. Communists had sometimes been expelled in a 'criminally frivolous way'. Nevertheless vigilance was still the order of the day. There were still communists who had to be 'unmasked'. They had protected themselves so far by expelling other members to ensure that no accusation of lack of vigilance could be levelled at them. They were careerists and had to be removed. Those unjustly expelled could be re-admitted to the party. Presumably the reason for the sudden ending of the party purges was that serious damage was being done to the effectiveness of party cadres in implementing central policy.

Stalin and the top leadership appear to have believed that there was growing political opposition to their rule. The inevitable oncoming war fuelled uncertainty. This was a potent mix as the leadership sought to protect themselves and the country from fifth columnists in an increasingly dangerous domestic and international environment.

4

The Great Fatherland War, 1941–45

THE ATTACK

Operation Barbarossa (Red Beard) was launched at 3.30 (Moscow time) on the morning of Sunday 22 June 1941 across a wide front. There were three main groups to the German attack. Army Group North headed for the Baltic States and Leningrad, Army Group Centre struck towards Belorussia and Moscow, and Army Group South thrust towards Ukraine and Kiev. The *Wehrmacht* had 3.2 million men at its disposal and Finnish, Hungarian, Slovak, Romanian, Italian and Spanish troops joined in later.

The Red Army, numbering some 2.9 million men, and the Red Air Force were quite unprepared for the onslaught. Despite precise information about the imminent attack from defecting German soldiers and the British government – both ignored – front commanders were under strict instructions not to take any action. Hence when the Germans attacked they had to ask for orders.

Stalin was stunned by the turns of events. Just why he should have trusted Hitler to keep to the terms of the Non-Aggression Pact and not attack the USSR has never been satisfactorily explained. It is all the more puzzling given his suspiciousness, verging on paranoia, of the motives and actions of Soviet citizens. Stalin worked round the clock but his commanders did not tell him the full horror story of what was happening at the front. On 23 June he approved the setting up of **Stavka**, a General Staff responsible for all land, sea and air operations. On 27 June, with German forces near Minsk, the true magnitude of the danger dawned on him. He took himself off to his dacha and read a play about Ivan the Terrible. The Politburo was left to its own devices. It set up the State Committee of Defence (GKO), on 30 June. It had a wider brief, supervising the military, political and economic life of the country. Its members then drove out to Stalin's dacha to plead with him to return and take charge. He was surprised at their faith in him. He returned to the Kremlin on 1 July as supreme war leader.

Stavka: General Staff of the Red Army and Navy during the Great Patriotic War (1941–45).

Stalin had sufficiently composed himself by 3 July 1941 to address the nation and to tell the terrible truth about the war [**Doc. 16, p. 128**]. He appealed to everyone in the name of Mother Russia to fight the invader to the death. If the Red Army was forced to retreat, nothing of any value was to be left for the invader. A scorched earth policy was to be carried out.

GERMAN WAR GOALS

The Germans did not invade the Soviet Union because they feared imminent attack. It was thus not a preventive war on their part, but a continuation of the policy of aggression pursued since 1938. The immediate target was to attain a line running from Archangel to Astrakhan. From there German bombers could hit industrial targets in the Urals. This was not to be an ordinary occupation: communism was seen by Hitler as the main obstacle to his plans for world domination and the Soviet Union had all the raw materials and living space, *Lebensraum*, that Germany needed. The Russians were to be 'severely beaten' and reduced to a 'leaderless people performing labour'. Since socialism in the Soviet Union was ineradicable, the USSR was to be broken up into separate socialist states which would be dependent on Germany. A 'national Russian state' was not to be allowed to exist since it would inevitably be anti-German. The *Wehrmacht* was given orders to be ruthless: 'We are not waging war to conserve the enemy', declared the Führer. Himmler, head of the SS (*Schutzstaffel* or protection units), was even more frank: 'I am totally indifferent to the fate of the Russians and Czechs. . . . Whether they live well or are wracked by hunger only interests me in so far as we need them as slaves for our culture. Otherwise they don't interest me.' The *Generalplan Ost* stipulated that about 75 per cent of the Slav population was to be moved later to Siberia. Germans, Norwegians, Swedes, Danes and Dutch were to colonise the land vacated by the Slavs.

In the Caucasus the *Wehrmacht* supported national governments, which sprang up in the wake of the retreating Red Army. A Karachai national government, for instance, came into being. The experiment, however, was not repeated in the Slav areas. This policy was opposed by some German commanders. General Jodl, for example, wanted to appeal to the Russians over the heads of their leaders as a way of breaking up the Soviet Union.

THE PROGRESS OF THE WAR

The *Wehrmacht* knew that it could not conquer and occupy the whole of the Soviet Union. It needed to defeat the Red Army in a *Blitzkrieg*, a lightning war. The resources of the country in men and war material were so enormous that a long-drawn-out encounter would most likely favour the Soviets. Hence the tactics were to advance rapidly and encircle and destroy huge concentrations of men and equipment. This required great mobility and almost total control of the air. This the *Luftwaffe* had secured early on. The Soviet forces' main hope was to slow down the German advance. Every hold-up, every hour's delay, gave more time for an effective defence to be organised. Hence Stalin's appeal for every citizen to defend Mother Russia to the last drop of blood [**Doc. 16, p. 128**].

The first stage of Operation Barbarossa was completed successfully but then the Germans hesitated. Hitler thought of striking at Leningrad, the General Staff wanted to push on to Moscow, but on 21 August Hitler surprised everyone by deciding to go south to take Ukraine. There the *Wehrmacht* could live off the land, which it could not do in the north. Then, on 17 September 1941, with Leningrad at his mercy, Hitler withdrew his armour and bombers to strengthen the forces in the south in their bid to take the Crimea and the Baku oilfields. Leningrad was now to be starved into submission.

Then Hitler decided to attack Moscow, and on 30 September 1941 he launched 'Operation Typhoon'. As the advance German units reached the outskirts of the capital, the government repaired to Kuibyshev, in the Urals, but Stalin made for his dacha. Troops were preparing to blow it up. He told them: 'We will not surrender Moscow.' Meanwhile the underground stopped, the NKVD and police left the streets, the bakeries stopped producing bread, and the communists tore up their party cards. Incredibly the Germans did not realise this, and once gone the opportunity never recurred. German losses were mounting. By the end of November 1941, 164,000 *Wehrmacht* troops were dead. Together with the wounded, this meant that about 25 per cent of the German forces in the Soviet Union were now casualties. These figures were dwarfed by Soviet losses. Between June and December the Red Army lost 2.7 million killed and 3.4 million taken prisoner. No wonder the German High Command thought, quite erroneously, that the Red Army had no more reserves.

The Red Army counter-attacked during the night of 5 December 1941 and, when it discovered how weak the German defences were, it launched an offensive over a 1,000 kilometre front. Had Hitler not demanded that every German soldier hold his ground, disaster might have overtaken the *Wehrmacht*. Even so it was thrown back 200–300 kilometres in places.

The successful defence of Moscow was due in large part to the incisive leadership of **Zhukov**. He was fortunate to have some fresh Siberian troops at his disposal and he held them back until they could have the maximum effect. Stalin had been able to withdraw about half his Far Eastern troops, together with about 1,000 tanks and 1,000 aircraft, to bolster the capital's

Zhukov, Marshal Georgy Konstantinovich: The most prominent and successful Red Army commander during the Great Fatherland War. After a successful career he became commander of Soviet occupation forces in Germany. Stalin was wary of his popularity and in April 1946 demoted him but after Stalin's death he returned to Moscow as Deputy USSR Minister of Defence.

defences. The vital information which permitted this move came from Richard Sorge, a German communist spy in Tokyo, who had discovered that the Japanese were not going to strike against Siberia but against the US in the east and the British and French in the south. Had Japan decided to attack Siberia from its base in northern China it is difficult to see how the Soviet Union could have survived. Hitler had not even informed Japan of the planned attack on 22 June 1941. His reason was that he did not wish Japan to share in the glory of routing the Red Army! The Soviet Union was fortunate that the Anti-Comintern Pact only existed on paper and was not a military alliance.

The battle for Moscow was a turning point in the war. Was the failure of the *Blitzkrieg* due more to the *Wehrmacht's* shortcomings than to the strengths of the Red Army? The Germans were not prepared for a winter war. Hitler had only expected a short campaign, leaving 15–20 divisions in the USSR. The clinging mud meant that tracked vehicles were necessary, but most German vehicles were wheeled. German carts fell apart and their horses died in thousands, while the mangy Russian animal carried on. When the frosts came the Germans had no warm clothing and little anti-freeze for their vehicles; Soviet tanks did not need this since they ran on diesel. Jackboots offered little protection at −30 C, and between 27 November 1941 and 31 March 1942 over a quarter of a million German soldiers succumbed to frostbite.

German estimates of Soviet strength were woefully inaccurate. Yet even had his generals come up with correct estimates, Hitler would have dismissed them out of hand as being pro-Soviet. He had an *idée fixe* about Slavs being *Untermenschen*, or inferior beings, and was unwilling to alter his opinion in the light of contrary information. The Germans committed many tactical mistakes. If they had taken Moscow, this would have put the nerve centre of the country out of action since all communications went through the capital. Leningrad, the city of Lenin and of revolution, would also have been a great psychological victory.

The *Wehrmacht* believed itself so strong that it did not concern itself with the political war. The 'commissar order' of 6 June 1941, which required every Red Army political commissar to be shot, was short-sighted and criminal. It was soon extended to include other party and government officials, and also Jews. The Germans were quite incapable of handling the large numbers of prisoners they took and many prisoners died of hunger and disease. Of the 5.7 million Soviet prisoners taken during the war 3.4 million died in captivity [**Doc. 16, p. 130**]. The Soviets captured 2.39 million German prisoners and of these 356,000 died. Hence over 2 million returned to Germany. They took 1.1 million others, mainly Hungarians, Romanians and Austrians, and of these 162,000 died.

Allowing prisoners of war to die was self-defeating since it stiffened Soviet resolve, and the propaganda about death awaiting every Red Army man who surrendered turned out to contain much truth. Many non-Russians had welcomed the Germans as liberators, preferring them to Soviet rule, but the Germans squandered this goodwill by their brutality.

However, German mistakes in 1941 pale into insignificance when compared with their successes. In the short run everything favoured the Germans. Neither Stalin nor the General Staff, *Stavka*, possessed any knowledge of modern warfare. They had to learn in the field, but this was costly, although eventually the lessons learnt were put to good effect. The price for Stalin's slaughter of the top echelons of the army had now to be paid. However, Stalin must be given credit for many of his principal appointments, especially that of Marshal Zhukov, who became commander of the western front in October 1941. He was given his head and eventually won Stalin's grudging admiration. During the first year of the war commanders could display more initiative than later.

During 1942 the *Wehrmacht* scored triumph after triumph, but victory was becoming increasingly difficult to achieve. In June 1942 Hitler launched his troops against Stalingrad, but near the city he split his forces, half to take the town, the other half to go southwards towards Baku. By early September German and Soviet troops were fighting in the streets of Stalingrad and one of the epic battles of history ensued. The *Wehrmacht* was tantalisingly close to victory on several occasions but the self-sacrifice and heroism of the defenders turned the tide. Hitler would not allow the Sixth Army to make a tactical retreat so as to avoid being encircled in a counter-attack, and he thereby sealed its fate. Romanian, Hungarian and Italian troops, whom the Red Army found easier to fight than the Germans, were cut to shreds. Field-Marshal Paulus and 24 generals surrendered, along with some 90,000 men. About 200,000 Germans perished in the ruins of Stalingrad; Soviet losses will never be known.

Stalingrad was a turning point. For the first time the Soviets had defeated the German army in a pitched battle and the psychological effect was immense. The *Wehrmacht* was not invincible after all. Yet from the German point of view the battle had been unnecessary. Stalingrad was not of primary stategic importance, for the Volga could have been cut between the city and Astrakhan with the same effect and minimal loss.

The initiative, however, still lay with the *Wehrmacht*, and it decided to repair its reputation in the east. Hitler chose Kursk and committed all his heavy tanks to what became the greatest tank battle in history to that date. The Soviets made a similar commitment, and when they discovered the exact time of the attack, on the morning of 4 July 1943, struck first and put a significant number of German guns out of action. On 13 July Hitler broke off the engagement after the *Wehrmacht* had failed on several occasions to achieve a decisive breakthrough. Kursk, therefore, was also a turning point. The tactical initiative now passed to the Red Army.

As the tide slowly turned, the way was open for the advance on Berlin. This was checked from time to time but in the end became irresistible. The year 1944 saw a complete transformation of the situation. By late March the Soviets were approaching Czechoslovakia and Romania. A tremendous Soviet offensive was launched on 22 June 1944 over a 700-kilometre front, just two weeks after the successful Anglo-American landings in Normandy. The *Wehrmacht's* losses mounted alarmingly and its performance between June 1944 and May 1945 was poor, except for the struggle to hold East Prussia. The Soviets did not make a beeline for Berlin. They switched troops to the south to assist the push into the Balkans. Romania was separated from Germany in August 1944 and war was declared on Bulgaria, although technically the country had never declared war on the Soviet Union. In the course of the autumn the Red Army also penetrated into Hungary and Yugoslavia.

Stalin was determined to get to Berlin first. Capturing the capital of Hitler's Third Reich would be a brilliant prize. However, the military reason was not the most important one. The real prize was in the Kaiser Wilhelm Institute, in Berlin Dahlem. Stalin had launched a two-prong attack on Berlin and set Marshals **Konev** and Zhukov against one another to get there first. Reckless attacks were launched on well-ensconced defences but Stalin was not concerned about casualties. On 24 April 1945, Soviet troops entered the institute and seized 250 tonnes of metallic uranium and 3 tonnes of uranium oxide. The institute was the centre of German nuclear research. This haul was to prove of great value in the building of the Soviet Union's own atomic bomb.

Why was it that the German forces did so well until Kursk and then fell away; or to phrase the question differently, why did the Red Army prove irresistible after July 1943?

The Germans started off with the incalculable benefit of tactical surprise. Man for man they were better than the Soviets and so was their equipment. This gradually changed as Stalin and his generals learned how to fight a modern war, and the Soviet success in the tank battle of Kursk demonstrated that they had mastered the art. The *Luftwaffe* controlled the skies in the early stages, but a war has to be won on the ground. The Soviets were prepared to sustain heavy losses for tactical gain. Whereas German personnel could not be replaced (the *Wehrmacht* was already short of 625,000 men by April 1942) the Soviets had abundant reserves (but even so were running short in 1945). The vaunted German military discipline proved a disadvantage when things started to go badly. The *Wehrmacht's* chain of command was strictly hierarchical, with unquestionable orders handed down from above. Such a system is fine if the supreme commander is providing first-class leadership,

Konev, Marshal Ivan Stepanovich: One of the most successful Red Army commanders during the Great Fatherland War. Commander of the Kalinin Front, October 1941– December 1942. He commanded the Steppe Front, 1943–44 and became a Marshal of the Soviet Union in 1944. He was First Deputy People's Minister of Defence and commander of Soviet ground forces, 1946–50.

but Hitler made too many mistakes. Seasoned commanders would arrive at the Führer's HQ telling themselves that they were going to put Hitler right, and would leave on cloud nine believing a miracle was about to occur. The personal oath of loyalty which officers swore to Hitler inhibited the vast majority from acting decisively against him. The German military system did not produce men who would put their country first and everything else second. Tactically, the Germans were very rigid. As the war progressed, the Red Army learned to anticipate the moves the Germans were likely to make and were thus able to counter them more and more effectively. German NCOs were not trained to use their own initiative; hence, by the end of the war, the *Wehrmacht* was almost incapable of springing a tactical surprise. Given their experience and resources the Germans should have performed much better after June 1944. Even their most bitter enemies were surprised by the speed with which the great German war machine broke down.

The Red Army only fought on one front, while the *Wehrmacht* was engaged on several. Things became more difficult for the Germans after the Anglo-American landings in North Africa in November 1942. Thereafter Hitler had constantly to switch his resources. Troops had to be kept in France to guard against an Allied landing there, and as it turned out too many men were stationed in France at a time when they were desperately needed on the eastern front. One of the reasons which led Hitler to pull out of the battle of Kursk was the news of the Allied landings in Sicily.

Lend-Lease: US military and food aid to Allies during the Second World War; authorised by Congress in March 1941 to aid Great Britain, it was extended to include China in April and the USSR in September 1941; about 22 per cent of aid or US$10,000 million went to the Soviet Union.

Lend-Lease aid was important, despite the efforts of Soviet writers to play down its significance. Khrushchev, once out of office, revealed how important American Dodge trucks and gun mountings had been to the Soviet war effort (Khrushchev, 1971: 199). They helped to make the Red Army mobile in 1943 and speeded up its advance. But the main contribution to the supply of war material was made by Soviet industry. Prodigious achievements were recorded as the whole nation was girded for war; the result was that the Soviet war machine gradually out-produced the German, and the longer the war lasted the greater the difference became. For instance, the Soviets produced twice as many rifles and sub-machine guns as the Germans during the war and finally out-produced them in every major category of weapon. Some of the Soviet material was superior to the German from the very beginning; this applied especially to certain types of tank and to the Katyusha rocket.

Morale and willpower are always very important during wartime. During 1941 the Red Army either fought very poorly or just surrendered. This rapidly changed, and after Stalingrad Soviet morale was very high. The Germans made life more difficult for themselves because of their brutality and their maltreatment of prisoners. They made the war a savage one from the start. The Red Army paid them back in kind and gradually the German soldier began to fear 'Ivan', as the Soviet soldier was known. If a German soldier

misbehaved himself elsewhere he was sent to the eastern front as a punishment. The average Soviet soldier was better able physically to endure war
than the German.

The number of Soviet war losses has always been an emotive and contro-
versial issue. Stalin, in March 1946, put the figure at 7 million but Khrushchev
raised it to 20 million. Gorbachev, on the 45th anniversary of the war's end
in 1990 announced that research had produced a figure of 26–27 million.
In 1993 it was estimated that military losses during the war were 8.7 million,
of whom 289,000 died from accidents or were executed by the Red Army.
Corrections to these figures provide another estimate: 7.8 million dead, of
whom 5.5 million died at the front, 1.1 million from wounds in hospital, and
1.2 million in German captivity (Ellman and Maksudov, 1994: 674).

THE ECONOMY

By November 1941 about half the population and one-third of productive
capacity had been lost or was threatened. Enormous efforts were made to
dismantle factories and by November 1941 over 1,500 had been moved
eastwards. Women and the unskilled had to be used to fill the gaps left by
the fighting men, but they succeeded in raising production in 1942 to 59 per
cent and by 1944 to 79 per cent of the GDP in 1940.

Food production suffered, as much of the arable land fell under German
control. Grain output in 1942 was 36 per cent and in 1944 64 per cent of
that of 1940. Horses, where available, were sent to the army, so that women,
who had to shoulder most of the burden, were left to farm under the most
primitive conditions. Where there were no animals, women had to be yoked
to the plough. The cow population in 1942 was only half that of 1940. The
Soviet Union simply went hungry during the war years [**Doc. 17, p. 130**].

CULTURE

The two years which followed the invasion were an Indian summer for Soviet
letters. A torrent of writing about the war engulfed the reader. Deeply patriotic and violently anti-German, it painted a picture of fortitude, heroism,
self-sacrifice and suffering. The long agony of the Leningrad siege – when the
terrible winter of 1941–42 claimed 600,000 civilian deaths, mostly the result
of starvation and cold – produced particularly moving literature. The common soldier was not forgotten and his qualities of wit, humour and perse-
verance were celebrated in print and on the stage.

Someone had to be held responsible for the dreadfully poor leadership of the Red Army, and in his novel *The Front*, published in *Pravda* in August 1942, Aleksandr Korneichuk put the blame fairly and squarely on the shoulders of the older generation of war leaders. The younger generation, more technically able, would, he asserted, turn the tide.

Russia's national history was glorified and the heroes of the past who had served Russia at vital moments – Aleksandr Nevsky, Kutuzov, Peter the Great and the like – rallied the forces again from the grave. This glorification of the past continued a trend which had already been perceptible in the 1930s.

Writers had great leeway when it came to deciding how to treat their subjects, but in late 1943 the party began again to exert some authority. The person who felt the full force of the party's ire was Mikhail Zoshchenko, a noted satirist. His *Before Sunrise* was stated to be too pessimistic, too subjective and short on patriotism. Konstantin Fedin also came in for some harsh treatment. The offending work was volume two of his **Gorky** anthology, and such was the furore that volume three was never published.

Writers seized the opportunity afforded them by the war of depicting real people in real situations. Heroes and heroines came to life on the page and were a far cry from the nebulous beings of the late 1930s.

Gorky, Maxim: Seen by many as the father of Soviet literature, he became the most famous communist writer in the world, while living, of all places, in fascist Italy. He returned to Moscow in 1931 and his death may have been due to natural causes or Stalin may have helped him into the next world.

THE PARTY

The war changed the composition of the party. During the war over 5 million candidate members and 3.6 million new members joined the ranks of the party; of these, 3.9 million candidate members and 2.5 million members were serving in the army and navy. By 1945 one-quarter of the men and women in the armed forces were communists and a further 20 per cent were members of the *Komsomol*. This meant that service men and women accounted for just over half of party members at the end of the war. This was a new phenomenon, for in June 1941 only 15 per cent of the military had been enrolled in the party.

THE NATIONALITIES

The multinational nature of the Soviet Union was a potential weakness on the eve of the German invasion. The decimation of the national élites during the purges and the travails of collectivisation had left behind a reservoir of resentment among many non-Russians. Over a million Soviet citizens, including 250,000 Cossacks, fought on the German side against the Red

Army. Stalin did not afford Soviet Germans the luxury of choice. He dissolved the Volga German autonomous republic in August 1941 and packed off all the Germans, communists included, to the east [**Doc. 18, p. 132**].

Since some nationalities welcomed the German invaders, they were accused of collaboration and deported. This involved the Karachai in October–November 1943, the Kalmyks in December 1943, the Chechens and Ingushi in February 1944, the Crimean Tatars in June 1944, the Greeks also in 1944, as well as the Meskhetians and the Balkars (though there is some doubt about the date in the case of the last two). In all, about 3.3 million people were deported or resettled between 1941 and 1948. All these nations were rehabilitated after 1956, demonstrating the fact that their suffering had been for nothing. After rehabilitation these nationalities were allowed to return to their ancestral homes with two exceptions, the Volga Germans and the Crimean Tatars. Some Germans, however, left the Soviet Union to settle in East or West Germany.

THE GRAND ALLIANCE

No formal alliance involving Great Britain, the USA and the USSR was ever concluded. When Winston Churchill heard of the German attack he moved quickly to propose aid to the Soviet Union. There was no immediate response from the Soviet side, but with Stalin back at the helm everything changed. An Anglo-Soviet diplomatic agreement was reached on 12 July 1941, and on 18 July Stalin wrote to Churchill proposing a second front in France and another in the Arctic. When the Soviet leader met Harry Hopkins, President Roosevelt's personal envoy, at the end of July, he had already drawn up a long list of needed equipment. On 3 September 1941 Stalin asked Churchill for 30,000 tonnes of aluminium by the beginning of October and a minimum *monthly* aid of 400 aeroplanes and 500 tanks. He also wanted a second front in the Balkans and France in 1941. On 13 September 1941 he proposed that Great Britain should land 25–30 divisions at Archangel or ship them to the southern part of the USSR via Iran to cooperate militarily on Soviet soil with the Red Army. Asking for foreign troops on Soviet soil underlines how desperately pessimistic Stalin was about the situation. The US extended a $1,000 million credit in November 1941 and included the USSR in the Lend-Lease Act.

Hitler committed a major error of judgement when he declared war on America on 11 December 1941. Had he not done so it is more than possible that the USA would have restricted itself to fighting Japan before committing combat troops to the European theatre.

An Anglo-Soviet treaty was signed in London on 26 May 1942 but it had taken six months to negotiate. One sticking-point was that the Soviets wanted the frontiers of 22 June 1941 to be recognised. This would have meant Poland ceding territory, but the Polish government-in-exile in London would countenance no such thing. The Americans were also against making binding agreements about post-war frontiers. This highlighted the problem of Poland, which was to become one of the most bitter during the war. Even when the Soviet Union was waging a life and death struggle with the *Wehrmacht*, Stalin was still thinking about future territorial gains.

One of the few occasions on which Stalin lost his temper in the presence of a western statesman was in August 1942 in Moscow, when Churchill informed him that Anglo-American forces would not invade northern France but North Africa in November 1942. Stalin's reaction was to taunt Churchill with the suggestion that British troops were afraid of fighting Germans. The British Prime Minister swallowed this insult. Indeed, on the Anglo-American side there were some feelings of guilt about the fact that it was the Red Army which was bearing the brunt of the *Wehrmacht's* onslaught. Stalingrad was a turning point in relations. Until then the Soviet Union had been begging for aid and was very fearful of the future. Afterwards, as the tide of war began to turn, Stalin became very self-confident in his dealings with Allied statesmen. He knew that time was on his side and that if the Red Army overran eastern Europe it would be Moscow which would decide the shape of the western frontiers of the Soviet Union.

The first time the Big Three – the UK, the USA and the USSR – came together was at Tehran in November 1943, and it was a striking success for Soviet diplomatic skill as Churchill and Roosevelt competed with one another to please Stalin. They did not take a firm line on Poland, and indeed it was Churchill who suggested that perhaps Poland could be compensated for loss of land in the east by the acquisition of some German territory in the west. The second front in France was firmly set for 1944.

By the time the Big Three met again at Yalta, in the Crimea, in February 1945, the military situation had so changed that the USSR was preparing the final assault on Berlin. Eastern and south-eastern Europe had been almost completely overrun. Finland had left the war in September 1944. A Polish provisional government had been recognised by Moscow on 5 January 1945. In May 1944 Churchill had conceded the Soviet Union a key role in Romania and Bulgaria, and when he visited Moscow in October 1944 he widened the agreement to embrace Hungary and Yugoslavia, in which countries the USSR and the West were to have equal influence. Greece was to fall within the British sphere. Stalin merely put a large tick against the percentages proposed by the British Prime Minister. Since both parties were aware of the fact that there were no Anglo-American troops in the countries involved, Churchill was tacitly conceding that the Soviets would play the leading role in them. In Greece, British troops were present, and this would tip the scales there.

Although Stalin did not get everything he wanted at Yalta, he could derive some satisfaction from the meeting. The Polish frontier was to be moved westwards, with the final details being worked out at the peace conference after the war. This was guaranteed to make post-war German–Polish relations very tense, with Berlin attempting to recover the lost territories. In such circumstances Poland would need an ally interested in maintaining the new frontier. The USSR could play this role and in so doing bind Poland to itself. Another gain from Yalta was that the Soviet Union was to receive southern Sakhalin and the Kurile islands in exchange for going to war with Japan after Germany had been defeated.

Neither side completely trusted the other to fight Germany to a finish. The western Allies were not certain as late as the summer of 1944 whether, once the Red Army reached the German frontier, it would stop. Stalin, in his turn, suspected that the western Allies might conclude a separate peace with Berlin, thus freeing the *Wehrmacht* to pit all its strength against the Soviet Union. One of the reasons why Churchill was willing to concede so much in 1944–45 was the fear that if some agreement were not reached the victorious Red Army might sweep forward so fast that Moscow would become the arbiter of the fate of all Europe. His concessions to Moscow were an attempt to salvage as much as possible for the west.

The Red Flag flying over the *Reichstag* in Berlin on 2 May 1945 symbolised the new situation. The Soviet Union had become the leading power in Europe and was also a world power. It was only later that Moscow and Washington came to accept this. On VE Day, 8 May 1945 (9 May 1945 in Moscow, because of the time difference), the Soviet Union was unsure of itself and uncertain how long it would be staying in Germany. Washington expected the USSR to be economically weak and to need up to 20 years to recover fully. Britain was expected to be the leading power in Europe, but was economically in no position to sustain such a role.

5

High Stalinism, 1945–53

INTERNAL POLICY

The war raised Stalin's stature to new heights; afterwards he basked in the reflected glory of military success. The years which separate 1945 from his death on 5 March 1953 saw the cult of his personality reach astounding heights. He became the true charismatic leader. There was always an air of mystery about him. He was not given to much internal travel, and Khrushchev maintained that he only knew the country and agriculture from film which, of course, had been deliberately touched up. Stalin was also sparing in his public appearances. In a pre-television era most citizens knew him only from newspaper photographs. The films in which he appeared presented him in heroic colours with no sign of the pock marks on his face. Like many short men – he was only about 1.6 metres in height – he was acutely conscious of the fact, and portraits and films give the deliberate impression of a taller man.

Stalin moved quickly after victory to break up the key institutions which had fought the war and hence wielded great power. The State Defence Committee (GKO) was dissolved on 4 September 1945 and its functions were distributed among various commissariats. Demobilisation had begun in June 1945 and the party launched a campaign to raise the ideological level of its members (McCauley, 1993: 178). This was of pressing importance since many members had been enrolled on the battlefield. Since most soldiers were from the countryside their formal education had been modest. The military hierarchy was also downgraded. Marshal Zhukov left Germany for the Odessa Military District and lost his position on the party CC; other high-ranking officers followed him into less important posts. There were practically no promotions to the senior ranks between the end of the war and Stalin's death.

The upper reaches of the party took on a new life. From December 1945 the Politburo began to meet fortnightly. The CC convened in March 1946 and elected a new Politburo, Secretariat and **Orgburo**. Shortly afterwards, in August 1946, the Politburo ruled that the Orgburo was to supervise all party affairs and to meet at least once a week. All this did not mean that the supreme organs of the party had been reinvested with the authority they had possessed in the 1920s. Stalin was in name only a secretary of the CC, but in reality he still held the reins of power. As time passed the frequency of meetings decreased. The party favoured a flowering of Marxist-Leninist ideology, but Stalin held back since there was no guarantee that it could be kept fully under control. Ideology was important to Stalin but only as something which was decreed from on high.

War experience changed the population, especially those who had served at the front. They become more assertive – this is very evident in the camps where there were many confrontations and conflicts – and no longer were willing to remain passive. Whereas the pre-war culture was influenced by the Civil War, culture after 1945 was indelibly marked by the titanic struggle against Germany. Veterans were proud of their contribution and this gave them the moral self-confidence to challenge bureaucrats and demand their due. This self-assertiveness is one of the reasons for the violent attacks on foreign culture and influence associated with Zhdanov. Foreign experience and practice were to be excluded from debate.

Interpreting Stalin's thought was particularly difficult as he was never a man to waste words. There are only three items for 1947 and two for 1949 in his collected works. *Pravda* editorials called for everything to be done in a Stalinist spirit and declared that a Stalinist attitude to work was needed, but all this was not very helpful if one's task was to repair combine harvesters. The worker who discovered the technical solution to a problem was praised for demonstrating Stalinist initiative.

The Americans thought that the war had profoundly changed the USSR. The Comintern had been dissolved in May 1943 and this led many to think that Moscow was giving a low priority to revolution. In reality the USSR did not need the Comintern any more, since it could coordinate communist policy in the CC Secretariat. Washington yearned for a stable world order, with the great powers all pulling together to create a brave new world. Potential trouble spots could be defused by mutual agreement, and no one power would selfishly use international tension for its own ends. There were many idealists in the American government who believed that, if sufficient concessions were made, Moscow would come to see that things had changed and would play the world game according to American rules. Stalin could never bring himself to believe that this offer was genuine. Presumably, had the boot been on the other foot and had the USSR enjoyed an atomic monopoly, Stalin would have squeezed as many concessions out of Washington as he could. So far as he was concerned the American propositions were a trap, since the

Orgburo: Organisational Bureau of the CC; handled all matters of an organisational and administrative nature, domestic and foreign, except those deemed important enough to be passed over to the Politburo; abolished in 1952.

USA, being so much stronger than the USSR, had no need to offer concessions. In this Stalin was far less perceptive than, for instance, Maxim Litvinov, the former Foreign Minister, who favoured a much more positive approach to the USA.

Had Stalin decided to meet the Americans half way it would have meant dismantling part of the Stalinist system. American technology, capital, ideas, culture and political values would have penetrated the Soviet Union, loosening up the rigid hierarchical structure which was fundamental to Stalinism. The Soviet leader was pessimistic about the capacity of the USSR to resist an inflowing American tide. The origins of the Cold War are complex but the fact that the Soviet Union felt itself inferior to the USA is of crucial importance. If the USSR was not a match for the USA then it was certainly not one for the USA and its allies. Moscow could never admit this to itself, or to the world. Hence it was necessary to give the impression that the country was strong and that America was not half so strong as it thought it was. The violence of the verbal polemics testifies to Moscow's nervousness; they bit deep into the American soul, caused great offence, and further exacerbated the situation. Neither Britain nor France took the rhetoric as seriously as America; they had learned from their historical experience and had developed an imperial, not to say imperious, hauteur towards the criticism of others.

Negotiating with the Soviets was seldom a rewarding exercise, for the Soviet Union had practically no experience of the outside world and had few experts and specialists versed in the thought and practices of the capitalist powers. Very little authority was delegated to Soviet negotiators; their brief was to hold on to what the Soviet Union had and attempt to gain further advantage. Soviet negotiators tried to seize the initiative at meetings by exaggerated criticisms of the other side, openly challenging its good faith. This put their opponents on the defensive and forced them to justify themselves – an unpleasant position for people who assumed beforehand that they, and not the Soviets, held the stronger hand. The USSR never brought any good will to the negotiating table, for it took it for granted that its protagonists were out to score off it and to reduce its power. Since the USSR often found itself ranged against France, Great Britain and America, it found no difficulty in believing that the western powers were in collusion against it.

Stalin acquired some diplomatic skill. He was extraordinarily quick at grasping the essentials of a situation, be it political, economic or technical. He could formulate a response very succinctly and was a master of tactics, talents which he had developed in the political infighting of the 1920s. One of his strengths was that he never allowed sentiment to cloud his judgement; he liked Roosevelt, for instance, but this did not distract him from the task of getting the better of him.

Had the Soviet population been given a choice they would have marched along the road of cooperation with the western allies. Rumours were rife during the war that things were going to be better after victory, and this implied that the Stalinist system was to be modified. However, such thoughts were far from Stalin's mind in 1945; instead, he set out to recreate the atmosphere of the late 1930s. Soviet soldiers who had been in German prison camps were often marched straight off to Siberian labour camps on their return home. Stalin feared two things: that they might turn on him, and that they might contaminate the Soviet population with their experiences. After all, about 800,000 Soviet citizens had served in the German forces during the war. Every prisoner of war was regarded as having let the Soviet Union down.

Stalin pointed the way ahead in a major speech on 9 February 1946. He maintained that victory had demonstrated the vitality of the Soviet social system and of the Soviet state. Industrialisation had proved its worth and without collectivisation the age-old backwardness of agriculture would not have been overcome. He then enumerated the economic targets not for 1950 but for 1960. The future was going to be hard.

Party membership grew slowly and it was only about 20 per cent higher in 1953 than it had been in 1945. The new recruits were first and foremost the decision-makers, the men and women needed to build the USSR; engineers, technicians, members of the intelligentsia, skilled industrial workers and leading cadres in agriculture. Hand in hand with careful selection of new recruits went purges; about 100,000 members were expelled annually during the last years of Stalin.

Intellectually, the Soviet Union turned in on itself after the war, and foreign learning and achievements were scorned. The man who spearheaded this process was Andrei Zhdanov, who had been the party leader in Leningrad during the dreadful siege. Literature was the first to be attacked. The journal *Leningrad* was closed down after being accused of publishing material which was 'permeated with the spirit of servility towards everything foreign'. Then Zhdanov called Mikhail Zoshchenko, a leading satirist, the 'scum of the literary world' and declared that he could not decide whether Anna Akhmatova, a leading poetess, was a nun or a whore. 'Kowtowing to the west', or praising anything foreign, was condemned.

The theatre and the cinema came in for similar treatment, and in agriculture T.D. Lysenko played the role of Zhdanov. Philosophy was also harshly criticised.

The object of this exercise was not to convince writers, academics and scientists that Zhdanov's views – and by extension Stalin's – were correct, but to frighten them. It was an assault on the mind. Along with this went the glorification of all things Russian; anything worth discovering had been discovered by a Russian; relativity theory, quantum mechanics and genetics, which had not been fathered by Russians, were derided as nothing more than pseudoscience. Russian nationalism became even more prominent than during the 1930s. It was synonymous with Soviet patriotism and heralded the downgrading of the achievements of the non-Russian nations in the USSR. One group of citizens who came in for much criticism because of the international situation were the Jews. Jewish theatres and journals were closed down and Jewish intellectuals were arrested. The years 1948–53 were black ones indeed for Soviet Jewry.

The world communist movement also split in 1948. Tito, the Yugoslav leader, was unceremoniously drummed out of the Communist Information Bureau (**Cominform**) in June 1948. The Cominform had been set up at Szklarska Poreba, in Poland, in September 1947 and embraced most communist parties in Europe. Zhdanov had been the main speaker at its founding Congress and had divided the world into two camps, the socialist and the imperialist, with countries such as Indonesia and India outside both. As far as the Soviet Union was concerned, Tito had thought and acted too independently, even though Tito regarded himself as a loyal Stalinist. Stalin thought that he could bring Tito down very quickly and that Yugoslavia would then return to the fold. This did not happen, and in the Soviet view the Yugoslavs passed over into the camp of the enemy.

Zhdanov died in August 1948. This benefited his main political rival, Georgy Malenkov, who soon afterwards became involved in the framing and subsequent execution of leading Leningrad party and Soviet officials, known as the 'Leningrad Affair'. This erupted in July 1949 and proved fatal among others, for M.I. Rodionov, Prime Minister of the RSFSR, and N.A. Voznesensky, the leading economist of the time. Just why all these key officials were executed is still unclear. What is certain is that everyone feared for his political life. There were a considerable number of top party and central government changes and the atmosphere was charged with mutual suspicion and recrimination. People disappeared, denunciations flowed in to the police, and the dreadful, claustrophobic atmosphere of the late 1930s returned. **N.A. Bulganin**, Soviet Prime Minister between 1955 and 1958, once confessed to Khrushchev: 'It has happened that a man goes to Stalin on his invitation as a friend. And when he sits with Stalin he does not know where he will be sent next, home or to gaol.' When someone was arrested, the usual response was to pour calumny on him. At the same time the cult of Stalin's personality reached new heights [**Doc. 20, p. 136**].

If Stalin was hard to men, he was equally hard to women. Milovan Djilas, a prominent Yugoslav communist, records a conversation about the misbehaviour of Soviet troops [**Doc. 21, p. 137**], which shows that Stalin did not spare a thought for the feelings of the victims of their assaults. This was typical of the attitude towards women during Stalin's last years, which was that the apogee of their calling was to bear children. However, with millions

Cominform: Communist Information Bureau; established in 1947 and disbanded in 1955.

Bulganin, Marshal Nikolai Aleksandrovich: A political marshal who occupied many high-ranking posts connected with defence and security. His task at the beginning of the Second World War was to ensure that the military obeyed Stalin and implemented his orders. He was Minister for the Armed Forces 1947–49, then becoming Deputy Prime Minister until Stalin's death.

of men dead there were simply not enough males to go round. The law was therefore changed and the paternity suit disappeared. Henceforth a man was not to be held legally responsible for offspring born out of wedlock. The literature of this period portrays the problems which occurred when soldiers returned from active service. Women who had filled men's shoes during wartime had simply to step down. The woman who devoted herself completely to the party and neglected her husband and children now became an object of censure. The male was king, and never had the law and the state been so openly on his side.

Djilas thought he perceived a rapid decline in Stalin's mental faculties by 1948 [**Doc. 22, p. 138**]. If this is true then it would be one explanation for the mayhem which overtook the USSR between 1948 and 1953. There was no love lost between Stalin and the Jews. When his daughter Svetlana fell in love with an older man who happened to be a Jew, Stalin had him labelled a British agent and dispatched him to an Arctic labour camp. It is striking how many of the political opponents he destroyed were Jews – Trotsky, Zinoviev, Kamenev, Sokolnikov, Radek, to name only a few. However, it is not quite true to say that under high Stalinism there were no Jews in the CC; Kaganovich, for instance, was a member.

It was very difficult for top party and government officials to acquire information. The Politburo and CC probably never met as full bodies between 1947 and 1952. Stalin's tactic was to convene small groups to discuss key policy questions and to supervise their implementation. The XIXth Party Congress in October 1952 appears to have been convened on the initiative of the CC, which had met in August. Stalin was not well enough to deliver the main report, so Malenkov stood in for him. Khrushchev, in delivering the CC report, was very frank about the behaviour of the little Stalins up and down the country. 'There are quite a few officials who consider that they are not subject to the law. Conceited enough to think that they can do as they please, these officials turn the enterprises or institutions under their control into their own fief where they introduce their own "order" and their own "discipline". There are many scandalous practices of this kind wherever such bureaucrats with a party card in their pockets are active.' The Politburo and the Orgburo were abolished. The new supreme body was the Presidium, which contained more than twice as many full and **candidate members** as the old Politburo. The CC and the Secretariat also doubled in size. There was an uneasy feeling that the 'old man' was preparing a new purge. Even Molotov's wife was in exile and such was her husband's nervousness that he did not dare to bring the matter up with his leader. The fact that she was Jewish may have had something to do with her disgrace.

The most startling news of the late Stalin era was carried in *Pravda* on 13 January 1953. A 'Doctors' Plot' had been discovered in the Kremlin medical centre. Most of the specialists, inevitably Jews, were connected with an

Candidate member: (a) Before a person could become a full member of the Communist Party he had to serve a probationary period during which he was called a candidate member; (b) candidate members of the Central Committee and Politburo might attend meetings, speak but not vote.

American Jewish organisation. There were plans afoot, so it was said, to wipe out the top Soviet leadership. Medical murders had been committed, with Zhdanov among the victims, and it was given out that documentary evidence to support all these allegations existed. But on 23 February 1953 the whole campaign was dropped. The reason soon became apparent; Stalin was nearing his end. He suffered a stroke during the night of 1–2 March and died on 5 March 1953. At the time he was struck down his personal physician, Professor Vinogradov, was not at hand. He was in leg irons in the Lubyanka prison and was being beaten regularly on Stalin's personal orders. Inside a month the 'doctors' plot' was declared to have been a fabrication and the surviving doctors were rehabilitated.

The years 1948–53 saw millions of Soviet citizens on the move. Besides those going to labour camps and into exile there were repeated round-ups of former prisoners and exiles. Legally these persons had served their sentences and were innocent. However, their residence permits could be cancelled and they could be made to move. Local authorities were simply ordered to clear their town of 'suspicious elements'. Anyone with a record fell within this category, as did everyone else the urban authority wanted to be rid of. Possible suspects had to get out of town very quickly to avoid arrest, for neighbours and landladies immediately reported anyone whom they suspected. The only time to move was at night. The family of the ex-prisoner was automatically in disgrace and his wife automatically lost her job. Nadezhda Mandelstam describes one wife who managed to retain her job by concealing her marriage. Her husband, a violinist, kept perpetually on the move up and down the Volga earning a few roubles here and there by giving lessons. Whenever he could he sneaked back to see his wife, after dark of course. He became so skilled at reading political signals that he was never arrested. Had he been a Jew he would almost certainly have been picked up. However, the strain and lack of proper nourishment eventually told on him and he contracted tuberculosis. He could not teach his son to play the violin since he could never go near the boy for fear of giving him the disease.

ECONOMIC POLICY

Material wartime losses were immense: 70,000 villages and 98,000 *kolkhozes* were wholly or partly wiped out; 1,876 *sovkhozes* were destroyed; 17 million head of cattle and 7 million horses were driven away; 65,000 kilometres of railway track were rendered useless, as well as half of all the railway bridges in occupied territory. In the towns 1.2 million homes had been demolished, and 3.5 million in the country [**Doc. 19, p. 135**]. The fourth FYP (1946–50) set out the way of putting the country back on its feet. Wonders were, in fact, achieved even when account is taken of the way in which the official figures are exaggerated by the continued use of 1926–27 prices [**Doc. 7, no. 5, p. 113**]. The plan for national income – the approximate equivalent of Gross National Product (GNP) in western statistics – was officially fulfilled [**Doc. 7, no. 1, p. 113**]. However, agriculture suffered from drought in 1946, as well as a dearth of mechanical equipment, and consequently never approached the planned targets [**Doc. 7, no. 11, p. 113**]. The poor state of the rural sector meant that the movement of young men and women to the cities, in search of employment, was greater than envisaged [**Doc. 7, nos 16 and 17, p. 113**]. Hence total money wages were far in excess of the plan [**Doc. 7, no. 18, p. 114**] and real wages did not rise as quickly as intended [**Doc. 7, no. 19, p. 114**]. Agricultural incomes were miserably low, and large numbers of farmers were saved from starvation only by the possession of a cow [**Doc. 24, p. 140**]. However, the more effort put into cultivating the private plot and looking after the cow, the less time there was for social labour on the *kolkhoz*. This was a perennial problem for the authorities, and the policy of the late Stalin era was increasingly harsh. Yet as the taxes and procurements on the private plot increased, after 1949, so farmers reduced their output and livestock numbers. This was at a time when food was desperately short and private plots were responsible for half the total output of agriculture.

Now is an opportune moment to take a closer look at Stalinist economic planning [**Doc. 27, p. 143**]. A unique system evolved in which the impression was given that a master FYP was being carried out. In reality there was no master plan, merely a mass of lower-level plans which the centre tried to coordinate. How could there have been an overall plan if the FYP was adopted only after the beginning of the period during which the plan was meant to operate? The targets for what each enterprise, each steel mill, each power station had to produce always demanded more than the economy was capable of producing. Hence there had to be a multitude of adjustments, usually in favour of heavy industry. It was quite normal for a factory to receive emendations every day. All economic units throughout the country were really part of one vast company, USSR Limited. Information was therefore of key importance if the centre – **Gosplan** and the economic ministries – was to take rational economic descidions. Many of the failures were due to decisions being based on inadequate information. The Stalinist economic system was efficient from the point of view of control; it was also very successful in concentrating resources in key sectors so as to fulfil priority goals; but in all other respects it was very inefficient and wasteful. Giving priority to certain products meant disrupting the whole economy. Labour discipline and labour productivity are closely linked and here the great optimism of the early 1930s proved misplaced. Workers could be frightened into turning up for work but not into consistently giving of their best.

Gosplan: State Planning Commission of the USSR Council of Ministers; responsible for drafting economic plans and checking on their implementation; founded February 1921.

The key economic official was the first secretary, that is the top party man of an *oblast*. The more important the *oblast* was, industrially speaking, the greater the responsibility of its first secretary. These officials needed technical training and most were engineers. Under Stalin the *oblast* first secretary was responsible for everything in his area and hence had considerable power. He could even take technical decisions without consulting the relevant ministry in Moscow. During the war, first secretaries in the Urals and Siberia, areas vital to the Soviet war effort, were expected to coordinate their efforts and they developed close horizontal collaboration. If one got into trouble at the local level the others would come to his aid. N.S. Patolichev, first secretary in Chelyabinsk *oblast* in the Urals and later the USSR Minister for Foreign Trade, describes such an incident in his memoirs. In 1942 an order signed by Stalin arrived dismissing the top official of the South Urals railway and putting him on trial. Patolichev was convinced of the man's innocence because of his close working relationship with him. As a result he telephoned his two top contacts in Moscow and asked them to intercede with Stalin. They did so, with the result that the official was simply relegated to a minor post. Patolichev eventually secured his reinstatement, and the man in question later became deputy chairman of the USSR State Committee on Foreign Relations. This incident underlines certain realities of Soviet party life. The first secretary of an *oblast* had considerable autonomy of decision and because of his great responsibilities he needed to develop close ties with others in the same position and with those who played key roles in ensuring that economic plans were met. The first secretary, in practice, was more important than some ministers. However, he was almost helpless when dealing with Stalin. Patolichev ran the risk of losing his job for defending the dismissed man. When Patolichev was promoted to the post of CC secretary in 1946 Stalin asked him whom he would like to have as his assistants. He chose three of the secretaries who had worked with him closely in the Urals since he knew and trusted them. Patolichev also approached someone who had worked with him in Yaroslavl *oblast*, his previous post. This episode neatly illustrates how careers could be built in the Soviet Union. If an official linked himself to a rising star he could rise with him; if he was connected with someone who was going down, he was liable to fall with him. The really skilled official was the one who knew when to change horses.

FOREIGN POLICY

The Soviet Union became a world power in 1945 but could not quite believe it. The western Allies recognised that Moscow had legitimate security interests on its western frontiers and accepted that the regimes which came to power in Poland, Czechoslovakia, Hungary, Romania and Bulgaria could not be anti-Soviet. They did not expect them to be communist but anticipated regimes which might contain communists but whose overall outlook would owe more to western political thinking than to Moscow's views on the subject.

The key country as far as the USSR was concerned was Germany. Even if Moscow neutralised eastern and south-eastern Europe it would be to no avail if Germany became hostile once again. Soviet thinking about post-war Germany began as early as 1943 and by 1944 commissions comprising leading members of the Communist Party of Germany (KPD), then in exile in the Soviet Union, were busily working out plans for German development. It was only at Yalta (February 1945) that Stalin knew for certain that the advance of the Red Army would give it control of a part of Germany. The behaviour of the Soviet reparations and dismantling squads, not controlled by the military in the Soviet zone of Germany but directly under Moscow, angered the Germans. This hurt the prospects of the communists, led by Walter Ulbricht, and boosted support for the Social Democrats (SPD). The latter wanted the factories and equipment which were being seized by the Soviets – on the grounds that they had belonged to Nazi criminals – nationalised and used as the base of a socialist economy. At the Potsdam Conference, in July–August 1945, it was agreed that Germany should be denazified, demilitarised and democratised, and that the USSR should get huge reparations, though the exact sum was not determined. Germany was divided into three zones (increased to four when France became an occupying power) and Berlin was given its own control council under three (later four) power control. A major drawback, not clearly seen at the time, was that Berlin was 180 kilometres inside the Soviet zone.

Relations between the USSR and the western Allies in 1945 were good. In 1946, however, they became strained and during and after 1947 they were bad. There were many reasons for this. From early 1946 the western Allies became concerned about the expansion of Soviet power. The event which marked a watershed took place in the Soviet zone in April 1946, when two political parties, the KPD and the SPD, were compelled to unite in the Socialist Unity Party (**SED**). This was mainly due to Soviet concern about the popularity of the SPD. The SED was technically an all-German party, but the other occupying powers would not legalise it in their zone. It was the most powerful party in Germany and as such was feared by France, Britain and America. Many social democrats in East Germany and the vast majority of social democrats in West Germany opposed the fusion. One may regard the fusion as a mistake since it produced an issue which could be used against the Soviet Union; it also meant that Marxist socialism or even Christian socialism suddenly became less attractive in West Germany, and this pushed parties to the right, establishing a gulf which had not existed in 1945.

SED: Socialist Unity Party; ruling communist party in the German Democratic Republic; founded in April 1946.

The Soviets pushed through many reforms in their zones without consulting their allies. They were the first to license political parties, again a unilateral decision. Gradually they realised that short of a war the western Allies could not force them into concessions they did not wish to make. They therefore used their zone as a testing ground. If a reform was acceptable there, it was presumably acceptable elsewhere in eastern and south-eastern Europe.

In eastern and south-eastern Europe there were small indigenous communist parties, led in the main by former Moscow émigrés. Had the membership of these parties been free to act they would have gone for a socialist revolution in 1944–45. However, they were held back by Moscow until 1947. The initial Soviet goal was to carry through democratic revolutions involving parliaments and a multi-party system. Tactically this was an astute move, since the countries concerned were very weak economically, and would find it difficult to satisfy the Soviet demand for reparations; had they gone communist all the resentment of the population would have been directed towards local communists and their Soviet protectors. Stalin knew that the indigenous communist parties had to be cleansed of 'sectarians' and 'adventurers', in short of all those elements which would not accept uncritically the tactics which Moscow proposed. It was not only in the east that the Soviet communists held back fraternal parties from attempting to seize power. Western parties were also affected. Moscow considered it prudent at a time when there were American troops in France and Italy not to be seen to be fomenting revolution. This circumspection lasted until 1947, but by then the most propitious moment for revolution had passed. It is reasonable to assume that there was a general directive to all communist parties to collaborate and to work within the parliamentary system but not to attempt a revolution in 1945 and 1946.

The exception to the above rule was the Communist Party of China. There Mao Zedong was wont to adopt his own counsel, and indeed when the People's Republic of China was proclaimed on 1 October 1949 it came as an unpleasant surprise to Stalin. He would have preferred the communists to come to power in Beijing when he judged it opportune. He also wanted a Chinese leadership which was willing to follow Moscow's directives to the letter. Mao and his associates were certainly not such men.

The Cominform's task was to supervise the transformation of eastern and south-eastern Europe into people's democracies. This process occupied the period 1947–49, during which the various states gradually adopted Soviet political institutions and became, in effect, satellites of their powerful neighbour and guardian.

The western powers, by 1947, had become alarmed at the expansion of Soviet power. Hitherto it had been assumed that the main task was to contain a resurgent Germany, but by 1947 the West perceived that the Soviet

Union posed the main threat. Policy therefore switched from containing Germany to containing the USSR. The Marshall Plan, the Truman Doctrine (promising help to any regime threatened by communists), the fusing of the American and British zones to form Bizonia, and the currency reform which split Germany economically by introducing new money in West Germany in June 1948, were some of the measures adopted. They, in turn, caused Moscow to seek ways of welding the countries of eastern and south-eastern Europe more closely to it. The Berlin Blockade was the Soviet Union's desperate gambit to force the western powers to go back on their currency reform, but it was self-defeating. The blockade increased hostility to Moscow in all zones of Germany and outside. By the time the blockade was lifted in May 1949 the western zones were well on their way to becoming the Federal Republic of Germany. The currency reform was the key event in the division of Germany, but the Berlin Blockade led many opponents of the establishment of a West German state to change their minds.

The Soviet Union's prime need after the war was security. Soviet foreign policy between 1945 and 1953 was a failure if its objective was to prevent the capitalist world uniting against the USSR. The coming into being of the North Atlantic Treaty Organisation (NATO) in 1949 was the western response to a perceived threat from the Soviet Union. Communism was thought to be on the march and had to be kept at bay. Who was responsible for the Cold War? All the leading powers bear some responsibility. So far as Russia was concerned, it had been the practice ever since Peter the Great to seek security by extending the land frontiers of the country. This was partly the result of not having a fixed western frontier, although Peter himself practised it against Persia in the early eighteenth century. The Soviets had always been very nervous about relying on the goodwill of their near neighbours and felt that they had to control these countries wherever possible in order to increase their own security. When Moscow took over a contiguous state, the one next to it became the next source of Soviet security needs. In other words Soviet insecurity was such that gradually more and more states had to be brought within the Soviet orbit. Along with this way of thinking went a peculiarly insensitive appreciation of the feelings of small nations, since Moscow's assumption was that Soviet interests must always take precedence.

Having shed blood in the liberation of south and south-eastern Europe, the Soviet Union felt that it had the moral right to a leading role there. Historically the Russians have either played an important role in other Slav states or have seen themselves as the guardians of them. Misunderstandings arose from the fact that the western Allies deliberately refrained from polemics with Stalin during the war since they regarded their primary task as the defeat of fascism. However, in so doing they negotiated poorly, and Roosevelt especially paid little attention to the consequences of the obligations he entered into. If London and Washington had been tougher from the beginning there would almost certainly have been less friction after 1945. The Soviets felt that America, the key capitalist power (since Great Britain could not act on its own without American support), had acknowledged at the various wartime conferences that eastern and south-eastern Europe should come within the Soviet zone of influence. The USSR felt aggrieved when the Americans and the British began trying to wrest the area away from it. The western Allies, in their turn, felt let down, since promises made by the Soviets – for example, the holding of free elections in Poland – had not been kept. The peace treaties with Bulgaria, Romania and Hungary had not provided for occupation forces. Now that they were, in fact, occupied by Red Army units, America felt betrayed and Great Britain, with public opinion now flowing strongly against the Soviets, felt guilty.

When the western Allies failed to achieve their goals by political and diplomatic means, they began to regard the Soviet Union as an opponent, and a very formidable one. The lack of reliable information about the real state of the Soviet economy and military power led to exaggerated fears about Soviet intentions and power. From underestimating Moscow in 1945 Washington swung over to overrating Moscow in and after 1947. The USSR read American intentions correctly in 1945 and assumed that it would be free from attack. This permitted it to demobilise about 9 million men, and according to Khrushchev the armed forces had declined to 2.8 million by 1948. Then the Berlin Blockade, the formation of NATO, and the onset of the Korean war led to a build-up.

The Soviets felt that they could not make any major concessions, for once the floodgates were open a rout could easily develop. Stalin knew that given a free vote no country would stay within the Soviet orbit – hence his determination to hold on to what had been gained in eastern and south-eastern Europe, and to secure for the Soviet Union a position from which it could only be dislodged by a world war (which was, of course, unthinkable).

Part 3

ASSESSMENT

6

Stalin: Personality and Power

Stalin destroyed many documents and materials at the height of his power. Presumably his reasoning was that they shed too much light on his thinking and personality. As an inveterate collector of information, he may have surmised that someone else, ill-disposed towards him, could use the papers as evidence against him. This neatly sums up Stalin's personality and modus operandi. Reveal as little as possible and confuse the opposition. Critical decisions and orders should not be written down, they should be delivered orally. If the order concerns one person or a small group of persons, it can be given orally. However, if it involves a large group, for instance, party officials or NKVD officers, it has to be put down on paper. The historian is thankful for this since it provides invaluable insights into the decision-making process during Stalin's time. As someone who was conscious of his place in history, Stalin wanted to be painted a hero and to leave an indelible mark on Soviet society. He saw himself as a revolutionary whirlwind which would sweep Russia from being a run-of-the-mill European power to become its leading force. The world would then follow Europe. More important than this would be the transformation of Russian society from an underdeveloped bourgeois to a socialist and then to a communist society. The wheel of history had to turn quickly. Since there was no time to waste, change had to be accelerated. The most opportune implement was force. Those who resisted were rejecting a brilliant tomorrow, a paradise on earth. The most effective way of dealing with them was to exterminate them. They were parasites, vermin and a disease on the body politic. It was a service to humankind to dispose of them. Maxim Gorky once remarked perspicaciously that Lenin treated workers, and indeed people, as a miner treats ore. Stalin was of the same mould. Anything was justified which pushed the revolution forward. If some innocents were killed in the process this was a small price to pay for progress. After all, the masses were important, the individual was not.

On the one hand, Stalin, at the pinnacle of the Soviet Union, is not difficult to understand. He saw himself as an agent of history, acting rationally, not

only in the interests of the Soviet working class, but also of the world proletariat. A heady mix which can lead to vanity, if not megalomania. On the
other hand, he was an intensely private person, hiding his emotions, a
superb actor who could read the weaknesses and frailties of others and play
on them to his own advantage. He never kept a diary, but then neither did
Lenin nor any leading Bolshevik. Private thoughts were not important in the
struggle to build a new world. Some decisions of the Politburo were deemed
so important they were not recorded in the minutes. Others were simply
recorded as decisions. The work of members of the party secretariat was
deemed secret and not put down on paper.

Stalin controlled his drinking but liked to force his companions to drink
to excess. He did not need to know any Latin to realise that *in vino veritas*,
drink loosens the tongue. The British politician, Rab Butler, has related how
he coped with the problem of drink. Winston Churchill, a great bibber, plied
him with the best brandy and insisted that he kept drinking with him. When
Churchill was not looking or lighting up a cigar, Butler poured the spirits
down his shoe. No comrade dared to do the same when Stalin replenished
his glass for the umpteenth time. Stalin liked Georgian wine but usually
ate traditional Russian food. However, he had a penchant for bananas. When
he was served unripe bananas, in 1949, he had the minister of the food
industry sacked! He was a night owl, like many of the world's powerful leaders, and obliged his colleagues to spend interminable nocturnal
vigils with him. According to Khrushchev, Stalin loved watching cowboy
films. He always played the role of the sheriff! Another reason for having his
colleagues round him was that when they were at his dacha they could not
plot against him. His pipe was a constant companion but he had to give up
smoking in 1952.

Stalin was attracted to women and they to him. He was married twice and
had several offspring. He forced himself on some women but some, such as
Lavrenty Beria's wife, were capable of keeping him at a safe distance. Nikita
Khrushchev thought he espied dolly birds in the Kremlin. As a Georgian,
Stalin preferred dark-eyed, dark-haired beauties. He did not share Fidel
Castro's view that sex is all right for a revolutionary but love is not. The
Cuban dictator thought that love weakens the drive of a revolutionary. Stalin
expected his cohorts to stay with their wives and be good husbands. This
said, he did have a liaison with a very young native woman when in exile in
the frozen north. The son became a military officer. Unlike some members of
his Politburo, there are no reports of any homosexual act by Stalin. After
1945 he gradually withdrew from his family and towards the end of his
life hardly saw his grandchildren. Many top leaders, Mikhail and Raisa
Gorbachev spring to mind, had wives or consorts who played an important
part in their success. There was no strong woman behind Stalin. However,

his second wife committed suicide. One of the factors which tilted the balance of her mind was the brutal collectivisation policy.

Stalin was born on 6 December 1878 in Gori, Georgia. The Georgian Orthodox Church used the Julian calendar which means that, according to the Gregorian calendar, he was born on 18 December 1878. His birth certificate, his christening certificate, his seminary school records and his graduation certificate all bear the same date. The documents of the Tsarist secret police, the *Okhrana*, give 6 December 1878 as his date of birth. In December 1920, Stalin filled in a long questionnaire for the Swedish newspaper, *Folkets Dagblad*, and again gave as his date of birth as 6 (18) December 1878. However, in late 1921, the date of his birth was changed to 21 December 1879 (9 December 1879 old style). Subsequently, this latter date was always given as his date of birth. No one has yet explained why Stalin changed his date of birth to render himself one year and three days younger. He once remarked that he had done nothing outstanding, compared with others, before the revolution. Perhaps changing his date of birth was a symbolic way of distancing himself from the years before 1917. He never allowed anyone to write a biography of his activities before October 1917. Indeed, his private secretary, Tovstukha, the keeper of his personal archive until 1935, withdrew from archives as many documents about his activities before 1917 as he could find. They were then passed on to the boss, most of them never to be seen again. Stalin had collaborated with the *Okhrana* and this painful fact had to be glossed over or suppressed.

According to one account (Beria, 1999: 20) Stalin did not love his mother. She was given to affairs and it was rumoured that Stalin was not her husband's son. There was a lot of domestic violence before her husband abandoned the family. Stalin suffered much at his father's hands. He did not introduce his children to his mother until they were in their teens, even though they spent summers in Georgia. He did not attend her funeral in 1937.

Stalin's left arm was slightly withered because of an infected ulcer and this exempted him from service in the Tsarist army in 1916. Understandably, he was very sensitive about this physical defect and since children can be very cruel he suffered at their hands. Smallpox left pock marks on his face and, in future years, he had them brushed out on his portraits. He was sent to an Orthodox seminary but soon lost his faith in God. This was replaced by faith in Marx and his chief Russian disciple, Lenin. In exile, Stalin was confronted several times by fellow Bolsheviks who accused him of being an *Okhrana* agent. To them, it could not just be coincidence that he escaped arrest so many times. How could he have travelled to Petrograd and then abroad several times without being arrested? Stalin's usual answer was to make counter-accusations. The lessons and skills he learnt as an illegal political actor in Russia served him well in future conflicts within the party.

Although Stalin spoke and wrote Georgian fluently, and crafted some poems as well, he began to identify more and more with Russia. During the purges he did not spare the Georgians. He chose traditional Russian names for his children and they did not learn Georgian. Stalin saw himself in the lineage of Ivan the Terrible and Peter the Great. The writer Aleksei Tolstoy, researching a biography of Peter the Great, informed Stalin that he had unearthed some documents which suggested Peter's father was a Georgian king. He thought he would ingratiate himself with Stalin by telling him this. Instead Stalin was appalled and forbade Tolstoy to mention the matter ever again.

Much taken by uniforms, Stalin loved, after 1945, to try out new ones. He always attempted to conceal the fact that he was getting older but kept his weight in check. He did this by regular visits to the sauna since he was no lover of physical exercise. He liked to mount the steps at the Lenin Mausoleum at the double, causing his heavier colleagues some embarrassment. He was quite vain and expected every household to have a portrait of him in a prominent place. He once visited Beria's dacha and immediately went round it looking for a portrait. He was not pleased when he did not find one.

He was very condescending towards his colleagues about they way they looked and dressed. Malenkov, who looked like a pastry cook who had eaten too many of his own pastries, was a constant butt. He was to lose some of his flabby fat by going to the sauna and taking exercise. He did take up horse riding but it did not help. Khrushchev was shaped like a barrel but Stalin regarded him as a hopeless case. He kept on telling Mikoyan he did not know how to knot his tie. Kaganovich was to shave off his beard. 'I don't want a rabbi near me', was Stalin's comment. Bulganin was also to remove his facial hair but managed to make do with a goatee. Lavrenty Beria had to wear a hat and a tie which displeased him greatly. Needless to say, Stalin thought his pince-nez inappropriate. 'It makes you look like a Menshevik', was his wry comment. He was long on humiliation and short on compassion. Voroshilov was told on occasions: 'Shut up, you idiot!' **Budenny** was treated a little better but he was even dimmer than Voroshilov. Stalin never forgot a slight and could wait years before exacting revenge. He loved humiliating his cohorts and seeing them sweat. As he grew older he became more capricious. He had a great fear of death and one can speculate about his growing moroseness. Fear of judgement by a higher power? Near the end he appears like a ruler sacrificing victims in order to assuage the wrath of the gods.

Because he was a short man himself, Stalin liked to surround himself with dwarfs. Ezhov was only about five feet tall and Poskrebyshev, his secretary, was so short that when he sat at table the only part visible was his head. He was very ugly but a good and faithful servant.

Budenny, Marshal Semen Mikhailovich: He became one of Stalin's favourite military men. A cavalry man, mechanised warfare in 1941 totally bewildered him. Stalin shunted him sideways. His intellect may have saved him during the purges.

Stalin could deploy great personal charm when required. He had a great ability to find topics of conversation which would put people at ease. He was interested in their problems. He was well read. Certain authors he loved, such as Emile Zola. He once told Beria's son that the best way to know someone was to ask him what he read. He always went to a person's library to check which books were there. He leafed through them to discover whether they had actually been read. He revealed that he read 500 pages a day and that his time was mapped out days ahead (Beria, 1999: 143).

Stalin's skill at chess was put to good use. He could always plan two moves ahead and was very resourceful in promoting friction among his subordinates. He often told one comrade a lie about another to sow discord. He made it his business to get to know all leading party and state officials and invited them for private chats. There were many overlapping party and state agencies and this permitted Stalin to balance one against the other. In the field of aviation several research bureaux competed against one another on the same project. He was a brilliant organiser and immediately penetrated to the core of a problem. He could formulate tasks very swiftly and issue precise orders about how to implement them. He had no equal as a politician and was a master of intrigue. He easily outfoxed Trotsky, who regarded intrigue as being beneath him.

He had a superb mind and was methodical to a fault. He did not rush into decisions and often appeared cold and impersonal. Vladimir Semonov, who first served in the Soviet embassy in Berlin in 1940, related, in private conversation, how Stalin operated. He was called into Stalin's presence after the war and addressed him as comrade Stalin. The boss did not like to be called Iosef Vissarionovich. Semenov was asked to sit while Stalin circled him, keeping his slightly yellow eyes fixed on him all the time. He had information that there were defence plants in Berlin-Zehlendorf, then part of the British sector. Semenov told him that Berlin-Zehlendorf was a residential area and that there were no plants there. Stalin began to swear, which made Semenov anxious. The boss put him at ease by saying that the information was clearly false. He then asked Semenov's opinion about something else. Stalin listened attentively and when he had finished commented: 'But comrade Semenov you told me on such and such a date something completely different.' Semenov replied that the situation had changed and Stalin accepted his new analysis. This reveals that Stalin was extremely well versed in German affairs and had an encyclopaedic memory.

Foreign observers also gave him high marks. President Harry Truman liked the way Stalin looked him straight in the eye when he was speaking to him. Averell Harriman, Roosevelt's envoy in Moscow, was struck by his high intelligence, shrewdness and fantastic grasp of detail. 'Better informed than Roosevelt, more realistic than Churchill . . . the most effective of the war leaders', was his verdict. (Harriman was not naive. He knew that Stalin was a 'murderous tyrant' who was capable of 'ghastly cruelty'.) General Sir Alan Brooke (Lord Alanbrooke), Chief of the Imperial General Staff and a man of high intelligence, concluded that Stalin's grasp of strategy was due to a 'brain of the highest calibre'. General Charles de Gaulle, wartime French resistance leader, saw Stalin in a different light. He 'was consumed by a desire for power. Trained by a life of plots to conceal his faculties and nature, to do without illusions, pity or sincerity, to see in every man an obstacle or a danger, to him everything was manoeuvre, mistrust and obstinacy.' Stalin did not rate the French very highly either.

Stalin did not promote men (there were no women) of high intelligence to leading positions. Neither could he fill his innermost circle with idiots. He had to sow uncertainty and fear among them in order to maintain the upper hand, playing one group off against another to his mutual advantage. This required great skill, patience and endless hours of work. He checked up on those closest to him. He often arrived unannounced at their homes and set about working out the family hierarchy. Close contact among Politburo families was discouraged for fear that it could lead to coalition building. He was always checking on the whereabouts of Politburo members. Friendships among top officials were not allowed to develop. Hence he frowned on the Russian love of parties which started late and ended in the early hours; they could produce loose talk. Not that Stalin was short of gossip – everything was bugged and the transcripts landed on his desk. If Beria made a derogatory remark about Stalin, which was part of his style, Malenkov would trot round to the boss and blab. Character assassination was a fine art in Kremlin politics and this was the way the boss liked it. There was precious little co-operation as each official was competing for Stalin's favour. He was suspicious of everyone's motives and expected all others to be the same.

Since it could be suicidal to report failure to him, how did Stalin decipher the truth? Can one say that he was misled? He had several sources of information on the same matter: his own personal chancellery, the NKVD, the government apparatus, his own personal envoys and so on. He then studied the reports and drew his own conclusions. This was a very important problem when he was dealing with the purges. Yagoda, and even more so Ezhov, presented mounting evidence of plots, conspiracies and opposition. A case can be made that he was misled into believing that there was more opposition than really existed. The trouble is that he was often the instigator himself, demanding that large numbers be arrested and found guilty. Some scholars used to think that the terror had got out of control and that he was also a victim. This is not a sustainable point of view given the evidence in the archives. The NKVD was never out of control and it never subordinated the party to its power. Caught up in the frenzy of the purges, Stalin gradually realised that he could wipe out all opposition, including those former colleagues who had parted company with him, such as Bukharin. There was often a policy reason behind the killing. Rykov and the right opposed the militarisation of the economy and fought for balanced budgets (income and expenditure on a par). Their demise meant that no one could reiterate these arguments. The fear of war and the need to prevent a fifth column emerging explains, to some extent, the murder of the national contingents. The NKVD complained to Stalin that the 1936 constitution permitted former oppositionists to vote in upcoming elections. It was concerned about their impact. Stalin then let the NKVD loose against former Mensheviks, SRs and anarchists. The problem was solved by exterminating them before they could exercise their newly granted right to vote. All the 'superfluous' people such as former *kulaks*, criminals, recidivists and so on, of no use in the building of a socialist society, could be disposed of like vermin. The problem was that, in 1940, Moscow was again full of thieves and criminals. The solution adopted was simple – shoot the lot.

Stalin devoted an enormous amount of time to editorial work. He read books, film scripts and plays before publication and made changes. In fact, he was a superb editor and publisher. The same applied to party publications where every CC and Politburo resolution was corrected by him. The speeches of his colleagues were submitted to him and he made many suggestions and improvements. Indeed he was very concerned with style and a change of language heralded a change of policy. He did not like vague expressions such as 'proletariat' and replaced it with 'workers' or 'labourers'. Interestingly enough, he excised references to 'Bolsheviks', 'Bolshevism' and 'revolutionary Bolshevism'. Another expression which he found obsolete was the 'dictatorship of the proletariat'. He comes across as a strict schoolmaster, deriding sloppy language and fuzzy thinking. Stalin resumed his habit of repairing to Sochi for about two months each autumn in 1945. Officially he was on vacation but he still worked prodigiously. At least 20 or 30 documents or other materials arrived and the same number left Sochi daily.

He paid great attention to the British Labour Party. He edited the minutes of meetings he had with Labour leaders in July 1946 and October 1947. In order to make the text lighter he inserted, in parentheses, 'smiling' or 'laughter'. Nevertheless, his recorded comments are sharper than in the original discussions. He instructed Harry Pollitt, the leader of the Communist Party of Great Britain, to draft a new party programme and then edited it. He insisted on its stating that Labour was nothing more than the 'left wing of the Conservative Party'. He changed the programme's title from 'For a People's Parliament and a People's Britain' to 'For a Progressive Workers' Government and People's Democratic England'. He told Pollitt, in January 1951, he had spent so much time on the draft because he wanted it to be a model for the

Canadian and Australian parties as well. In Malenkov's draft report to the XIXth Party Congress, in 1952, he repeatedly replaced the adjective 'social-ist' with 'democratic'. The 'socialist' camp becomes the camp of 'peace and democracy'. He was keen to emphasise the responsibility of the US for the woes of the world. He crossed out a reference to the 'aggressive policy of the Anglo-American bloc' and inserted the 'aggressive policy of the leading circles of the USA' (Naimark, 2002: 1–15). In other drafts he excised refer-ences to the Soviet Union being willing to fight and to its nuclear weapons.

Vyacheslav Molotov, appointed Foreign Minister in 1939, was a stubborn man who stood up to Stalin. He was regarded as competent by the boss but when war came in 1941 Stalin became involved in day-to-day affairs and supervised Molotov very closely. When Molotov flew to London, in 1942, to negotiate the Anglo-Soviet treaty, Stalin demanded to know every detail. He introduced changes in policy and instructed his Foreign Minister how to conduct himself. Stalin addressed Molotov with the second person singular, a mark of intimacy, and signed himself *Instantsiya* (the boss). He was also sharply critical of Molotov at times. After the war, Stalin sometimes provided Molotov with instructions twice a day, told him what negotiating position to take, what opposition he could expect to encounter and how to deal with it. He did not want Molotov to become a popular foreign minister in the West and kept him on a tight leash. He overruled Molotov's acceptance of mem-bership of the USSR Academy of Sciences. Molotov had been too enthusi-astic in his acceptance letter. Stalin had his Foreign Minister's Jewish wife banished from Moscow. (But he did the same to the Jewish wives of Poskrebyshev and Voroshilov.) Clearly Stalin was keen to demonstrate that he was in charge. The tension between Stalin and Molotov was visible in late 1945 and the latter had abjectly to concede that he had committed errors during various negotiations. On one occasion he actually broke down in tears but this did not mollify Stalin. Molotov was sacked as Foreign Minister in 1949.

One of the few passions, apart from politics, which Stalin and Trotsky shared was cartoons. Stalin was a great doodler. At a Politburo meeting, in 1930, he drew a cartoon of the Minister of Finance, who is depicted naked and suspended from a rope by his genitals. A note is attached: 'To all mem-bers of the Politburo, for all his present and future sins, Bryukhanov is to be hung by his balls. If they hold up he should be considered not guilty but if they give way he should be drowned in a river.' The famous cartoonist, Boris Efimov, relates how, in 1947, he was hauled out of a meeting by his elbows and taken to see Andrei Zhdanov. He informed him that Stalin wanted a cartoon ridiculing the American military build-up in the Arctic. The next day Stalin phoned him. The boss did not bother to say 'Hello, how are you?' but got down to essentials straight away. He wanted Eisenhower drawn arriving at the North Pole with a large army. He is asked why they are there, given that everything is peaceful. 'Can't you see we are being threatened?', retorts Eisenhower. Efimov came up with the idea of drawing a poor Eskimo family and a bedraggled penguin. Stalin corrected it by adding Alaska and the North Pole and entitled it 'Eisenhower to the Defence'. After it was published Efimov got telephone calls poking fun at the penguin. People delighted in pointing out that penguins were only to be found at the South Pole. When Efimov informed them that Stalin had approved the drawing, they clammed up.

7

The Judgement

Stalinist socialism was a child of the Enlightenment. It was an attempt to fashion a new, just and prosperous society on earth. It was inspired by European secular thinkers such as Hegel and Kant. Their work can be seen as secular versions of Judeo-Christian thinking. For instance, in Kant's *Kritik der reinen Vernunft (Critique of Pure Reason)* 'Vernunft' is a secular word for God. It is no accident that Kant's main discipline was mathematics. Kant, like many others, was inspired by Sir Isaac Newton's mathematics. Hegel's convoluted prose can be summed up quite simply: paradise on earth is inevitable, sooner or later. The guarantee for this was the ability of man to reason. The Enlightenment toyed with the idea of a science of society. The race was on to discover the laws of mathematics which would reveal the evolution of the human race. Higher mathematics – a form of philosophy with numbers – was held to be the key. Higher mathematics is beyond the comprehension of most and so this implied that there were special people, imbued with great insight, who could plot the route to the promised land. Their disciples, like Old Testament prophets, could claim special knowledge which afforded them the right to lead the people forward. The Jews considered themselves the people of God, a chosen people. Karl Marx, although he would turn in his grave if one claimed that he was influenced by the prophets, also conceived of a chosen people. In his case it was the working class. They were the saviours of humankind. Marxism is an eclectic mix of morality and materialism – the oppressors will be punished and the oppressed will inherit the earth.

The religious and secular versions of the kingdom of heaven on earth have intoxicated generations throughout the ages. The wonderful thing about these visions is that not only are they desirable, they are inevitable.

The first time the secular vision was tested was the French Revolution. It produced two opposites: great humanitarian thinking but also savage violence. The latter arose from the fact that there were those who did not share the vision of the men who held power in the state. Such were seen as yesterday's men and women holding up the progress of humankind to a better tomorrow. If they stood in the way, they could be annihilated. The greater good came before any feeling of morality. Indeed a new morality was born. Whatever served to push the revolution forward was held to be good. Crimes could be committed in the name of revolution. Of course, they were not held to be crimes, merely necessary acts.

Why should a revolution, imbued with such noble aspirations as the French Revolution, have descended into such base violence? The justification of violence comes from the religious visions of a perfect society. The Middle East has given birth to three great world religions: Judaism, Christianity and Islam. All of them preach peace but contain justifications for violence. In the Old Testament it is written that God ordered the extermination of peoples. There is the philosophy of an eye for an eye, a tooth for a tooth. This carried over into Christianity, where some of Christ's followers believed they had the right to kill in his name. During the Spanish Inquisition, some held that, if the heathen refused to convert to Catholicism, the body could be killed to save the soul. Then there is St Augustine's concept of the just war. In Islam, the *jihad* is a holy war against the infidel who has insulted God. Hence all three religions are, at the same time, potentially profoundly pacific and potentially profoundly violent.

This dichotomy was carried over into Enlightenment thought. Marx did not preach violence but he regarded it as inevitable. The dictatorship of the proletariat would be imposed violently, with the bourgeoisie being put to the sword. His followers reveal the same dualism as the great religions: a pacific wing and a violent wing. The German social democrats, by 1914, had come to regard the arrival of socialism as inevitable. There might even be a coalition of the bourgeoisie and the working class to usher it in. This is the evolutionary thinking which so enraged Lenin. Coming from an underdeveloped state, and without any experience of modern industry, he regarded the violent overthrow of the bourgeoisie as inevitable. The Russian ruling class would never see reason.

Another reason why Russian socialism is so bloodstained is that political assassination was also the norm before 1914. As George Bernard Shaw once remarked: 'Russia is an autocracy tempered by assassination.' Thousands of officials and politicians were murdered before 1914. It would appear that this was the Russian way of forcing change.

Stalin was caught up in the heady vision of transforming Russian society. Marx's 'antagonistic contradictions' (groups which opposed the greater good of society) would be overcome in order to produce a conflict-free, harmonious society. In order to do this, purification was necessary. Everything which slowed down the march of progress could be eliminated. Those who could not, or would not, contribute to the building of the new were classified as 'yesterday's people'. As such they had to be exterminated. Lenin spoke of vermin – he meant humans – and Stalin continued the trend. A healthy society had to exterminate vermin. It was a historical necessity. After the war, Stalin wrote that there were 'weeds' sprouting in the stone walls of the socialist edifice. As every gardener knows, weeds have to be extirpated.

Institutions to catalogue, list, regulate, map the progress of and supervise each person were needed. Enormous effort was put into monitoring and controlling the population – all deemed necessary to measure the progress achieved in creating the moral–political unity of society. It is instructive that terror intensified after the victory of socialism was proclaimed in 1936. This was because Stalin wanted to purify society quickly and reach the promised land, if possible, in his lifetime. After 1945, he devoted much thought to introducing a moneyless economy.

Stalin's ruthless pursuit of the new millennium went through various stages. The elimination of the *kulaks* was necessary since private property could not exist in the new socialist world. Peasants had to work for the common good not for their own good. As a class the *kulaks* had to be exterminated. They were the class enemy, as were the remnants of other groups, such as the sons of priests. Individualism had to be rubbed out as each person had to work harmoniously with others for the common benefit of society. Each new campaign created a new enemy. Before the 1936 constitution, the vilest term was 'class enemy'; afterwards it became 'enemy of the people'. The advantage of the latter phrase was that it included members of the Communist Party. All Old Bolsheviks, who did not convert to Stalinism, were to be mown down. A particular target was Trotsky and his followers. They were hunted down with ruthless zeal. This reveals that Stalin regarded them as the greatest threat to his hegemony.

Another target which exercised Stalin greatly was nationalism. In order to create the new conflict-free, harmonious society, everyone had to come to think of themselves as forming part of a socialist nation. That nation would be based on the great Russian nation and Russian would be the language of the new world. A major problem was that the borderlands of the Soviet Union were peopled mainly by non-ethnic Russians. Deportation was one solution but Stalin could not deport 50 million Ukrainians. When the Baltic States were incorporated, hundreds of thousands of the educated were deported in order to remove the leading lights of each nation. The Cossacks, ethnic Russian in origin but living mainly outside Russia, were fiercely independent and refused to give up their distinctive traditions. Stalin repressed them savagely. No wonder 250,000 fought with the Germans against the Red Army. They were ferociously efficient in killing Russian soldiers. Two more nationalities exasperated Stalin: the Chechens and the Crimean Tatars. In deporting them to Central Asia, he hoped to wipe out their culture. They were not permitted Chechen-language schools or to honour their traditions. The modern struggle to the death between Russians and Chechens goes back a long way. Another special target were the Jews. Their claim to be a chosen people riled Stalin and other Russian communists. After all, Russians were the chosen people.

There was a ruthless logic to Stalin's policies. If someone's class, nationality, culture or religion prevented them from full commitment to the building of the new society, they had to be eliminated. If they were perceived to be unreformable, they had sentenced themselves to death. Enormous efforts were devoted to propaganda under Stalin in order to teach everyone the new way. A favourite term was 'moral–political unity', meaning a harmonious society. Stalin, in using this term, also issued a stern warning. There were those who were mouthing the new thinking but harboured the seeds of old thinking in their minds. If they did not do away with the vestiges of the old thinking, they would be done away with.

Many of Stalin's closest associates were intoxicated by the vision of the new society. Some, like Molotov, revelled in the violence which was part and parcel of it. To him, Bolshevism meant struggle: without struggle there was no need for Bolsheviks. But this could lead to innocents being killed. He showed no mercy. 'Let innocent heads roll.' What were a few lives, if the moral–political unity of society was promoted? Understandably, he was disgusted by Khrushchev, who wanted a quieter life.

Part of the brilliance of the Stalinist model was that everyone was expected to participate in it. There were to be no passive bystanders. Each person was to be engaged in purifying himself or herself and checking that others were doing the same. Each new wave of cleansing instituted by the leadership was to be executed by the people themselves. They were to choose, from among their midst, who was to be executed, imprisoned or deported. They were empowered but at the same time were powerless. One can regard this aspect as an indication of Stalin's political genius. He was able to remove all those he perceived to be a brake on his massive social-engineering project and he enlisted the whole population to help him do it!

Part 4

DOCUMENTS

Document 1   THE PARTY

Stalin here spells out systematically his understanding of the role of the Communist Party. This document was originally published in 1924 and is one of the foundation stones of Leninism which Stalin, more than anyone else, developed.

What are the specific features of this new party?

1. *The Party as the vanguard of the working class.* The Party must be, first of all, the *vanguard* of the working class. The Party must absorb all the best elements of the working class, their experience, their revolutionary spirit, their selfless devotion to the cause of the proletariat. But in order that it may really be the vanguard, the Party must be armed with revolutionary theory, with a knowledge of the laws of the movement, with a knowledge of the laws of revolution. Without this it will be incapable of directing the struggle of the proletariat, of leading the proletariat. The Party cannot be a real party if it limits itself to registering what the masses of the working class feel and think, if it drags at the tail of the spontaneous movement, if it is unable to overcome the inertness and the political indifference of the spontaneous movement, if it is unable to rise above the momentary interests of the proletariat, if it is unable to elevate the masses to the level of the class interests of the proletariat. The Party must stand at the head of the working class; it must see farther than the working class; it must lead the proletariat, and not follow in the tail of the spontaneous movement. . . .

No army at war can dispense with an experienced General Staff if it does not want to court certain defeat. Is it not clear that the proletariat can still less dispense with such a General Staff if it does not want to give itself up to be devoured by its mortal enemies? But where is this General Staff? Only the revolutionary party of the proletariat can serve as this General Staff. The working class without a revolutionary party is an army without a General Staff. The Party is the General Staff of the proletariat. . . .

2. *The Party as the organized detachment of the working class.* The Party is not only the vanguard detachment of the working class. If it desires really to direct the struggle of the class it must at the same time be the organized detachment of its class.

3. *The Party as the highest form of class organization of the proletariat.* The Party is the organized detachment of the working class.

This organization is the Party of the proletariat. . . . the Party, as the best school for training leaders of the working class, is, by reason of its experience and prestige, the only organization capable of centralizing the leadership of the struggle of the proletariat, thus transforming each and every non-Party organization of the working class into an auxiliary body and transmission belt linking the Party with the class. The Party is the highest form of class organization of the proletariat. . . .

4. *The Party as the instrument of the dictatorship of the proletariat.* . . . The Party is not only the highest form of class association of the proletarians; it is at the same time an *instrument* in the hands of the proletariat *for* achieving the dictatorship where that has not yet been achieved and *for* consolidating and expanding the dictatorship where it has already been achieved. . . .

The proletariat needs the Party *for* the purpose of achieving and maintaining the dictatorship. The Party is an instrument of the dictatorship of the proletariat.

5. *The Party as the embodiment of unity of will, incompatible with the existence of factions.* The achievement and maintenance of the dictatorship of the proletariat is impossible without a party which is strong by reason of its solidarity and iron discipline. . . . Iron discipline does not preclude but presupposes conscious and voluntary submission, for only conscious discipline can be truly iron discipline. But after a contest of opinion has been closed, after criticism has been exhausted and a decision has been arrived at, unity of will and unity of action of all Party members are the necessary conditions without which neither Party unity nor iron discipline in the Party is conceivable. . . .

But from this it follows that the existence of factions is incompatible either with the Party's unity or with its iron discipline.

6. *The Party is strengthened by purging itself of opportunist elements.* The source of factionalism in the Party is its opportunist elements. . . . Our Party succeeded in creating internal unity and unexampled cohesion of its ranks primarily because it was able in good time to purge itself of the opportunist pollution, because it was able to rid its ranks of the Liquidators, the Mensheviks. Proletarian parties develop and become strong by purging themselves of opportunists and reformists, social-imperialists and social-chauvinists, social-patriots, and social-pacifists. The Party becomes strong by purging itself of opportunist elements.

Source: J. Stalin, *Problems of Leninism* (Moscow, Foreign Language Publishing House, 1945), pp. 97–109.

THE RIGHT DEVIATION   **Document 2**

Published in April 1929, this condemnation of Bukharin and his supporters is a good example of Stalin's political style. Note how he blackens the Right by asserting that support for them means betrayal of the revolution. By 1929 he was in a position to decide what was in the best interests of the revolution.

The fight against the Right deviation is one of the most decisive duties of our party. If we, in our own ranks, in our own party, in the political General Staff

of the proletariat, which is directing the movement and is leading the proletariat forward – if we in this General Staff tolerated the free existence and the
free functioning of the Right deviationists, who are trying to demobilize the
party, to demoralize the working class, to adapt our policy to the tastes of
the 'Soviet' bourgeoisie, and thus yield to the difficulties of our construction
– if we tolerated all this, what would it mean? Would it not mean that we
want to send the revolution down hill, demoralize our socialist construction,
flee from difficulties, surrender our positions to the capitalist elements? Does
Bukharin's group understand that to refuse to fight the Right deviation is to
betray the working class, to *betray* the revolution?

Source: Ibid., pp. 371–2.

Document 3   DIZZY WITH SUCCESS

This is part of an article which appeared in Pravda *on 2 March 1930.
Collectivisation was supposed to be voluntary but officials herded peasants
into collectives against their will. To reduce the mayhem in the countryside
and to ensure that the spring sowing was done, Stalin called a temporary halt.
It was only tactical, as collectivisation was stepped up later in the year.*

But what really happens sometimes? Can it be said that the voluntary principle and the principle of allowing for local peculiarities are not violated in a
number of districts? No, unfortunately, that cannot be said. We know, for
example, that in a number of the Northern districts of the grain-importing
belt, where there are comparatively fewer favourable conditions for the
immediate organization of collective farms than in the grain-growing districts, not infrequently efforts are made to *substitute* for preparatory work in
organizing collective farms the bureaucratic decreeing of a collective farm
movement from above, paper resolutions on the growth of collective farms,
the formulation of collective farms on paper – of farms which do not yet
exist, but regarding the 'existence' of which there is a pile of boastful resolutions. Or, take certain districts in Turkestan, where there are even fewer
favourable conditions for the immediate organization of collective farms than
in the Northern regions of the grain-importing belt. We know that in a number of districts in Turkestan attempts have already been made to 'overtake
and outstrip' the advanced districts of the U.S.S.R. by the method of threatening to resort to military force, by the method of threatening to deprive the
peasants who do not as yet want to join the collective farms of irrigation
water and of manufactured goods.

What is there in common between this Sergeant Prishibeyev 'policy' and
the party's policy which rests on the voluntary principle and allows for local

peculiarities in collective farm construction? Obviously, they have not, nor can they have, anything in common.

Source: Ibid., pp. 421–2.

HARSH REALITIES   **Document 4**

This (a) is from a letter by Stalin, in August 1930. He is ordering more exports at a time when the world market is depressed. In 1929, the Soviet Union exported 200,000 tonnes of grain but, in 1930, 4.8 million. The impact it had is graphically illustrated (b) by a worker's letter to Pravda, *in September 1930 (not published, of course).*

Mikoyan reports that grain collections grow and every day we export   **(a)** 1–1.5 million poods [16.38 poods = 1 kg] of grain. I think this is too little. We need to raise (NOW) daily exports to a minimum of 3–4 million poods. If not, we risk not finishing our new metallurgical and machine-building (Avtozavod, Chelyabzavod, and others) plants . . . In short, we need furiously to force the export of grain.

Source: Reprinted in Elena Osokina, *Our Daily Bread* (Armonk, NY, M.E. Sharpe, 2001), p. 44.

The building of socialism is not done by Bolsheviks alone. It should not be   **(b)** forgotten that many millions of workers are participating in the building of socialism. A horse with its own strength can drag seventy five poods, but its owner has loaded it with a hundred poods, and in addition he's fed it poorly. No matter how much he uses the whip, it still won't be able to move the cart.

   This is also true for the working class. They've loaded it with socialist competition, shock work, overfulfilling the industrial and financial plan, and so forth. A worker toils seven hours, not even leaving his post, and this is not all he does. Afterwards he sits in meetings or else attends classes for an hour and a half or two in order to increase his skill level, and if he doesn't do these things, then he's doing things at home. And what does he live on? One hundred and fifty grams of salted mutton; he will make soup without any of the usual additives, neither carrots, beets, flour nor salt pork. What kind of soup do you get from this? Mere 'dishwater'.

Source: Reprinted in Lewis Siegelbaum and Andrei Sokolov, *Stalinism as a Way of Life* (New Haven, CT, Yale University Press, 2000), pp. 39–40.

Document 5   THE BREAKNECK SPEED OF INDUSTRIALISATION

Those who favoured a slowdown in industrialisation were answered by Stalin in 1931. He had a long memory for past Russian defeats, something one would not have expected of a Soviet leader. Note that past German defeats have been omitted.

It is sometimes asked whether it is not possible to slow down the tempo a bit, to put a check on the movement. No, comrades, it is not possible! The tempo must not be reduced! On the contrary, we must increase it as much as is within our powers and possibilities. This is dictated to us by our obligations to the workers and peasants of the U.S.S.R. This is dictated to us by our obligations to the working class of the whole world.

To slacken the tempo would mean falling behind. And those who fall behind get beaten. But we do not want to be beaten. No, we refuse to be beaten! One feature of the history of old Russia was the continual beatings she suffered for falling behind, for her backwardness. She was beaten by the Mongol Khans. She was beaten by the Turkish beys. She was beaten by the Swedish feudal lords. She was beaten by the Polish and Lithuanian gentry. She was beaten by the British and French capitalists. She was beaten by the Japanese barons. All beat her – for her backwardness: for military backwardness, for cultural backwardness, for political backwardness, for industrial backwardness, for agricultural backwardness. She was beaten because to do so was profitable and could be done with impunity. Do you remember the words of the pre-revolutionary poet: 'You are poor and abundant, mighty and impotent, Mother Russia.' These words of the old poet were well learned by those gentlemen. They beat her, saying: 'You are abundant,' so one can enrich oneself at your expense. They beat her, saying: 'You are poor and impotent,' so you can be beaten and plundered with impunity. Such is the law of the exploiters – to beat the backward and the weak. It is the jungle law of capitalism. You are backward, you are weak – therefore you are wrong; hence, you can be beaten and enslaved. You are mighty – therefore you are right; hence, we must be wary of you.

That is why we must no longer lag behind.

In the past we had no fatherland, nor could we have one. But now that we have overthrown capitalism and power is in the hands of the working class, we have a fatherland, and we will defend its independence. Do you want our socialist fatherland to be beaten and to lose its independence? If you do not want this you must put an end to its backwardness in the shortest possible time and develop genuine Bolshevik tempo in building up its socialist system of economy. There is no other way. That is why Lenin said during the October Revolution: 'Either perish, or overtake and outstrip the advanced capitalist countries.'

We are fifty or a hundred years behind the advanced countries. We must make good this distance in ten years. Either we do it, or they crush us.

Source: J. Stalin, *Problems of Leninism* (Moscow, Foreign Language Publishing House, 1945), pp. 455–6.

FAMINE AND THE NOUVEAUX RICHES   **Document 6**

This NKVD report highlights the desperate food situation in Voronezh oblast.   **(a)**

Leningrad raion, Azov-Black Sea krai, has been plagued by disorganized peasant migrations from Voronezh oblast. In December and November 1937, 150 people arrived . . . Most of them have no [internal] passports or documents, nor do they have permission to leave the collective farm. The local organizations need more workers on their kolkhozes and have allowed the new peasants to stay. Those which cannot find work live in railway stations or in migrant camps in the fields. They are begging. The migrants explained that Voronezh oblast has suffered a very bad harvest and that the peasants are starving, since they are forced to live on 200 grams of bread per workday. The influx of peasants is continuing.

Source: Reprinted in Elena Osokina, *Our Daily Bread* (Armonk, NY, M.E. Sharpe, 2001), p. 158.

This NKVD report about the village of Donshino, Volga-River oblast, in   **(b)**
January–February 1937, lists 60 people dead, 27 of them from hunger.

The Kinyakin family of non-kolkhoz peasants: Kinyakin himself died in December 1936. In January 1937, his 36 year old wife died, followed by his 15 year old daughter and 13 year old son.

The Potemkin family of non-kolkhoz peasants: Potemkin himself left the village in search of work while his wife and six children remained in the village. Four of them died in January, the rest of them are bloated with hunger.

The Lyubaev family of non-kolkhoz peasants: Lyubaev and his 17 year old daughter died; his wife and the other two children are bloated.

The Vedyasov family of non-kolkhoz peasants: Vedyasov, his 37 year old wife, 15 year old daughter, and 8 year old son all died.

Source: Ibid., p. 159.

(c) *A person could not become a millionaire in Soviet Russia by producing and selling goods but he could through theft and speculation. Great ingenuity was displayed in stealing goods. Assistants reclassified poor goods as high quality; wrote off goods as damaged and sold them privately; they put in loss claims and wrote off large quantities of goods. Those employed in warehouses did not need to steal; they simply bought goods at state prices and sold them on the black market. All this activity required many hands to be greased to continue. The NKVD had hundreds of informers in the trade system. Below is one report, dated 1937.*

Many state trade employees in the city of Moscow regularly engage in organized theft – they are not punished but are respected people. Their example influences many other people, and gradually it has become a tradition, an inalienable right for a trade employee to be a thief – that's normal. They must have valuable things and get them regularly: they must build dachas; they must go on sprees; they must have lovers; etc. Unfortunately, many people look at the big-time tradeworker-thieves with the same lack of concern as people used to view the quartermasters who embezzled state funds.

Source: Ibid., p. 184.

(d) *Famine returned in 1946–47 and below is an extract from a report by party Central Committee inspectors about the situation in Mariupol, Ukraine. Industry was a privileged sector and this highlights the plight of other sectors.*

In the municipal industries of Mariupol, the number of workers ill of dystrophy has recently increased significantly. City doctors concluded on 1 March [1947] that there are 3,789 cases of dystrophy in five factories in Mariupol . . . Their examination has established that the increase in illness is related to a significant degree to the fact that the Ministry of Trade has, in the course of the last five months, systematically reduced the supply of grain and food products to the factories.

Source: Reprinted in Elena Zubkova, *Russia After the War* (Armonk, NY, M.E. Sharpe, 1998), p. 48.

———————◀●▶———————

FULFILMENT OF THE PRINCIPAL GOALS OF THE STALINIST FIVE-YEAR   **Document 7**
PLANS, 1928–50

The following table estimates to what extent the principal goals of the Five-Year Plans were achieved. Jasny, Bergson, Nutter, Kaplan, Moorsteen, Johnson and Kahan are western economists. Figures are given in percentages.

	First Five-Year Plan (1928–1932) (1)	Second Five-Year Plan (1933–1937) (2)	Fourth Five-Year Plan (1946–1950) (3)
National Income			
1. Official Soviet estimate (1926/27 prices)	91.5	96.1	118.9
2. Jasny estimate (1926/27 'real' prices)	70.2	66.5	
3. Bergson estimate			89.9
4. Nutter estimate			84.1
Industrial Production			
5. Official Soviet estimate (1926/27 prices)	100.7	103.0	116.9
6. Jasny estimate	69.9	81.2	
7. Nutter estimate	59.7	93.1	83.8
8. Kaplan and Moorsteen estimate	65.3	75.7	94.9
9. Official Soviet estimate, producer goods (1926/27 prices)	127.6	121.3	127.5
10. Official Soviet estimate, consumer goods (1926/27 prices)	80.5	85.4	95.7
Agricultural Production			
11. Official Soviet estimates (1926/27 prices)	57.8	62.6–76.9	89.9
12. Jasny estimate	49.6	76.7	
13. Nutter estimate	50.7	69.0	76.4
14. Johnson and Kahan estimates	52.4	66.1–69.0	79.4
Transport			
15. Railway freight traffic (ton–km)	104.0		113.2
Employment			
16. National economy, workers and employees	144.9	93.4	116.1
17. Industry, workers and employees	173.9		118.9

	First Five-Year Plan (1928–1932) (1)	Second Five-Year Plan (1933–1937) (2)	Fourth Five-Year Plan (1946–1950) (3)
Wages (workers and employees, nat. economy)			
18. Average money wage	143.9	173.6	127.8
19. Average real wage, official Soviet estimate	31.9	102.6	89.1
20. Average real wage, Zaleski estimate	26.0	65.8	
Labour Productivity, Industry			
21. Official Soviet estimate	65.1		100.7
22. Jasny estimate	41.8		
23. Nutter estimate	36.3		
24. Kaplan and Moorsteen estimate			80.0
Cost of Production			
25. Industry (current prices)	146.1	121.2	134.2
Investment			
26. In constant prices	54.0		122.0

Source: E. Zaleski, *Stalinist Planning for Economic Growth 1933–1952*, (Basingstoke, Macmillan, 1980), p. 503, copyright © 1980 by the University of North Carolina Press, used by permission of the publisher.

Note: Khanin (in Harrison, 1993) estimates industrial growth over the years 1928–41 at 10.9 per cent annually (officially 17 per cent) and national income growth at 3.2 per cent (officially 13.9 per cent).

Document 8   MANDELSTAM'S POEM ABOUT STALIN (NOVEMBER 1933)

Osip Mandelstam was arrested in May 1934 for composing this poem, which he had recited at a gathering. Stalin got to know about it and was offended by the unflattering reference to him. This was enough to lead to Mandelstam's arrest and eventual death in a labour camp.

We live, deaf to the land beneath us,
Ten steps away no one hears our speeches,
But where there's so much as half a conversation

The Kremlin's mountaineer will get his mention.[1]
His fingers are fat as grubs
And the words, final as lead weights, fall from his lips,
His cockroach whiskers leer
And his boot tops gleam.
Around him a rabble of thin-necked leaders –
Fawning half-men for him to play with.
They whinny, purr or whine
As he prates and points a finger,
One by one forging his laws, to be flung
Like horseshoes at the head, the eye or the groin.
And every killing is a treat
For the broad-chested Ossete.[2]

Source: N. Mandelstam, *Hope Abandoned* (London, Collins Harvill, 1971), p. 13.

---

[1] In the first version, which came into the hands of the secret police, these two lines read:

   All we hear is the Kremlin mountaineer,
   The murderer and peasant-slayer.

[2] 'Ossete'. There were persistent stories that Stalin had Ossetian blood. Ossetia is to the north of Georgia in the Caucasus. The people, of Iranian stock, are quite different from the Georgians.

(A) INTERROGATION TECHNIQUES   **Document 9**

Osip Mandelstam (M. in the text) was subjected to various types of treatment, here described by Nadezhda Mandelstam, his wife. The police could always rely on a steady flow of denunciations. It was one way of exacting revenge for past wrongs. Informers were everywhere as well.

At the very first interrogation M. had admitted to being the author of the poem on Stalin, so the stool pigeon's task could not have been merely to find out something that M. was hiding. Part of the function of these people was to unnerve and wear down prisoners under interrogation, to make their lives a misery. Until 1937 our secret police made much of their psychological methods, but afterward these gave way to physical torture, with beatings of the most primitive kind. After 1937 I never again heard of anyone being held in solitary confinement cells, with or without stool pigeons. Perhaps people picked out for such treatment after 1937 did not leave the Lubianka alive. M. was put through the physical ordeal which had always been applied. It consisted mainly of not being allowed to sleep. He was called out every night and kept for hours on end. Most of the time was spent not in actual questioning, but in waiting under guard outside the interrogator's door. Once, when there was no interrogation, he was wakened all the same and taken to see a woman who kept him waiting at the door of her office for many hours, only to ask him at the end of it whether he had any complaints. Everybody knew how meaningless it was to make complaints to the prosecutor, and M. did not avail himself of this right. He had probably been called to her office simply as a formality, and also to keep him awake even on a night when the interrogator was catching up on his own sleep. These night birds lived a preposterous life, but all the same they managed to get some sleep, although not at the times when ordinary mortals did. The ordeal by deprivation of sleep and a bright light shining right in the eyes are known to everybody who has gone through such interrogations.

The work of undermining a person's sanity was carried on quite systematically in the Lubianka, and since our secret police is a bureaucratic institution like any other, all the procedures involved were probably governed by precise instructions. Even though the personnel were specifically selected for the job, one cannot ascribe what went on to their wicked nature, since the same people could overnight have become kindness itself – if so instructed. There were rumours among us that Yagoda had set up secret laboratories and staffed them with specialists who were carrying out all kinds of experiments with drugs, hypnosis, phonograph records and so forth. It was impossible to check such stories, and they may have been a product of our morbid imaginations, or tales deliberately put about to keep us all on tenterhooks.

The interrogator's arrogance was reflected not only in his manner, but also in occasional very superior remarks that smacked of the literary drawing room. The first generation of young Chekists, later to be removed and destroyed in 1937, was distinguished by its sophisticated tastes and weakness for literature – only the most fashionable, of course. In my presence Christophorovich said to M. that it was useful for a poet to experience fear ('you yourself told me so') because it can inspire verse, and that he would 'experience fear in full measure.' Both M. and I noted the use of the future tense. In what Moscow drawing rooms had Christophorovich heard this kind of talk?

Apart from people who were forced into cooperating, there were hosts of volunteers. Denunciations poured into every institution on a quite unmanageable scale. Before the Twentieth Congress [1956] I heard an inspector of the Ministry of Education address a meeting at the Chuvash Teachers' Training College, where I was then working, and ask the staff to stop writing denunciations, warning them that anonymous ones would no longer be read at all. Can it be true that they no longer read anonymous denunciations? I find it hard to believe.

Because of this system of 'interviews', people developed two kinds of phobia – some suspected that everybody they met was an informer, others that they might be taken for one.

One final question: was it my fault for not getting rid of all our friends and acquaintances, as did most good wives and mothers at that time? My guilt is lessened only by the fact that M. would in any case have given me the slip and found a way of reading his outrageous poem – and in this country all real poetry is outrageous – to the first person he met. He was not one to put a gag on himself and lead a life of voluntary seclusion.

Source: Ibid., pp. 75–6.

(B) AUNT LESIA   **Document 9**

This report is by Chrystia Freeland, a Canadian journalist, describing the arrest and travail of her favourite great-aunt, Oleksandra Blavatska, or Aunt Lesia.

My favourite great-aunt spent 10 years in Stalinist labour camps for two crimes: buying a funeral wreath and playing the harp at a dinner party. The funeral wreath was purchased in 1944 when Aunt Lesia was 19 years old. . . . It was for Metropolitan Sheptytsky, head of the Ukrainian Catholic Church. He was revered . . . 'as the holiest of holies' for his defiance of both the Nazis and the Soviets during the Second World War. . . . 'We bought a beautiful wreath with red linden at the centre, as was the Ukrainian custom. . . . And on a black band draped across the wreath we wrote: "To the unforgettable defender of Ukrainian youth, from the students of the Soviet Trade Institute." The Bolsheviks – not known for their sense of humour – could never forgive me for that.'

The day after the funeral she was expelled from the Institute and the mid-night interrogations at KGB headquarters, which began for Lesia as soon as the Red Army took over the western Ukrainian city of Lviv, intensified. But a dinner party a few months later was the last straw. When a delegation of Soviet Ukrainian writers came to Lviv they were entertained by Lesia's mother, the city's most accomplished hostess in the old days of the Austro-Hungarian, and later Polish, rule. While Mrs Blavatska charmed the writers by chatting in French, her daughter, the only harpist in the city (the harp was a ploy to get Lesia into the Conservatory after she had been expelled from the Trade Institute) provided a musical accompaniment.

A few weeks later, Lesia was arrested on her way to the Conservatory and she began an education of a different sort. Over the next decade she progressed from KGB interrogation cells to a tour of Soviet labour camps. Along the way, she gave birth to my second favourite aunt Vira, 'Faith', who spent her early childhood separated from her mother in a Soviet orphanage.

'The KGB cell had an open window and it was winter, so there was ice and snow on the floor. It was full of rats. It was exactly seven steps wide: I know because I paced back and forth all day and all night.' After 18 days in the isolation cell, Lesia collapsed. 'I was young and I loved to dance but I told myself that if I was ever again able to walk I would never dance. I've kept that promise.' Unconscious, Lesia was carried into a larger, crowded jail cell, where she spent two months, and then she was sentenced. 'Because I was so young and they really couldn't find anything at all to accuse me of I was given what we called a child's sentence, just 10 years of hard labour and five years of exile in Siberia.' The journeys between the camps were the worst part. 'A hundred prisoners would be herded into locked cattle cars with a hole in the middle to act as a toilet. Every day we were given one slice of salted herring, a piece of bread and a bottle of water. . . . I couldn't bring myself to eat the herring and maybe that was what saved me.'

Early in her sentence, when she was in a labour camp in Estonia, Lesia was conned by more savvy inmates into selling part of her food ration in exchange for promised assistance to escape. 'That was, of course, very stupid, because no one ever escaped Stalin's camps. But I was tricked and I sold them some of my food. My body began to decay and one day the work captain said he would no longer accept me, so I got even less food. Slowly, I began to die.' Saved by a sympathetic doctor in the prison infirmary, Lesia recovered and was sent to the labour camp in Mordova, in north-western Russia, where she would serve most of her sentence. Vira, born in the Estonia prison, was initially kept together with other children in a camp adjacent to her mother's but when the children were 18 months old they were sent to an orphanage in Siberia. 'If the caretaker at the orphanage was very kind, once a year she would send me a letter about my daughter. Three times the prison warders called me and asked me to give her up for adoption, but each time I refused and began a hunger strike. Eventually they gave up.' While Vira grew up, her mother devoted herself to survival. 'It was a very select camp: we had the prima ballerina of the Minsk ballet, Hitler's private secretary, a few Parisians and some Moscow girls who had married diplomats.' . . . Lesia preserved her body with a rapidly acquired public cunning . . . and her soul with small acts of private defiance. She proudly shows me the relic of one such gesture: a misshapen gold wedding band, her mother's, which Lesia hid from the prison warders during a decade of body searches by wearing it under a dirt encrusted bandage on one of her toes. 'For 10 years I didn't take that bandage off. It was so dirty and disgusting and rotten it made my skin crawl to look at it. But the guards couldn't bear to examine it too closely either, so I still have my mother's wedding ring. I think I might be one of the only people who ever managed to hide something from Stalin's police.' . . .

One last question: how did you survive? 'I'm not sure. We former political prisoners often tell each other that the experience has warped us all somehow. That's probably true, but I think I still appear to be quite normal. Maybe it was because my mother was such a strong disciplinarian and always insisted on good manners. Even in the labour camps, I never learned to swear, although many did; I never learned to smoke, although many did; and unlike the more cosmopolitan girls from the big cities, I never became a lesbian.'

Source: *Financial Times* (London), 13–14 August 1994.

BUKHARIN   **Document 10**

Bukharin, Rykov and Yagoda were the most prominent defendants during the third great Show Trial. While in prison, Bukharin wrote several letters to Stalin. On 10 December 1937, he wrote the following letter, explaining why he had decided to plead guilty to the charges laid against him. He, and other senior communists, could not bring themselves to reject the party even though they knew that the charges, to which they were pleading guilty, were completely baseless. They did this for the good of the party. Bukharin was not a Jew.

Iosif Vissarionovich,

This is perhaps the last letter I shall write to you before my death. That's why, although I am a prisoner, I ask you to permit me to write this letter without resorting to officialese, all the more since I am writing this letter to you alone: the very fact of its existence or non-existence will remain entirely in your hands. I've come to the last page of my drama and perhaps of my very life, I agonized over whether I should pick up pen and paper – as I write this, I am shuddering all over from disquiet and from a thousand emotions stirring within me, and I can hardly control myself. But precisely because I have so little time left, I want to *take my leave* of you in advance, before it's too late, before my hand ceases to write, before my eyes close, while my brain somehow still functions.

In order to avoid any misunderstandings, I will say to you from the outset that, as far as the *world at large* is concerned a) I have no intention of recanting anything I've written down; b) In *this* sense (or in connection with this) I have no intention of asking you or pleading with you for anything that might derail my case from the direction in which it is heading. But I am writing to you for your *personal* information. I cannot leave this life without writing to you these last lines because I am in the grip of torments which you should know about.

1. Standing on the edge of the precipice, from which there is no return, I tell you on my word of honour, as I await my death, that I am innocent of those crimes which I admitted to at the investigation . . .

2. I had no 'way out' other than that of confirming the accusations and testimonies of others and of elaborating on them. Otherwise it would have turned out that I had not 'disarmed'.

3. Apart from extraneous factors and apart from argument 2 above, I have formed, more or less, the following conception of what is going on in our country:

There is something *great and bold about the political idea* of a general purge. It is a) connected with the pre-war situation and b) connected with the transition to democracy. This purge encompasses 1) the guilty; 2) persons under suspicion; and 3) persons potentially under suspicion. This business could not have been managed without me. Some are neutralized one way, others in another way, and a third group in yet another way. What serves as a guarantee for all this is the fact that people inescapably talk about each other and in doing so arouse an *everlasting* distrust in each other. (I'm judging from my own experience. How I raged against Radek, who had smeared me, and then I myself followed in his wake . . .) In this way, the leadership is bringing about a *full guarantee* for itself.

For God's sake, don't think that I am engaging here in reproaches, even in my inner thoughts. I wasn't born yesterday. I know all too well that *great* plans, *great* ideas, and *great* interests take precedence over everything, and I know that it would be petty for me to place the question of my own person *on a par* with the *universal-historical* tasks resting, first and foremost, on your shoulders. But it is here that I feel my deepest agony and find myself facing my chief, agonizing paradox . . .

6. . . . Once, most likely during the summer of 1928, I was at your place, and you said to me: 'Do you know why I consider you my friend? After all, you are not capable of intrigues, are you?' And I said: 'No, I am not.' At that time, I was hanging around with Kamenev . . . Believe it or not, but it is *this* fact that stands out in my mind as original sin does for a Jew. Oh, God, what a child I was! What a fool! And now I am paying for *this* with my honour and my life. For this, forgive me Koba. I weep as I write . . . I ask you for forgiveness, though I have already been punished to such an extent that everything has grown dim around me and darkness has descended upon me.

7. When I was hallucinating, I saw you several times and once I saw Nadezhda Sergeevna [Stalin's late wife]. She approached me and said: 'What

have they done with you, Nikolai Ivanovich? I'll tell Iosif to bail you out.' This was so real that I was about to jump and write a letter to you and ask you . . . bail me out! . . . Oh, Lord, if only there were some device which would make it possible for you to see my soul flayed and ripped open! If only you could see how attached I am to you, body and soul, quite unlike certain people . . . No angel will appear now to snatch Abraham's sword from his hand. My fatal destiny shall be fulfilled . . .

(a) It would be a thousand times easier for me *to die* than go through the coming trial. I simply don't know how I'll be able to control myself . . .

(b) If I'm to receive the death sentence, then I implore you beforehand, I entreat you, by all that you hold dear, not to have me shot. Let me drink poison in my cell instead. (Let me have morphine that I can fall asleep and never wake up.) For me, this point is extremely important. I don't know what words I should summon up in order to entreat you to grant me this as an act of charity . . . Have pity on me! . . . So if the verdict is death, let me have a cup of morphine. I *implore* you . . .

Source: Reprinted in J. Arch Getty and Oleg V. Naumov, *The Road to Terror* (New Haven, CT, Yale University Press, 1999), pp. 556–9.

OPERATIONAL ORDER NO. 00447: 30 JULY 1937   **Document 11**

This is the decree, signed by Ezhov, but penned by Stalin, which aimed at liquidating all 'anti-Soviet elements' still alive.

It has been established . . . that a significant number of former kulaks who had earlier been subjected to punitive measures and who had evaded them, who had escaped from camps, exile, and labour settlements, have settled in the countryside. This also includes many church officials and sectarians who had formerly been put down, former active participants of anti-Soviet armed campaigns. Significant cadres of anti-Soviet political parties (SRs, Georgian Mensheviks . . .) as well as cadres of former active members of bandit uprisings, Whites, members of punitive expeditions, repatriates, and so on remain nearly untouched in the countryside. Some of the above-mentioned elements, leaving the countryside for the cities, have infiltrated enterprises of industry, transport and construction. Besides, significant cadres of criminals are still entrenched in both countryside and city. These include horse and cattle thieves, recidivist thieves, robbers, and others who have been serving their sentences and who had escaped and are now in hiding . . . The organs of state security are faced with the task of mercilessly crushing this entire gang of anti-Soviet elements . . .

I therefore ORDER THAT AS OF 5 AUGUST 1937, ALL REPUBLICS AND REGIONS LAUNCH A CAMPAIGN OF PUNITIVE MEASURES AGAINST FORMER KULAKS, ACTIVE ANTI-SOVIET ELEMENTS, AND CRIMINALS . . .

I   GROUPS SUBJECT TO PUNITIVE MEASURES

1. Former kulaks who have returned home after having served their sentences and who continue to carry out active, anti-Soviet sabotage.
2. Former kulaks who have escaped from camps or from labour settlements, as well as kulaks who have been in hiding from dekulakization, who carry out anti-Soviet activities.
3. Former kulaks and socially dangerous elements who were members of insurrectionary, fascist, terroristic, and bandit formations, who have served their sentences, who have been in hiding from punishment, or who have escaped from their places of confinement and renewed their criminal, anti-Soviet activities.
4. Members of anti-Soviet parties (SRs . . .)
5. Persons unmasked by investigators . . . and who are the most hostile and most active members of White Guard–Cossack insurrectionary organizations . . .
6. . . . bandits, Whites, sectarian activists, church officials and others, who are presently held in prisons, camps, labour settlements and colonies . . .
7. Criminals (bandits, robbers, recidivist thieves, professional contraband smugglers . . .)
8. Criminal elements in camps and labour settlements who are carrying out criminal activities in them . . .

1. All kulaks, criminals, and other anti-Soviet elements subject to punitive measures are broken down into two categories:
    (a) To the first category belong all the most active of the abovementioned elements. They are subject to immediate arrest and, after consideration of their case by the troikas, to be shot.
    (b) To the second category belong all the remaining less active but nonetheless hostile elements. They are subject to arrest and to confinement in concentration camps for a term ranging from 8 to 10 years, while the most vicious and socially dangerous among them are subject to confinement for similar terms in prisons as determined by the troikas.
2. In accordance with the registration data presented by the people's commissariat of the republic NKVD and by the heads of krai and oblast [regional] boards of the NKVD, the following number of persons subject to punitive measures is hereby established:

	First Category	Second Category	Total
Azerbaidzhan SSR	1,500	3,750	5,250
Armenian SSR	500	1,000	1,500
Belorussian SSR	2,000	10,000	12,000
Georgian SSR	2,000	3,000	5,000
Kirghiz SSR	250	500	750
Tadzhik SSR	500	1,300	1,800
Turkmen SSR	500	1,500	2,000
Uzbek SSR	750	4,000	4,750
Bashkir ASSR	500	1,500	2,000
Buryat-Mongolian ASSR	350	1,500	1,850
Dagestan ASSR	500	2,500	3,000
Karelian ASSR	300	700	1,000
Crimean ASSR	300	1,200	1,500
Tatar ASSR	500	1,500	2,000
Azov-Black Sea krai	5,000	8,000	13,000
Far Eastern krai	2,000	4,000	6,000
West Siberian krai	5,000	12,000	17,000
Leningrad oblast	4,000	10,000	14,000
Moscow oblast	5,000	30,000	35,000
Sverdlovsk oblast	4,000	6,000	10,000
Chelyabinsk oblast	1,500	4,500	6,000
. . .			

Source: Ibid., pp. 473–6.

MOLOTOV   **Document 12**

Molotov argues that the elimination of the military élite was necessary, not because they were spies, but because they were a potential 'fifth column' during a war. They might have challenged Stalin's authority.

Let us assume [Stalin] made mistakes. But name someone who made fewer mistakes. Of all the people involved in historic events, who held the most correct position? Given all the shortcomings of the leadership of that time, [Stalin] alone coped with the tasks then confronting the country . . .

Stalin was, of course, distinguished by his rudeness. He was a very blunt person. But if not for his harshness I don't know how much good would have been accomplished. I think harshness was necessary otherwise there would have been even greater vacillation and irresolution . . .

1937 was necessary. Bear in mind that after the revolution we slashed right and left; we scored victories but tattered enemies of various stripes survived, and as we were faced by the growing danger of fascist aggression, they might have united. Thanks to 1937 there was no fifth column in our country during the war . . . It's unlikely those people were spies, but they were definitely linked with foreign intelligence services. The main thing, however, is that at the decisive moment they could not be depended on . . .

Stalin, in my opinion, pursued a correct line: let innocent heads roll, but there will be no wavering during and after the war. Yes, mistakes were made, but look Rokossovsky and Meretskov were freed . . . The terror was necessary, and it couldn't have been completed without mistakes. The alternative was to carry the internal political debates into the war years . . . Many people were wavering politically.

Source: Reprinted in Philip Boobbyer, *The Stalin Era* (London, Routledge, 2000), pp. 76–7.

———————◀●▶———————

Document 13   STEPAN PODLUBNY'S DIARY

Stepan Podlubny, a young worker of peasant origin, in Moscow, kept a diary between 1931 and 1939. It is an extraordinarily revealing source for understanding the tensions in the lives of those of non-proletarian origin, especially before 1936. He always lived in fear of being 'unmasked' and being rejected by the new society.

8 December 1932   My daily secretiveness, the secret of my inside – they don't allow me to become a person with an independent character. I can't come out openly or sharply, with any free thoughts. Instead I have to say only what everyone [else] says. I have to walk on a bent surface, along the line of least resistance. This is very bad. Unwittingly, I'm acquiring the character of a lickspittle, of a cunning dog: soft, cowardly and always giving in. How trite and how disgusting! It makes me sick to mention this, but that's the way it is. I'm afraid that this is exactly the character I'm developing.

23 December 1933   Youth, in other words the way in which youth views the world, can be divided into two groups. One group that enjoys great respect in the current order is a group of state parrots. They never have their own opinion. They do everything the way they are ordered to, without any thought. These people have a shallow understanding of science and they resemble each other like a flock of sheep. There is another category of

people, which I would call more or less liberal. Liberal in the sense that they occupy a different place and have evolved differently, perhaps due to their upbringing. Well, these are unconventional people with progressive views or so. It is very noticeable that the character of these people is deeper, more developed and more gifted than the first one. They do everything silently and have a critical opinion on everything. . . . They would never say anything without reason. In terms of their knowledge one can feel that they don't know things in general, like the first category, but they know the depths. They are profound people. Profound, because they look at life with clear, not dull, eyes, and aren't afraid to face the truth. Often they are among the lists of the people who, as it is said, don't belong to us.

12 February 1935   This is the onset of a time of such reaction and persecution . . . I can't describe it in a few words. It only reminds me of studying the history of the party in 1907: a raging black reaction, going on right now. A raging reaction, and the persecution of free thought. You have to fear not only your comrades, you must also be afraid of yourself. They just don't persecute you for conversations, but they even persecute you for hinting at unfavourable speech.

18 December 1937   Of course I know a lot of rumours about the arrests of various people. This doesn't come as a surprise to anybody these days. But to number mama, a half-illiterate woman, among the Trotskyites, that would never have occurred to me. Not even in my dreams would I be able to imagine this, as I know her very well.

Source: Reprinted in Sheila Fitzpatrick, ed., *Stalinism: New Directions* (London, Routledge, 2000), pp. 87, 96–7, 105, 109.

STALIN THE MIRACLE-WORKER   **Document 14**

Bukharin acted as the protector of the literary élite as long as he was at liberty. His intervention on Mandelstam's behalf reveals that Stalin's word was absolute.

In his letter to Stalin, Bukharin added a postscript saying he had been visited by [Boris] Pasternak, who was upset by the arrest of Mandelstam. The purpose of this postscript was clear: it was Bukharin's way of indicating to Stalin what the effect of M.'s arrest had been on public opinion. It was always necessary to personify 'public opinion' in this way. You were allowed to talk of one particular individual being upset, but it was unthinkable to mention the existence of dissatisfaction among a whole section of the community – say, the intelligentsia, or 'literary circles'. No group has the right to its own opinion about some event or other. In matters of this kind there are fine points of etiquette which nobody can appreciate unless he has been in our shoes. Bukharin knew how to present things in the right way, and it was the postscript at the end of his letter that explained why Stalin chose to telephone Pasternak and not someone else. . . .

Stalin began by telling Pasternak that Mandelstam's case had been reviewed, and that everything would be all right. This was followed by a strange reproach: why hadn't Pasternak approached the writers' organizations, or him (Stalin), and why hadn't he tried to do something for Mandelstam: 'If I were a poet and a poet friend of mine were in trouble, I would do anything to help him.'

Pasternak's reply to this was: 'The writers' organizations haven't bothered with cases like this since 1927, and if I hadn't tried to do something, you probably would never have heard about it.' Pasternak went on to say something about the word 'friend', trying to define more precisely the nature of his relations with M., which were not, of course, covered by the term 'friendship'. This digression was very much in Pasternak's style and had no relevance to the matter in hand. Stalin interrupted him: 'But he's a genius, he's a genius, isn't he?' To this Pasternak replied: 'But that's not the point.' 'What is it, then?' Stalin asked. Pasternak then said that he would like to meet him and have a talk. 'About what?' 'About life and death,' Pasternak replied. Stalin hung up. Pasternak tried to get him back, but could only reach a secretary. Stalin did not come to the phone again. Pasternak asked the secretary whether he could talk about this conversation or whether he should keep quiet about it. To his surprise, he was told he could talk about it as much as he liked – there was no need at all to make a secret of it. Stalin clearly wanted it to have the widest possible repercussions. A miracle is only a miracle, after all, if people stand in wonder before it.

Everybody could now clearly see what miracles Stalin was capable of, and it was to Pasternak that the honor had fallen not only of spreading the good tidings all over Moscow, but also of hearing a sermon in connection with it. The aim of the miracle was thus achieved: attention was diverted from the victim to the miracle-worker. It was extraordinarily symptomatic of the period that, in discussing the miracle, nobody thought to ask why Stalin should have rebuked Pasternak for not trying to save a friend and fellow poet while at the same time he was calmly sending his own friends and comrades to their death. Even Pasternak [who] had not thought about [his] contemporaries took Stalin's sermon on friendship between poets completely at its face value and was ecstatic about a ruler who had shown such warmth of spirit.

Source: N. Mandelstam, *Hope Abandoned* (London, Collins Harvill, 1971), pp. 145–7.

THE STALIN CULT BLOSSOMS **Document 15**

This extract is taken from a speech by A.O. Avdienko, a writer, to the VIIth Congress of Soviets in February 1935; the poem appeared in Pravda *in August 1936.*

Thank you, Stalin. Thank you because I am joyful. Thank you because I am well. No matter how old I become, I shall never forget how we received Stalin two days ago. Centuries will pass, and the generations still to come will regard us as the happiest of mortals, as the most fortunate of men, because we lived in the century of centuries, because we were privileged to see Stalin, our inspired leader. Yes, and we regard ourselves as the happiest of mortals because we are the contemporaries of a man who never had an equal in world history.

The men of all ages will call on thy name, which is strong, beautiful, wise and marvellous. Thy name is engraven on every factory, every machine, every place on the earth, and in the hearts of all men.

Every time I have found myself in his presence I have been subjugated by his strength, his charm, his grandeur. I have experienced a great desire to sing, to cry out, to shout with joy and happiness. And now see me – me! – on the same platform where the Great Stalin stood a year ago. In what country, in what part of the world could such a thing happen?

I write books. I am an author. All thanks to thee, O great educator, Stalin. I love a young woman with a renewed love and shall perpetuate myself in my children – all thanks to thee, great educator, Stalin. I shall be eternally happy and joyous, all thanks to thee, great educator, Stalin. Everything belongs to thee, chief of our great country. And when the woman I love presents me with a child the first word it shall utter will be: Stalin.

> O great Stalin, O leader of the peoples,
> Thou who broughtest man to birth.
> Thou who fructifiest the earth,
> Thou who restorest the centuries,
> Thou who makest bloom the spring,
> Thou who makest vibrate the musical chords . . .
> Thou, splendour of my spring, O Thou,
> Sun reflected by millions of hearts . . .

Source: Pravda, 28 August 1936, reprinted in T.H. Rigby, *Stalin* (Englewood Cliffs, NJ, Prentice-Hall, 1966), pp. 111–12.

———————◄●►———————

Document 16   (A) A CALL TO ARMS

The situation was desperate when Stalin delivered this radio speech on 3 July 1941. Right up to the moment of invasion the Soviet people had been assured that there would be no attack. Added to German destruction was the demand that if the Red Army had to retreat, a scorched earth policy was to be adopted.

Comrades, citizens, brothers and sisters, men of our Army and Navy! It is to you I am speaking dear friends!

The perfidious military attack by Hitlerite Germany on our Motherland, begun on 22 June, is continuing. In spite of the heroic resistance of the Red Army, and although the enemy's finest divisions and finest air force units have already been smashed and have found their graves on the field of battle, the enemy continues to push forward, hurling fresh forces to the front. Hitler's troops have succeeded in capturing Lithuania, a considerable part of Latvia, the western part of Byelorussia and part of Western Ukraine. The Fascist aircraft are extending the range of their operations. . . . Grave danger overhangs our country.

The Red Army, Red Navy and all citizens of the Soviet Union must defend every inch of Soviet soil, must fight to the last drop of blood for our towns and villages, must display the daring, initiative and mental alertness characteristic of our people. . . .

We must strengthen the Red Army's rear, subordinating all our work to this end; all our industries must be got to work with greater intensity, to produce more rifles, machine-guns, cartridges, shells, planes; we must organize the guarding of factories, power stations, telephonic and telegraphic communications, and arrange local air-raid protection.

We must wage a ruthless fight against all disorganizers of the rear, deserters, panicmongers and rumour-mongers; we must exterminate spies, sabotage agents and enemy parachutists, rendering rapid aid in all this to our extermination battalions. We must bear in mind that the enemy is treacherous, cunning, experienced in deception and the dissemination of false rumours. We must reckon with all this, and not fall victims to provocation. All who by their panic-mongering and cowardice hinder the work of defence, no matter who they may be, must be immediately hauled before a military tribunal.

In case of a forced retreat of Red Army units, all rolling-stock must be evacuated, the enemy must not be left a single engine, a single railway truck, not a single pound of grain or gallon of fuel. Collective farmers must drive off all their cattle and turn over their grain to the safe keeping of the State authorities, for transportation to the rear. All valuable property, including non-ferrous metals, grain and fuel that cannot be withdrawn, must be destroyed without fail.

In areas occupied by the enemy, partisan units, mounted and foot, must be formed; sabotage groups must be organized to combat enemy units, to foment partisan warfare everywhere, blow up bridges and roads, damage telephone and telegraph lines, set fire to forests, stores and transports. In occupied regions conditions must be made unbearable for the enemy and all his accomplices. They must be hounded and annihilated at every step, and all their measures frustrated.

Source: Soviet Foreign Policy during the Patriotic War: Documents and Materials, vol. 1, 22 June 1941–31 December 1943 (New York, Hutchinson, 1946).

(B) REAL BURDEN OF DEFENCE OUTLAYS, 1940–44 (BILLION ROUBLES AT   **Document 16**
1937 FACTOR COST)

The Soviet Union paid a heavier price in human and material resources during the war than any other belligerent country.

	1940	1941	1942	1943	1944
GDP	247.6	206.3	144.1	160.9	192.2
Net imports	0.0	0.0	9.0	30.9	35.6
Defence outlays:	45.3	66.9	110.1	133.8	145.3
Munitions	16.6	28.3	61.6	82.3	90.2
Pay	6.8	9.8	15.8	16.6	17.2
Food	9.9	14.1	16.1	19.0	19.1
Clothing, etc.	4.4	5.1	6.4	5.3	6.3
Fuel	1.5	2.1	2.4	2.7	3.1
Transport	0.9	1.1	1.4	2.6	3.0
Construction	2.4	2.6	2.0	1.1	1.5
Other, including repairs	2.7	3.8	4.5	4.2	4.8
Defence outlays, less net imports	45.3	66.9	101.1	102.9	109.7
Defence outlays, % of GDP:					
Domestic supply	18.0	32.0	70.0	64.0	57.0
Foreign supply	0.0	0.0	6.0	19.0	19.0

Source: M. Harrison, 'Soviet economic growth since 1928: The alternative statistics of G.I. Khanin', *Europe–Asia Studies*, vol. 45, no. 1, 1993, Table 4 and D-1, reprinted by permission of the publisher (Taylor & Francis Ltd, www.informaworld.com).

Document 16   (C) MILITARY LOSSES IN THE GREAT PATRIOTIC WAR (MILLIONS)

1.	Killed in action and died of injuries before reaching a hospital	5.227
2.	Died from injuries in hospitals	1.103
3.	Died from disease, accident or shot as punishment	0.556
	(of whom	
	died from diseases	0.267
	died from accidents and shootings	0.289)
4.	Missing and imprisoned (according to military reports and the data of the repatriation organs)	3.396
5.	Unaccounted for losses in the first months of war	1.163
6.	Total losses (1 + 2 + 3 + 4 + 5)	11.444

Less

7.	Previously surrounded and missing soldiers subsequently called up on liberated territory	0.940
8.	Returned prisoners of war	1.836
9.	Total (7 + 8)	2.776
10.	Net loss (6 − 9)	8.668
	of whom	
	not returned from imprisonment (died, killed, emigrated)	1.783
	armed forces	8.509
	frontier troops	0.061
	internal troops	0.098

Source: M. Ellman and S. Maksudov, 'Soviet deaths in the Great Patriotic War: A note', *Europe–Asia Studies*, vol. 46, no. 4, 1994, p. 674, reprinted by permission of the publisher (Taylor & Francis Ltd, www.informaworld.com).

Document 17   (A) GDP PER HEAD OF THE USSR IN INTERNATIONAL COMPARISON, 1913–40 ($ AND 1980 PRICES)

The Soviet Union was ahead of Japan in GDP per head in 1913 but behind in 1940. Apart from Japan, however, the USSR was growing faster than the other economies. This was partly due to the fact that mature economies grow more slowly than those which begin from a low base. Real GDP by sector of origin reveals that industry by 1944 contributed almost as much as in 1937 – a formidable achievement given the war and dislocation.

	1913	1928	1932	1937	1940
Japan	800	1150	1130	1330	1660
Russia (USSR)	900	900	930	1440	1440
Italy	1550	1780	1740	1960	2070
Germany	1960	2280	1880	2740	3190
France	2000	2550	2280	2590	2330
UK	2970	3110	2990	3610	3980
USA	3790	4690	3450	4570	4970

Source: R.W. Davies, M. Harrison and S.G. Wheatcroft, eds, *The Economic Transformation of the Soviet Union 1913–1945* (Cambridge, Cambridge University Press, 1994), p. 270.

———————◀◉▶———————

(B) REAL GDP BY SECTOR OF ORIGIN, 1937–44 (BILLION ROUBLES AND 1937 FACTOR COST)　　**Document 17**

	1937	1940	1941	1942	1943	1944
Agriculture	63.0	69.9	42.3	25.3	30.4	45.0
Industry:	65.4	73.8	70.3	51.1	59.2	66.5
defence industry	3.4	8.3	14.2	28.1	35.0	38.7
civilian industry	62.0	65.5	56.2	22.9	24.2	27.8
Construction	10.5	10.6	6.9	3.2	3.4	4.4
Transport, communications	16.8	19.3	17.8	10.2	11.8	13.7
Trade, catering	10.4	11.1	9.3	3.8	3.5	4.1
Civilian services	33.1	42.0	35.3	22.1	23.4	28.8
Military services:	3.7	7.3	10.4	16.6	17.3	17.9
army, navy	3.4	6.8	9.8	15.8	16.6	17.2
NKVD	0.3	0.5	0.6	0.8	0.7	0.7
NDP	202.9	234.0	192.3	132.4	149.1	180.5
Depreciation	9.4	13.6	14.0	11.7	11.8	11.7
GDP	212.3	247.6	206.3	144.1	160.9	192.2

Source: M. Harrison, 'Soviet economic growth since 1928: The alternative statistics of G.I. Khanin', *Europe–Asia Studies*, vol. 45, no. 1, 1993, Table 1, reprinted by permission of the publisher (Taylor & Francis Ltd, www.informaworld.com).

———————◀◉▶———————

Document 18   (A) PRIKAZ (DECREE) OF THE USSR PEOPLE'S COMMISSARIAT OF INTERNAL
AFFAIRS ISSUED IN 1941

*This is the decree (prikaz) deporting ethnic Germans from the Volga German
Republic, Saratov and Stalingrad* oblasts *mainly to Siberia and Kazakhstan.
They were accused of conspiring with the advancing* Wehrmacht *troops. Ethnic
Germans in the Red Army, the party and other institutions were also affected.
The Germans were absolved of all blame by Khrushchev but their republic was
never returned to them. They, together with the Crimean Tatars, are the only
two deported nationalities which did not receive their old territory back. In all,
about 52 nationalities were deported in the 1940s. Recent Russian estimates
put the number exiled or resettled between 1941 and 1948 at about 3.3 million
with another 215,000 being despatched later. Besides storing up hatred of
Russians and the Soviet regime, these deportations had an unexpected consequence. They forced disparate nationalities from the North Caucasus and
Transcaucasia to cooperate to survive. Some of the mafia gangs of the 1980s
and 1990s in Russia began in embryo in exile.*

001158. Contents: Measures on the Deportation of Germans from the Volga
German Republic and Saratov and Stalingrad Oblasts No.001158 August 27,
1941 Moscow

In order to execute the Decree of USSR Sovnarkom and CC RCP(B) on the
deportation of Germans from the Volga German Republic, Saratov and
Stalingrad oblasts, the following measures are to be carried out:

1. Send a USSR NKVD operational group headed by Comrade Serov, USSR
   Deputy People's Commissar of Internal Affairs, to the area. . . .
2. Entrust the following troikas [group of three] with the task of preparing
   and carrying out the operation in the oblasts. . . .
3. On arrival at the designated place, the three responsible officials are to
   organise the operation. Carry out the operation according to the appended
   instructions.
4. The operation is to begin on September 3 and is to be completed on
   September 20, 1941.
5. Send special USSR NKVD officers to each settlement area for German
   deportees and make them responsible for preparing the timely acceptance of columns with the deportees at the transfer points and in the
   settlement areas. . . .
6. To carry out the deportation operation, Comrade Obruchnikov, Deputy
   People's Commissar, is to send 1200 NKVD officers and 2000 militia
   officials to the Volga German Republic; 250 special NKVD officials
   and 1000 militia officials to Saratov Oblast; 100 NKVD officers and
   250 militia officials to Stalingrad Oblast.
7. To carry out the deportation operation by the NKVD troops, Major-
   General Apollonov is to send Brigade Commissar Krivenko and 7350

Red Army soldiers, under his command, to the Volga German Republic; Colonel Vorobeikov and 2300 Red Army soldiers, under his command, to Saratov Oblast; Brigade Commissar Sladkevich and 2500 Red Army soldiers, under his command, to Stalingrad Oblast.

Deputy People's Commissar Obruchnikov and Major-General Apollonov are to ensure that those sent officially arrive at the place designated for them not later than September 1, 1941.

8. To ensure the embarquement of German deportees on steamers in Astrakhan, Comrade Voronin, Head of the Stalingrad NKVD Administration is to provide an operational group to help the Astrakhan Section for Operatives.

9. On the basis of the information received by local NKVD organs from agents and operatives, identify anti-Soviet elements and arrest them before the operation and deport their families in the conventional manner.

10. Prior to the operation, explain the situation to Soviet and Party activists and warn the deportees that if they assume an illegal status, some members will be prosecuted and other family members will be subjected to repression [execution or imprisonment].

11. If some family members to be deported refuse to go to the settlement area, arrest such persons and transfer them forcibly to the settlement area.

12. Warn all NKVD personnel involved in the operation that the operation is not to be accompanied by noise or panic. If any delays, anti-Soviet actions or armed clashes occur, take decisive measures to eliminate them.

13. To coordinate the whole deportation, transfer and settling procedure, Comrade Chernyshov, USSR Deputy People's Commissar of Internal Affairs, Comrade Fedotov, head of the Red Army Administration and Comrade Sinegubov, Head of the Transport Administration are to be seconded to the USSR NKVD.

14. Comrade Serov, Deputy People's Commissar, is to inform the USSR NKVD* on the preparation and the progress of the operation beginning from September 1, 1941.

L. Beria, USSR People's Commissar of Internal Affairs,
General Commissar of State Security

[*According to the data of the USSR NKVD Section of Special Deportation Areas, 446,480 persons were deported from the regions mentioned in the *prikaz;* in addition to the Germans from the Volga German Republic, more than 800,000 citizens of German nationality who were living scattered throughout the country had been deported.]

Source: TsGAOR, f. 8331, op. 22, d. 542, l. 234.

Document 18   (B) THE USSR NKVD SECTION FOR COMBATTING BANDITRY

An extract from an Explanatory Note by Lavrenty Beria to Comrade J.V. Stalin, Comrade V.M. Molotov (USSR Sovnarkom) and Comrade G.M. Malenkov (CC, RCP (b)).

July 1944

In order to implement the decree of the State Committee of Defence, 602,193 inhabitants of the North Caucasus, of whom 496,460 were Chechens and Ingushi, 68,327 were Karachai and 37,406 were Balkars, were deported by the NKVD for permanent residence in Kazakhstan and Kirgizia, in February–March 1944.

Most of the special deportees (477,809 persons) were sent to Kazakhstan. However, the republican agencies of Kazakhstan did not devote due attention to the problem of providing special deportees from the North Caucasus with gardens and household plots. As a result, the living standards of special deportees in Kazakhstan and their engagement in socially useful labour have been unsatisfactory. Special deportees' families settled in kolkhozes were not allowed to join agricultural artels [cooperatives]. The provision of special deportees with household plots and gardens and also living quarters was inadequate. Special deportees settled in sovkhozes and assigned to industrial enterprises were unsatisfactorily employed in industrial enterprises. Cases of typhus, shortcomings in the provision of household plots and in living conditions, thefts and criminal offences were recorded.

In order to introduce proper order, Kruglov, USSR Deputy People's Commissar of Internal Affairs, and a group of officers were sent on an official visit in May 1944 to Kazakhstan. In July 1944 2,196 special deportees were arrested for various offences. All the cases were heard by special courts. 429 NKVD special komendaturas were established to supervise the residence conditions of the special deportees, combat escapes, provide NKVD operatives and provide as quickly as possible special deportees' families with household plots.

Special deportees were provided with better and larger household plots. Of 70,296 families settled in kolkhozes, 56,800 or 81 per cent became members of agricultural artels; 83,303 families (74.3 per cent) received household plots and gardens; 12,683 families lived in their own houses. The work of children's labour colonies was organised. In June 1944 1,268 children were placed there. More special deportees were employed. For example, of a total of 16,927 persons found capable of work, 16,396 were actually employed in Dzhambul oblast. In Akmolinsk oblast of 19,345 persons, 17,667 were actually working and of these 2,746 were old people and children.

Source: TsGAOR, f. 9479, op. 1, d. 228, l. 259–67.

THE COST OF HOSTILITIES: A BALANCE SHEET

Document 19

The euphoria [of victory] however, concealed an appalling bill of costs. Outstanding among these were the 27 million to 28 million premature deaths incurred by the Soviet population, which accounted for no fewer than one in seven of the prewar population, and up to half of global demographic losses attributable to World War II.

The bleeding wounds of victory were everywhere. The Soviet Army had lost nearly 9 million dead. No other army in history had achieved so much at such great cost. The civilian cost was still greater. Some 19 million civilians had perished before their time. One-third of the prewar capital stock had been destroyed, and twice that amount used up by wartime defence, economic conversion, and lost national income. . . .

In the years just after the war, the reinforced legitimacy of Stalin and Stalinist institutions ran strongly against other, weaker currents welling up from below. The war experience would also supply a smothered impulse to reform. There was a widespread desire for liberalisation and relaxation, in politics as in culture and economic affairs. Veterans of military service and war work, whose loyalty to the Soviet system had passed the severest test, may have expected the system to reward them with greater trust and increased rights of participation, not just free bus passes. Some also believed that the war had revealed the weaknesses of Stalinist dictatorship, above all in 1941–2, and the necessity of limiting the arbitrary powers of individual leaders. The war had given many the opportunity to exercise their own personal initiative and responsibility on a wider scale than in peacetime, as military commanders, factory managers, farmers, war administrators, war writers and reporters, and had taught them that mere unthinking obedience to superior orders was not enough.

For the time being, however, such beliefs and values would remain implicit or, if voiced *en clair*, dangerous to the individuals who held them. Among the political leadership there were only confused ideological shadings, without sharp distinctions between overall political alternatives or coherent programmes. In the absence of any clear challenge, Stalin would seek to restore everything as it was before the war to the rigid mould of personal dictatorship and rule from above by decree. And while he lived he would very largely succeed. Other nations – the two Germanies and Japan under Allied occupation, Britain under the Attlee government, France and Italy under new postwar constitutions – went through different postwar reforms. In the Soviet Union, in contrast, the prewar order of forced industrial accumulation, political dictatorship, and social mobilisation, would be restored. . . .

If not Stalin, then who can be credited with the great victory on the eastern front? Millions of ordinary people, infantrymen, officers, workers at the bench and in the field, managers, writers – even war administrators and

Party secretaries: these shouldered the main burdens, whether they did it well or badly. For the most part they were not born great heroes, and they were not innately brave or noble, although many of them did very brave things. They were marked out not by special personal qualities but by special circumstances, and an extraordinary history.

What enabled them to wage such a terrible war and emerge victorious? The answer to these questions is the same – everything in their history, their revolutionary and national traditions, their cultural ties and family roles, the social, economic and administrative webs which defined their place in Soviet life, the organs of state, the Party and its leaders, and Stalin too. All these are indispensable elements of the explanation of what made them fight, and why victory cost them so much.

Source: J.D. Barber and M. Harrison, *The Soviet Home Front 1941–1945* (Harlow, Longman, 1991), pp. 206–11.

Document 20   STALIN THE OMNISCIENT

Stalin is the brilliant leader and teacher of the Party, the great strategist of the Socialist Revolution, military commander, the guide of the Soviet state. An implacable attitude towards the enemies of Socialism, profound fidelity to principle, a combination of clear revolutionary perspective and clarity of purpose with extraordinary firmness and persistence in the pursuit of aims, wise and practical leadership, and intimate contact with the masses – such are the characteristic features of Stalin's style. After Lenin, no other leader in the world had been called upon to direct such vast masses of workers and peasants. He has a unique faculty for generalizing the constructive revolutionary experience of the masses, for seizing upon and developing their initiative, for learning from the masses as well as teaching them, and for leading them forward to victory.

Stalin's whole career is an example of profound theoretical power combined with an unusual breadth and versatility of practical experience in the revolutionary struggle.

In conjunction with the tried and tested Leninists who are his immediate associates, and at the head of the great Bolshevik Party, Stalin guides the destinies of a multi-national Socialist state, a state of workers and peasants of which there is no precedent in history. His advice is taken as a guide to action in all fields of Socialist construction. His work is extraordinary for its variety; his energy truly amazing. The range of questions which engage his attention is immense, embracing complex problems of Marxist–Leninist theory and school textbooks; problems of Soviet foreign policy and the municipal affairs of Moscow, the proletarian capital; the development of the Great Northern Sea Route and the reclamation of the Colchian marshes; the advancement of Soviet literature and art and the editing of the model rules for collective farms; and, lastly, the solution of most intricate theoretical and practical problems in the science of warfare.

Everybody is familiar with the cogent and invincible force of Stalin's logic, the crystal clarity of his mind, his iron will, his devotion to the party, his ardent faith in the people, and love for the people. Everybody is familiar with his modesty, his simplicity of manner, his consideration for people, and his merciless severity towards enemies of the people. Everybody is familiar with his intolerance of ostentation, of phrasemongers and windbags, of whiners and alarmists. Stalin is wise and deliberate in solving complex political questions where a thorough weighing of pros and cons is required. At the same time, he is a supreme master of bold revolutionary decisions and of swift adaptations to changed conditions.

Stalin is the worthy continuer of the cause of Lenin, or, as it is said in the Party: Stalin is the Lenin of today.

Source: G.F. Alexandrov, *et al.*, *Joseph Stalin: A Short Biography* (Moscow, Foreign Language Publishing House, 1947), pp. 198–201.

STALIN ON RED ARMY DISCIPLINE   **Document 21**

'Do you see what a complicated thing is man's soul, his psyche? Well then, imagine a man who has fought from Stalingrad to Belgrade – over thousands of kilometres of his own devastated land, across the dead bodies of his comrades and dearest ones! How can such a man react normally? And what is so awful in his amusing himself with a woman, after such horrors? You have imagined the Red Army to be ideal. And it is not ideal, or can it be, even if it did not contain a certain percentage of criminals – we opened up our prisons and stuck everybody into the army. There was an interesting case. An Air Force major wanted to have a woman, and a chivalrous engineer appeared to protect her. The major drew a gun: "Ech, you mole from the rear!" – and he killed the chivalrous engineer. They sentenced the major to death. But somehow the matter was brought before me, and I made inquiries – I have the right as commander in chief in time of war – and I released the major and sent him to the front. Now he is one of our heroes. One has to understand the soldier. The Red Army is not ideal. The important thing is that it fights Germans – and it is fighting them well; the rest doesn't matter.'

Soon afterwards when I returned from Moscow, I heard, to my horror, of a far more significant example of Stalin's 'understanding' attitude toward the sins of Red Army personnel. While crossing East Prussia, Soviet soldiers, especially the tank units, had regularly shelled and killed all the German civilian refugees – women and children. Stalin was informed of this and asked what should be done. He replied: 'We lecture our soldiers too much; let them have some initiative!'

Source: M. Djilas, *Conversations with Stalin* (London, Hart-Davis, 1962), pp. 101–2.

Document 22 STALIN IN 1948

I could hardly believe how much he had changed in two or three years. When I had last seen him, in 1945, he was still lively, quick-witted, and had a pointed sense of humour. But that was during the war and it had been, it would seem, Stalin's last effort and had taken him to his limit. Now he laughed at inanities and shallow jokes. On one occasion he not only failed to get the political point of an anecdote I told him about how he had got the better of Churchill and Roosevelt, but he even seemed to be offended, as old men sometimes are. I perceived an embarrassed astonishment on the faces of the rest of the party.

In one thing, though, he was still the Stalin of old: stubborn, sharp, suspicious whenever anyone disagreed with him. He even cut Molotov, and one could feel the tension between them. Everyone paid court to him, avoiding any expression of opinion before he expressed his, and then hastening to agree with him. . . .

Toward the end of the dinner Stalin unexpectedly asked me why there were not many Jews in the Yugoslav Party and why these few played no important role in it. I tried to explain to him that there were not many Jews in Yugoslavia to begin with, and most belonged to the middle class. I added, 'The only prominent Communist Jew is Pijade, and he regards himself as being more of a Serb than a Jew'.

Stalin began to recall: 'Pijade, short, with glasses? Yes, I remember, he visited me. And what is his position?'

'He is a member of the Central Committee, a veteran Communist, the translator of *Das Kapital*', I explained.

'In our Central Committee there are no Jews!' he broke in, and began to laugh tauntingly. 'You are an anti-Semite, you, too, Djilas, you, too, are an anti-Semite!'

I took his words and laughter to mean the opposite, as I should have – as the expression of his own anti-Semitism and as a provocation to get me to declare my stand concerning the Jews, particularly Jews in the Communist movement.

Source: Ibid., pp. 138–40.

SOVIET ATTITUDES TOWARDS YUGOSLAV CULTURE   **Document 23**

How little the views of the Yugoslavs were respected can be seen from an incident which happened to Tito while he was in Moscow. He says:

'The representatives of the Soviet press asked me to write an article for their papers. I did so, and when I got the text, I noticed that eight-tenths of my views had been completely altered according to the wishes of the editors. I was already familiar with such methods in the Soviet Union, but I never imagined that Soviet journalists could alter to their own formula the text of an article written by the Prime Minister of a friendly allied country. The same thing happened to Djilas, Mora Pijade, and Rato Dugonjis, the Secretary of the People's Youth of Yugoslavia. The latter had written an article about the Brtko–Banovisi railway which the youth of Yugoslavia had built by voluntary work. The editor of *Komsomolskaya Pravda* changed the article considerably, even shortening the railway from fifty miles to thirty-seven. Strange logic!'

In contacts with the most responsible Soviet representatives a tone of disparagement towards the Yugoslavs as a people was noticeable, disparagement of our culture, complete ignorance of our history and our way of life. For instance, Zhdanov once asked Djilas whether opera existed in Yugoslavia. There were twelve opera houses in Yugoslavia, and Yugoslav composers, Lisinski for instance, had been writing operas more than a century ago. It was not merely a matter of belittling our culture, our language, and our press in words, but also in deeds. The Soviet representatives in Yugoslavia proposed that we should include as many Russian songs in our radio programmes as possible. Had we accepted their suggestion there would have been two or three times as many Russian songs as Yugoslav. They also asked us to increase the number of Russian plays in our theatres. We have always esteemed Gogol, Ostrovsky, Gorki, but we refused to flood our theatres with third-rate modern Soviet plays. As for films, in 1946 they imposed on us a block booking contract, so that we had no choice of the films they sent; and we had to pay the rental in dollars, at three, four, or five times the prices we paid for films from the West. Thus we got Laurence Olivier's *Hamlet* for about two thousand dollars but for *Exploits of a Soviet Intelligence Agent* we had to pay some twenty thousand dollars.

Various Soviet representatives especially pounced on our press as one of the most powerful instruments of propaganda. Almost every week a representative of the Soviet Information Bureau would come round with several hundred articles written in Moscow on various topics, mostly about life in the Soviet Union, birthdays of Russian writers, composers, and scientists, or life in the collectives; there were also many articles about other countries, and he persistently asked for all this material to be published in our dailies and weeklies. Had we printed them all, we should have had almost no space left for our own journalists, who would soon have been out of work, leaving the people to be informed of world events only through the eyes of writers in Moscow.

On the other hand, we asked the Soviet government to publish at least something about Yugoslavia in the Soviet press, on a reciprocal basis. This was always avoided. Some articles waited a year for publication, then were returned without having seen daylight. The same thing happened with books. We published 1,850 Soviet books; they published two of ours.

Source: V. Dedijer, *Tito Speaks* (London, Weidenfeld and Nicolson, 1953), pp. 274–5.

Document 24   THE IMPORTANCE OF THE COW

This was why I dreamed of a cow. Thanks to the vagaries of our economic system, a family could support itself for many years by keeping a cow. Millions lived in wretched huts, feeding themselves from the products of their tiny plots of land (on which they grew potatoes, cabbage, cucumbers, beets, turnips and onions) and their cow. Some of the milk had to be sold to buy hay, but there was always enough left over to add a little richness to the cabbage soup. A cow gives people some independence and, without over-exerting themselves, they can earn a little extra to buy bread. The State is still in a quandary about this relic of the old world: if people are allowed to buy hay to feed their cow, then they do only the very minimum of work on the kolkhoz; if, on the other hand, you take their cows away, they will die of hunger. The result is that the cow is alternately forbidden and then permitted again.

Source: N. Mandelstam, *Hope Abandoned* (London, Collins Harvill, 1971), p. 301.

Document 25   A JEWISH SUCCESS STORY

It was Lezhnev who had asked M. to write *The Noise of Time* for *Rossia*, but then turned it down after reading it – he had expected a totally different kind of childhood story, such as he himself was later to write. His was the story of a Jewish boy from the shtetl who discovers Marxism. He was lucky with his book. At first nobody wanted to publish it – though it was probably no worse than others of its kind – but then it was read and approved by Stalin. Stalin even tried to phone Lezhnev to tell him, but Lezhnev was not at home at the moment Stalin called. When he learned what had happened, Lezhnev sat by his phone for a whole week, hoping that Stalin might ring back. But miracles, as we know, are not repeated. A week later he was informed that there would be no further telephone call, but that orders had been given for his book to be published (it was already being printed), that he had been made a member of the Party on Stalin's personal recommendation and appointed editor of *Pravda's* literary section. In this way Lezhnev, hitherto a nobody who could always be trampled underfoot as a former private publisher, was suddenly raised to the greatest heights and almost went crazy from joy and emotion. Of all the Haroun al Rashid miracles, this, incidentally, turned out to be the most enduring: Lezhnev kept his *Pravda* post, or an equivalent one, right up to his death.

On hearing all this, Lezhnev at last left his telephone and rushed off to the barber – his beard had grown considerably during the week of waiting. Next he called on us to present us with *The Dialectic of Nature* and to tell us about the great change that Marxism had brought into his life. None of this had ever entered his head in the days when he was editor of *Rossia*. From what he said, it appeared that he had read some newly discovered works by Engels, notably *The Dialectic of Nature*, and seen the light. He had even gone into a bookshop just now and bought a copy for us, because he hoped it would help M. to see the light as well. Lezhnev was an exceptionally sincere and well-meaning person. I was even a little envious of him at that moment – a genuine conversion to the true faith, which suddenly puts an end to all your troubles and at the same time starts bringing in a regular income, must be a remarkably agreeable thing.

Source: Ibid., pp. 241–2.

YOUTH, CULTURE AND HEALTH   Document 26

Some young people were not satisfied with official culture. They continued the (a)
Russian tradition of self-education and developed their own private culture
which they referred to as a 'catacomb' culture. Ernst Neizvestny, who became
a famous sculptor and had a furious row with Khrushchev over art, describes
his experience. Khrushchev's son commissioned Neizvestny to do a headstone
which would serve as a memorial to this father. It can now be seen in
Novodevichy cemetery, Moscow.

We did not pose any political questions; we did not in any event have political conceptions. I was not even in the Komsomol, although one of our friends was a member of the party. We all intended, however, to educate ourselves well, and the reading of, say, Trotsky, or Saint Augustine, or Orwell, or Berdiaev was punishable. Therefore we needed a conspiracy . . . Before *samizdat* [underground self-publishing which began in the 1960s], we procured and copied privately the whole circle of the *Verhkovtsy* [liberal thinkers of the *Landmarks* movement, 1909] . . . Besides this we listened to reports on theosophy, genetics, on subjects forbidden in the USSR. If the authorities had asked us whether we studied politics, we would have had to answer honestly: no.

Source: Reprinted in Elena Zubkova, *Russia After the War* (Armonk, NY, M.E. Sharpe, 1998), p. 113.

(b)   *Neizvestny and his friends were at one end of the cultural spectrum; the other end was made up of party officials and rank-and-file members. These are extracts from a party Central Committee report, prepared by officials sent out to various parts of the country to assess the impact of propaganda, in 1947. The experience was rather chastening. The first two interviews are with local party officials. The third is with a rank-and-file party member.*

First interview

Q. What political literature do you read?
A. Comrade Stalin's first volume.
Q. What in particular have you read in it?
A. I forget. I can't remember. I can't say.
Q. What else do you read?
A. I read Comrade Aleksandrov on bourgeois theories.
Q. What kind of fiction do you read?
A. I read *Ivan the Terrible*, a book by one of our writers. I don't like the book. It speaks well of the people but among the bourgeoisie and the capitalists there isn't one good person. That is all I have read this year.

Second interview

Q. Have you read the report of Comrade Zhdanov on the journals *Zvezda* and *Leningrad*?
A. No, I haven't read it.
Q. Which of the recent decisions of the Central Committee guide you in your work?
A. I cannot now name any.
Q. What English political parties do you know?
A. I don't remember.
Q. Who is the head of the government in Yugoslavia?
A. I don't remember. Tito is in the government either in Yugoslavia or Bulgaria.

Third interview

Q. Name the highest organ of government in the USSR.

A. The working class. The Central Committee? The All-Union Communist Party?

Q. What is Comrade Stalin's position in government?

A. He has many offices, I can't say.

Q. Who is the head of the Soviet government?

A. I don't know.

Q. What is Comrade Molotov's position in government?

A. He travels abroad.

Q. What is currently going on in Greece?

A. A gang is making war on the working class.

Source: Ibid., pp. 124–5.

The Doctors' Plot, in January 1953, had some unexpected side-effects, as this (c)
extract reveals. It is by Ya. I. Rapoport, the well-known pathologist, who was
one of the plot's victims.

The unlikeliest rumours spread among the public, including 'reliable' reports that in many maternity wards newborn infants were being killed or that some sick person died immediately after the visit of a doctor, who was then, naturally, arrested and shot. Visits to clinics declined sharply, and the pharmacies were suddenly forsaken. At the institute where I worked, a young woman came and demanded an analysis of an empty vial of penicillin. Her child had pneumonia, and immediately after she was given the penicillin, according to the mother, he grew worse. Allergic reactions to antibiotics are common enough, but she attributed the reaction to the work of poison allegedly contained in the penicillin, declaring that she would not give him any more medicine. When I told her that she would thus condemn him to death, she replied: 'Let him die from illness but not from poison that I give him with my own hands.'

Source: Ibid., pp. 137–8.

THE REALITY OF SOVIET PLANNING   **Document 27**

Zaleski here argues that the central national plan, from which all other plans
are derived, was a myth.

In describing the Soviet economy – a centrally planned economy – the tendency is to give planning priority over management. This would be correct if the central plan, broken down among economic units in an authoritarian fashion, were actually carried out. However, this study shows that the existence of such a central national plan, coherent and perfect, to be subdivided and implemented at all levels, is only a *myth*. What actually exists, as in any centrally administered economy, is an endless number of plans, constantly evolving, that are coordinated *ex post* after they have been put into operation. The unification of these innumerable plans into a single national plan, supposedly coherent, takes place rarely (once or twice during a five-year period and once for an annual or quarterly plan); furthermore, the attempt at unification is only a projection of observed tendencies resulting from extrapolating trends based on natural forces.

In view of the changing and often ephemeral nature of the plans, management emerges as the only constant in the system. The economic administration is built on a strict hierarchy descending from the ministry (or people's commissariat) to the enterprise, subject to strict discipline, obeying orders transmitted continuously. Under each management agency, from the Council of Ministers down to the enterprises, there is a planning commission with a consulting role. . . . Of course, higher-level 'consultants' (Gosplan) tend to take over certain management functions (material and equipment supply) or to intervene more or less directly in management, but then they become administrators just like the others and their 'planning' becomes management.

The priority of management over planning has been the dominant feature of the Soviet economy since Stalin's time. Since management is highly centralized, this feature is characteristic of the entire model. Therefore, it seems more nearly correct to call the economy 'centrally managed' rather than centrally planned.

Source: E. Zaleski, *Stalinist Planning for Economic Growth, 1933–1952* (Basingstoke, Macmillan, 1980), p. 484, copyright © 1980 by the University of North Carolina Press, used by permission of the publisher.

Document 28   WHAT IS STALINISM?

There are many different approaches to a study of the Stalinist system. There is the totalitarian or intentionalist approach which concentrates on politics and ideology, the strong state and strong leader; the Stalinist Marxist approach which views Stalinism as the dictatorship of the proletariat; the Trotskyist approach which emphasises the trend to Thermidorian bureaucracy and the emergence of a Leviathan state; the state capitalist approach which sees a nominally socialist state but run along capitalist lines (workers as wage labour); the new class approach of Djilas; the oriental despotism interpretation of Karl Wittfogel, who argues that traditions of deference to authority may have had their origins in the high levels of socio-political organisation required by a 'hydraulic society' in which the office of watermaster (controller of irrigation water) in arid lands was sovereign; the pluralist approach, which includes institutional pluralism; the corporatist interpretation; and finally the industrial society approach which concentrates on the primacy of industrialisation.

1. Commitment to a violent anti-capitalist revolution which *does not develop beyond* the replacement of the political power of the bourgeoisie by the power of *political bureacracy* and of private property by *state ownership* of the means of production. **(a)**
2. The leading force of the revolution and the backbone of the postrevolutionary society is a *monolithic, strongly disciplined, strictly hierarchical party* which has a *monopoly* of all economic and political power and *reduces all other* social organisations to its *mere transmissions*.
3. The state tends to exist even after the complete liquidation of a capitalist class. Its primary new function is a *rigid administrative* planning of all production and complete control of all political life. The state is officially a dictatorship of the working class; in reality it is *dictatorship of the party leadership or of one single leader.*
4. The new society is continued as a *collectivist welfare* society in which most forms of *economic and political alienation* would survive.
5. As a consequence of the centralist political and economic structure, smaller nations in a multi-national country are *denied self-determination* and continue to be *dominated* by the biggest nation.
6. *All culture is subordinated to the sphere of politics* and is strictly controlled and censored by the ruling party.

Source: Mihailo Marković, 'Stalinism and Marxism' in R. Tucker, ed., *Stalinism: Essays in Historical Interpretation* (New York, W.W. Norton, 1977), p. 300.

Stalinism was not simply nationalism, bureaucratisation, absence of democracy, censorship, police repression and the rest in any precedented sense. These phenomena have appeared in many societies and are rather easily explained. **(b)**

Instead Stalinism was excess, extraordinary extremism, in each. It was not, for example, merely coercive peasant policies, but a virtual civil war against the peasantry; not merely police repression, or even civil war style terror, but a holocaust by terror that victimised tens of millions of people for twenty five years; not merely a Thermidorian revival of nationalist tradition, but an almost fascist-like chauvinism; not merely a leader cult, but deification of a despot. . . . Excesses were the essence of historical Stalinism, and they are what really require explanation.

Source: Stephen F. Cohen, 'Bolshevism and Stalinism' in ibid., pp. 12–13.

(c)   The cult of the state and worship of rank, the irresponsibility of those who hold power and the population's lack of rights, the hierarchy of privileges and the canonisation of hypocrisy, the barrack system of social and intellectual life, the suppression of the individual and the destruction of independent thought, the environment of terror and suspicion, the atomisation of people and the notorious 'vigilance', the uncontrolled violence and the legalised cruelty.

Source: R.A. Medvedev, *On Socialist Democracy* (Basingstoke, Macmillan, 1975), p. 553.

(**d**)   (i)   A formally highly centralised, directive economic system characterised by mass mobilisation and an overriding priority on the development of heavy industry;

(ii)   A social structure initially characterised by significant fluidity, most particularly in the form of high levels of social mobility which brings the former lower classes into positions of power and privilege; subsequent consolidation of the social structure results in the dominance of rank, status and hierarchy;

(iii) A cultural and intellectual sphere in which all elements are meant to serve the political aims laid down by the leadership and where all areas of culture and intellectual production are politically monitored;

(iv) A personal dictatorship resting upon the use of terror as an instrument of rule and in which the political institutions are little more than the instrument of the dictator;

(v)   All spheres of life are politicised, hence, within the scope of state concerns;

(vi) The centralisation of authority is paralleled by a significant measure of weakness of continuing central control, resulting in a system which, in practice, is in its daily operations loosely controlled and structured;

(vii) The initial revolutionary ethos is superseded by a profoundly conservative, status quo, orientation.

Source: G. Gill, *Stalinism* (Basingstoke, Macmillan, 1990), pp. 57–8.

Further Reading

There has been an explosion of published material on Stalin and Stalinism since 1991. Many archives became accessible for the first time to western researchers (some have already closed again) and this has permitted the publication of valuable collections of documents. Often they are the result of collaboration of western and Russian scholars. Notable among these are J. Arch Getty and Oleg V. Naumov, *The Road to Terror: Stalin and the Self-Destruction of the Bolsheviks, 1932–1939* (New Haven, CT, and London, Yale University Press, 1999). This is invaluable for a study of the terror. Lewis Siegelbaum and Andrei Sokolov, *Stalinism as a Way of Life: A Narrative in Documents* (New Haven, CT, and London, Yale University Press, 2000) presents documents that offer penetrating insights into the lives of the average person during the hurricane which was Stalinism. Another volume which has resulted from the collaboration of Yale and Russian archives is Lars T. Lih, Oleg V. Naumov and Oleg V. Khlevniuk (eds), *Stalin's Letters to Molotov 1925–1936* (New Haven, CT, and London, Yale University Press, 1995). The letters before 1930 are more revealing than those afterwards. Other fine collections of documents are Philip Boobbyer, *The Stalin Era* (London and New York, Routledge, 2000); Christopher Read, *The Stalin Years: A Reader* (Basingstoke, Palgrave, 2002). Eastern Europe is covered in a fine collection of documents: Gale Stokes, *From Stalinism to Pluralism: A Documentary History of Eastern Europe since 1945* (2nd ed.) (New York, Oxford University Press, 1996).

Biographies of Stalin are legion but Isaac Deutscher, *Stalin* (2nd ed.) (Oxford, Oxford University Press, 1972) is still worth reading. His sympathies lie with Trotsky. Trotsky's own *The Revolution Betrayed* (New York, Pathfinder Press, 1972) tells us more about Trotsky than Stalin. This said, anything by Trotsky is worth reading because, although one may disagree with him, he puts his arguments brilliantly. More recent studies which provide stimulating reading include Robert Tucker, *Stalin in Power* (New York, W.W. Norton and Co., 1992); Edward Radzinsky, *Stalin* (London, Hodder and Stoughton, 1996) is not an academic study but is very entertaining; Dmitry Volkogonov, *Stalin* (London, Weidenfeld and Nicolson, 1991) is full and revealing. Stephen Cohen, **Bukharin and the Bolshevik Revolution** (New York, Alfred Knopf, 1973) is a sympathetic study of the 'darling of the party'; Derek Watson, **Molotov and Soviet Government** (Basingstoke, Macmillan, 1996) provides many insights into the relationship between Molotov and his master. Marc Jansen and Nikita Petrov, **Stalin's Loyal Executioner: People's Commissar Nikolai Ezhov 1895–1940** (Stanford, CA, Hoover Institution Press, 2002), based on archives, is very revealing; Amy Knight, **Beria: Stalin's First Lieutenant** (Princeton, NJ, Princeton University Press, 1993) is the leading study.

On Stalin's personality, **Beria, My Father Inside Stalin's Kremlin** (London, Duckworth, 1999) by Sergo Beria – Lavrenty Beria's son – provides fascinating insights and is the most revealing source available; Roman Brackman, **The Secret File of Joseph Stalin: A Hidden Life** (London, Frank Cass, 2001) is an extraordinary book and the fruit of a life's labours to understand what motivated Stalin. Brackman sees the terror as flowing from Stalin's obsession to eliminate all archival evidence and human testimony about his collaboration with the *Okhrana*, the Tsarist secret police. A very detailed but not very flattering picture of Stalin emerges. Brackman does not take into account Stalin's ideological desire to found a new society. Probably the best study of the Soviet Union under Stalin is Chris Ward, **Stalin's Russia** (London, Edward Arnold, 1999). See also John Channon (ed.), **Politics, Society and Stalinism in the USSR** (Basingstoke, Macmillan, 1997); J. Cooper, M. Perrie and E.A. Rees (eds), **Soviet History 1917–1953** (New York, St Martin's Press, 1995); Graeme Gill, **Stalinism** (Basingstoke, Macmillan, 1990).

On particular aspects of the Stalin period see: M. Brown, **Socialist Realist Painting** (New Haven, CT, and London, Yale University Press, 1998); Susan Davies, **Popular Opinion in Stalin's Russia** (Cambridge, Cambridge University Press, 1997); Vera Dunham, **In Stalin's Time** (Cambridge, Cambridge University Press, 1976), which provides a fascinating insight into the adoption of bourgeois values by Soviet families, based on published novels; J. von Geldern and R. Stites (eds), **Mass Culture in Soviet Russia** (Bloomington, IN, Indiana University Press, 1995); A. Kemp-Welch, **Stalin and the Literary Intelligentsia, 1928–39** (Basingstoke, Macmillan, 1991); P. Kenez, **Cinema and Soviet Society 1917–1953** (Cambridge, Cambridge University Press, 1992), which looks at an important propaganda source; N. Krementsov, **Stalinist Science** (Princeton, NJ, Princeton University Press, 1997); A. Luukkanen, **The Religious Policy of the Stalinist State, 1929–1938** (Helsinki, SHS, 1997); Vladimir Papernyi, **Architecture in the Age of Stalin** (New York, Cambridge University Press, 2002); K. Smith, **Remembering Stalin's Victims** (Ithaca, NY, Cornell University Press, 1996);

P.H. Solomon, *Soviet Criminal Justice under Stalin* (Cambridge, Cambridge University Press, 1996); R. Taylor and D. Spring, (eds), *Stalinism and Soviet Cinema* (London, Routledge, 1993); R. Thurston, *Life and Terror in Stalin's Russia, 1934–1941* (New Haven, CT, Yale University Press, 1996); Elena Zubkova, *Russia After the War, Hopes, Illusions, and Disappointments, 1945–1957* (Armonk, NY, and London, M.E. Sharpe, 1998), which catches the period very well and is highly informative.

Catherine Merridale, *Night of Stone: Death and Memory in Russia* (London, Granta Books, 2000) is a haunting study of suffering. It is a prize-winning book which has been called an 'epic and moving history'.

On opposition, see Judy Kutulas, *The Long War: The Intellectual People's Front and Anti-Stalinism 1930–1940* (Durham, NC, Duke University Press, 1995).

On the economy, see Paul R. Gregory, (ed.), *Behind the Façade of Stalin's Command Economy: Evidence from the Soviet State and Party Archives* (Stanford, CA, Hoover Institution Press, 2001), which provides a mass of material but no startling revelations; James Hughes, *Stalinism in a Russian Province: A Study of Collectivization and Dekulakization in Siberia* (Basingstoke, Macmillan, 1996); Stephen Kotkin, *Magnetic Mountain: Stalinism as a Civilization* (Berkeley, CA, University of California Press, 1995), which is a magnificent study of the founding and development of Magnitogorsk; Elena Osokina, *Our Daily Bread: Socialist Distribution and the Art of Survival in Stalin's Russia, 1927–1941* (Armonk, NY, M.E. Sharpe, 2001), which is a fine study of Stalin's attempt to replace the market with state-controlled supply which never really worked; Matthew J. Payne, *Stalin's Railroad: Turksib and the Building of Socialism* (Pittsburgh, PA, University of Pittsburg Press, 2001); E.A. Rees, *Stalinism and Soviet Rail Transport 1928–1941* (Basingstoke, Macmillan, 1995); D. Shearer, *Industry, State and Society in Stalin's Russia 1926–1934* (Ithaca, NY, Cornell University Press, 1996); Lynne Viola, *Peasant Rebels under Stalin* (New York, Oxford University Press, 1996).

On women, see Wendy Z. Goldman, *Women at the Gates: Gender and Industry in Stalin's Russia* (Cambridge, Cambridge University Press, 2002); Melanie Ilic, *Women in the Stalin Era* (New York, Palgrave, 2001).

On the coming of war, see John Erickson and David Dilks (eds), *Barbarossa: the Axis and the Allies* (Edinburgh, Edinburgh University Press, 1994); Silvio Pons, *Stalin and the Inevitable War: Origins of the Total Security State in the USSR and the Outbreak of World War II in Europe* (London, Frank Cass, 2002); Lennart Samuelson, *Plans for Stalin's War Machine: Tukhachevskii and Military–Economic Planning, 1925–1941* (Basingstoke, Macmillan, 2000); David R. Stone, *Hammer and Rifle: The Militarization of the Soviet Union, 1926–1933* (Lawrence, KA, University of Kansas Press, 2000).

On the military and war, the leading scholar is John Erickson: *The Soviet High Command: A Military–Political History 1918–1941* (3rd ed.) (Portland, OR, Frank Cass, 2001), which is the standard work; and *The Road to Stalingrad* (London, Weidenfeld and Nicolson, 1983) and *The Road to Berlin* (London, Weidenfeld and Nicolson, 1983). Antony Beevor, *Stalingrad* (London, Penguin, 1999) and *Berlin the Downfall 1945* (London, Viking, 2002) are outstanding and prize-winning military histories.

The best account of the Great Fatherland War is Richard Overy, *Russia's War* (Harmondsworth, Penguin, 1997). Albert Axell, *Zhukov* (London, Longman, 2002) is authoritative and includes new material; see also his *Stalin's War Through the Eyes of His Commanders* (London, Arms and Armour Press, 1997).

On Churchill's relations with Stalin, see David Carlton, *Churchill and the Soviet Union* (Manchester, Manchester University Press, 2000), who strives manfully to cope with Churchill's mercurial temperament. He concludes that President Harry Truman was a more effective anti-communist than the brilliant British Prime Minister.

The best source on the Stalin cult is Jeffrey Brooks, *Thank You, Comrade Stalin! Soviet Public Culture from Revolution to Cold War* (Princeton, NJ, Princeton University Press, 2001), which is richly illustrated and penetrating; see also Karen Petrone, *Life Has Become More Joyous, Comrades: Celebrations in the Time of Stalin* (Bloomington, IN, Indiana University Press, 2000).

A fine comparative study of Stalinism and National Socialism is I. Kershaw and M. Lewin (eds), *Stalinism and Nazism* (Cambridge, Cambridge University Press, 1997).

On the republics, see David R. Marples, *Stalinism in Ukraine in the 1940s* (New York, St Martin's Press, 1992). Amir Weiner, *Making Sense of War: The Second World War and the Fate of the Bolshevik Revolution* (Princeton, NJ, Princeton University Press, 2001) is a superb study of Vinnytsia, part of the Soviet Republic of Ukraine during the war.

On Russian nationalism and the nationalities, see Maureen Perrie, *The Cult of Ivan the Terrible in Stalin's Russia* (Basingstoke, Palgrave, 2001); Ronald Grigor Suny and Terry Martin (eds), *A State of Nations: Empire and Nation-Building in the Age of Lenin and Stalin* (Oxford, Oxford University Press, 2001).

On espionage, Richard J. Aldrich, *The Hidden Hand: Britain, America and Cold War Secret Intelligence* (London, John Murray, 2001) reads like a James Bond thriller.

On the totalitarian approach, see Robert Conquest, *Harvest of Sorrow* (London, Hutchinson, 1986), *Stalin and the Kirov Murder* (London, Hutchinson, 1989) and *The Great Terror* (London, Pimlico, 1992); Leonard

Schapiro, *Totalitarianism* (Basingstoke, Macmillan, 1972) and *The Origin of the Communist Autocracy* (Basingstoke, Macmillan, 1977).

On the social history approach, the outstanding scholar is Sheila Fitzpatrick. Of note among her many writings are: *The Cultural Front: Power and Culture in Revolutionary Russia* (Ithaca, NY, Cornall University Press, 1992); *Stalin's Peasants* (New York, Oxford University Press, 1994); *Everyday Stalinism* (New York, Oxford University Press, 1999); *Stalinism: New Directions* (London, Routledge, 2000) – this volume contains many seminal articles published during the 1990s, edited by Fitzpatrick.

Moshe Lewin also addresses social problems but relates them to the political, unlike Fitzpatrick and her school of authors, sometimes called the 'new cohort'. Lewin sees the 1930s as a disaster of epic proportions as the Stalinist state set up bureaucratic institutions to stabilise the quicksand society it had created by its own destructive campaigns. He sees Stalin as a historical demon with roots in the peasant culture. The new cohort regards the demonologising of Stalin as totally erroneous. See Moshe Lewin, *Russian Peasants and Soviet Power* (Evanston, IL, Northwestern University Press, 1968); *The Making of the Soviet System* (London, Methuen, 1985); 'Bureaucracy and the Stalinist State', in I. Kershaw and M. Lewin (eds), *Stalinism and Nazism* (Cambridge, Cambridge University Press, 1997).

On Stalinism as a civilisation, see Stephen Kotkin, *Magnetic Mountain: Stalinism as a Civilization* (Berkeley, CA, University of California Press, 1995).

More detailed biographies of the leading figures of the Stalin era are to be found in Martin McCauley, *Who's Who in Russia since 1900* (London, Routledge, 1997). A more detailed chronology is in Martin McCauley, *Russia since 1914* (Harlow, Longman, 1998).

References

Aldrich, R.J. (2001) *The Hidden Hand: Britain, America and Cold War Secret Intelligence*. London: John Murray.

Alexandrov, G.F. *et al.*, (1947) *Joseph Stalin: A Short Biography*. Moscow: Foreign Language Publishing House.

Barber, J.D. and Harrison, M. (1991) *The Soviet Home Front 1941–1945: A Social and Economic History of the USSR in World War II*. Harlow: Longman.

Beria, S. (1999) *Beria: My Father Inside Stalin's Kemlin*. London: Duckworth.

Boobbyer, P. (2000) *The Stalin Era*. London: Routledge.

Brooks, J. (2001) *Thank You, Comrade Stalin! Soviet Public Culture from Revolution to Cold War*. Princeton, NJ: Princeton University Press.

Carr, E.H. (1979) *The Russian Revolution from Lenin to Stalin*. Basingstoke: Macmillan.

Cohen, S. (1977) 'Bolshevism and Stalinism' in Tucker, R. (ed.), *Stalinism: Essays in Historical Interpretation*. New York: W.W. Norton.

Davies, R.W., Harrison, M. and Wheatcroft, S.G. (eds) (1994) *The Economic Transformation of the Soviet Union 1913–1945*. Cambridge: Cambridge University Press.

Dedijer, V. (1953) *Tito Speaks*. London: Weidenfeld and Nicolson.

Djilas, M. (1962) *Conversations with Stalin*. London: Hart-Davis.

Ellman, M. (1991) 'A note on the number of 1933 famine victims', *Soviet Studies*, vol. 43, no. 2.

Ellman, M. and Maksudov, S. (1994) 'Soviet deaths in the Great Patriotic War: A note', *Europe–Asia Studies*, vol. 46, no. 4.

Fainsod, M. (1954) *How Russia is Ruled*. Cambridge, MA: Harvard University Press.

Fitzpatrick, S. (ed.) (2000) *Stalinism: New Directions*. London: Routledge.

Getty, J. Arch and Naumov, O.V. (1999) *The Road to Terror: Stalin and the Self-Destruction of the Bolsheviks, 1932–1939*. New Haven, CT: Yale University Press.

Gill, G. (1990) *Stalinism*. Basingstoke: Macmillan.

Harrison, M. (1993) 'Soviet economic growth since 1928: The alternative statistics of G.I. Khanin', *Europe–Asia Studies*, vol. 45, no. 1.

Jansen, M. and Petrov, N. (2002) *Stalin's Loyal Executioner: People's Commissar Nikolai Ezhov 1895–1940*. Stanford, CA: Hoover Institution Press.

Khrushchev, N. (1971) *Khrushchev Remembers*, ed. S. Talbott. Boston, MA: Little, Brown.

Kotkin, S. (1995) *Magnetic Mountain: Stalinism as a Civilization*. Berkeley, CA: University of California Press.

McCauley, M. (1993) *The Soviet Union 1917–1991* (2nd ed.). London: Longman.

Mandelstam, N. (1971) *Hope Abandoned*. London: Collins Harvill.

Marković, M. (1977) 'Stalinism and Marxism', in Tucker, R. (ed.), *Stalinism: Essays in Historical Interpretation*. New York: W.W. Norton.

Medvedev, R.A. (1975) *On Socialist Democracy*. Basingstoke: Macmillan.

Naimark, N. (2002) 'Cold War studies and new archival materials on Stalin', *The Russian Review*, vol. 61, no. 1.

Nove, A. (1992) *An Economic History of the USSR*. Harmondsworth: Penguin.

Osokina, E. (2001) *Our Daily Bread: Socialist Distribution and the Art of Survival in Stalin's Russia, 1927–1941*. Armonk, NY: M.E. Sharpe.

Overy, R. (1997) *Russia's War*. Harmondsworth: Penguin.

Rigby, T.H. (1966) *Stalin*. Englewood Cliffs, NJ: Prentice-Hall.

Siegelbaum, L. and Sokolov, A. (2000) *Stalinism as a Way of Life: A Narrative in Documents*. New Haven, CT: Yale University Press.

Stalin, J. (1945) *Problems of Leninism*. Moscow: Foreign Language Publishing House.

Tucker, R. (1977) *Stalinism: Essays in Historical Interpretation*. New York: W.W. Norton.

Wade, R. (2000) *The Russian Revolution, 1917.* Cambridge: Cambridge University Press.

Zaleski, E. (1980) *Stalinist Planning for Economic Growth, 1933–1952.* Basingstoke: Macmillan.

Zubkova, E. (1998) *Russia After the War: Hopes, Illusions and Disappointments, 1945–1957.* Armonk, NY: M.E. Sharpe.

Index

Stalin, Josef (*continued*)
  family life 49, 92–3
  foreign observers' views of 95–6
  and ideology 28–9, 34, 49–50, 77
  information sources 96–7
  and Lenin 6, 26–9, 35, 58, 91
  and the 'Lenin enrolment' 29–30
  and nationalism 102–3
  and Operation Barbarossa 64–5, 66
  and party officials 58
  personality cult 33, 58–9, 76, 80, 127, 136–7
  and the purges 52
  and the Secretariat 24
  and Soviet foreign policy 8, 54–7, 84–8
  and Stalinism 3
  and the Teheran conference 74
  and the western allies 77–9, 85–8
  and the Yalta conference 74–5
Stalingrad, battle for 68
Stalinism 76–88, 144–6
  approaches to the study of 8–12
  and post-war economic policy 82–4
  and the Second World War 76–7
  success and failure of 3, 7
  in the Thirties 57–63
state functioning, and Stalinism 59–60
Supreme Soviet 50
Sverdlov, Yakov 20, 21, 35
Sweden 56

Tehran conference (1943) 74
terror and the purges 9, 10, 48–54, 60–3, 96–7
  denunciations 53–4
  deportations 62, 73, 102, 132–6
  'doctors' plot' 81–2, 143
  former prisoners and exiles 82
  interrogation techniques 115–17
  liquidation of the *kulaks* 62–3, 102, 121–3
  military officers 52, 61, 123–4
  'national operations' 61–2
  Show Trials 48–9, 50–2, 118–21
  see also deaths and executions
theft, and state employees 112
Timasheff, Nicholas 10
Timoshenko, Marshal S.K. 56
Tolstoy, Aleksei 94
totalitarianism 8–9
trade unions
  Bolshevik control of 21–2, 23
  and Stalinism 60
Transcaucasian republic 26–7

Tripartite Pact 56, 57
Trotsky, L. 24, 27, 28, 30, 31, 32, 33, 34, 35, 61, 81, 98, 102
  assassination of 52
  and the *Declaration of the 83* 32
  Lessons of October 30
  and NEP 25
  and the Red Army 17, 19
  and Stalinism 10, 95
Trotskyism 29, 62
Truman Doctrine 87
Truman, Harry 95
Tukhachevsky, Marshal M.N. 52

Ukraine 19, 20
United Opposition 31, 32, 33, 34
United States 3, 7
  and Lend-Lease 70, 73
  and Stalinism 77–8, 87–8
  wartime alliance with Soviet Russia 73, 74–5

village values 10
Vinogradov, Professor 82
violence, and Russian socialism 101–2
Volga Germans 73, 132–3
Voroshilov, Marshal K.E. 52
VSNKh (Supreme Council of the National Economy) 21
Vyshinsky, A.Y. 50, 52, 63

wages 45, 114
war communism 20–5
West Germany 86, 87
Winter War 56
women 80–1, 92–3
workers' detachments 23
working class
  and the Bolsheviks 4
  and Marx 100

Yagoda, G.G. 51, 52, 60–1, 96
Yakovlev, Aleksandr 52–3
Yalta conference (1945) 74–5
youth culture 141–2
Yugoslavia 56, 57, 69, 74, 80
  Soviet attitudes towards Yugoslav culture 139–40

Zhdanov, Andrei 48, 52, 62, 77, 79, 80, 82, 98
Zhukov, Marshal G.K. 66–7, 68, 76
Zinoviev, G.E. 26, 27, 28, 29, 30, 31, 32, 81
Zoshchenko, Mikhail, *Before Sunrise* 72